C-3291   CAREER EXAMINATION SERIES

This is your
PASSBOOK for...

Electric Station Operator

Test Preparation Study Guide
Questions & Answers

NATIONAL LEARNING CORPORATION®

COPYRIGHT NOTICE

This book is SOLELY intended for, is sold ONLY to, and its use is RESTRICTED to individual, bona fide applicants or candidates who qualify by virtue of having seriously filed applications for appropriate license, certificate, professional and/or promotional advancement, higher school matriculation, scholarship, or other legitimate requirements of education and/or governmental authorities.

This book is NOT intended for use, class instruction, tutoring, training, duplication, copying, reprinting, excerption, or adaptation, etc., by:

1) Other publishers
2) Proprietors and/or Instructors of "Coaching" and/or Preparatory Courses
3) Personnel and/or Training Divisions of commercial, industrial, and governmental organizations
4) Schools, colleges, or universities and/or their departments and staffs, including teachers and other personnel
5) Testing Agencies or Bureaus
6) Study groups which seek by the purchase of a single volume to copy and/or duplicate and/or adapt this material for use by the group as a whole without having purchased individual volumes for each of the members of the group
7) Et al.

Such persons would be in violation of appropriate Federal and State statutes.

PROVISION OF LICENSING AGREEMENTS – Recognized educational, commercial, industrial, and governmental institutions and organizations, and others legitimately engaged in educational pursuits, including training, testing, and measurement activities, may address request for a licensing agreement to the copyright owners, who will determine whether, and under what conditions, including fees and charges, the materials in this book may be used them. In other words, a licensing facility exists for the legitimate use of the material in this book on other than an individual basis. However, it is asseverated and affirmed here that the material in this book CANNOT be used without the receipt of the express permission of such a licensing agreement from the Publishers. Inquiries re licensing should be addressed to the company, attention rights and permissions department.

All rights reserved, including the right of reproduction in whole or in part, in any form or by any means, electronic or mechanical, including photocopying, recording, or by any information storage and retrieval system, without permission in writing from the Publisher.

Copyright © 2024 by
National Learning Corporation

212 Michael Drive, Syosset, NY 11791
(516) 921-8888 • www.passbooks.com
E-mail: info@passbooks.com

PUBLISHED IN THE UNITED STATES OF AMERICA

PASSBOOK® SERIES

THE *PASSBOOK® SERIES* has been created to prepare applicants and candidates for the ultimate academic battlefield – the examination room.

At some time in our lives, each and every one of us may be required to take an examination – for validation, matriculation, admission, qualification, registration, certification, or licensure.

Based on the assumption that every applicant or candidate has met the basic formal educational standards, has taken the required number of courses, and read the necessary texts, the *PASSBOOK® SERIES* furnishes the one special preparation which may assure passing with confidence, instead of failing with insecurity. Examination questions – together with answers – are furnished as the basic vehicle for study so that the mysteries of the examination and its compounding difficulties may be eliminated or diminished by a sure method.

This book is meant to help you pass your examination provided that you qualify and are serious in your objective.

The entire field is reviewed through the huge store of content information which is succinctly presented through a provocative and challenging approach – the question-and-answer method.

A climate of success is established by furnishing the correct answers at the end of each test.

You soon learn to recognize types of questions, forms of questions, and patterns of questioning. You may even begin to anticipate expected outcomes.

You perceive that many questions are repeated or adapted so that you can gain acute insights, which may enable you to score many sure points.

You learn how to confront new questions, or types of questions, and to attack them confidently and work out the correct answers.

You note objectives and emphases, and recognize pitfalls and dangers, so that you may make positive educational adjustments.

Moreover, you are kept fully informed in relation to new concepts, methods, practices, and directions in the field.

You discover that you are actually taking the examination all the time: you are preparing for the examination by "taking" an examination, not by reading extraneous and/or supererogatory textbooks.

In short, this PASSBOOK®, used directedly, should be an important factor in helping you to pass your test.

ELECTRIC STATION OPERATOR

DUTIES:

An Electric Station Operator receives intensive on-the-job and classroom training, and assists in the local control operation of electric and auxiliary equipment in hydroelectric generating, receiving and distributing stations; does routine inspection, cleaning, meter reading, and occasional switching under direction.

THE EXAMINATION:

The written test will be of the multiple choice type and will be designed to test for knowledge, skills, and/or abilities in such areas as: electricity; arithmetic; physics and general science; spatial relationships; mechanical aptitude and hand tools; reading comprehension; and other necessary knowledge and abilities.

HOW TO TAKE A TEST

I. YOU MUST PASS AN EXAMINATION

A. *WHAT EVERY CANDIDATE SHOULD KNOW*

Examination applicants often ask us for help in preparing for the written test. What can I study in advance? What kinds of questions will be asked? How will the test be given? How will the papers be graded?

As an applicant for a civil service examination, you may be wondering about some of these things. Our purpose here is to suggest effective methods of advance study and to describe civil service examinations.

Your chances for success on this examination can be increased if you know how to prepare. Those "pre-examination jitters" can be reduced if you know what to expect. You can even experience an adventure in good citizenship if you know why civil service exams are given.

B. *WHY ARE CIVIL SERVICE EXAMINATIONS GIVEN?*

Civil service examinations are important to you in two ways. As a citizen, you want public jobs filled by employees who know how to do their work. As a job seeker, you want a fair chance to compete for that job on an equal footing with other candidates. The best-known means of accomplishing this two-fold goal is the competitive examination.

Exams are widely publicized throughout the nation. They may be administered for jobs in federal, state, city, municipal, town or village governments or agencies.

Any citizen may apply, with some limitations, such as the age or residence of applicants. Your experience and education may be reviewed to see whether you meet the requirements for the particular examination. When these requirements exist, they are reasonable and applied consistently to all applicants. Thus, a competitive examination may cause you some uneasiness now, but it is your privilege and safeguard.

C. *HOW ARE CIVIL SERVICE EXAMS DEVELOPED?*

Examinations are carefully written by trained technicians who are specialists in the field known as "psychological measurement," in consultation with recognized authorities in the field of work that the test will cover. These experts recommend the subject matter areas or skills to be tested; only those knowledges or skills important to your success on the job are included. The most reliable books and source materials available are used as references. Together, the experts and technicians judge the difficulty level of the questions.

Test technicians know how to phrase questions so that the problem is clearly stated. Their ethics do not permit "trick" or "catch" questions. Questions may have been tried out on sample groups, or subjected to statistical analysis, to determine their usefulness.

Written tests are often used in combination with performance tests, ratings of training and experience, and oral interviews. All of these measures combine to form the best-known means of finding the right person for the right job.

II. HOW TO PASS THE WRITTEN TEST

A. NATURE OF THE EXAMINATION

To prepare intelligently for civil service examinations, you should know how they differ from school examinations you have taken. In school you were assigned certain definite pages to read or subjects to cover. The examination questions were quite detailed and usually emphasized memory. Civil service exams, on the other hand, try to discover your present ability to perform the duties of a position, plus your potentiality to learn these duties. In other words, a civil service exam attempts to predict how successful you will be. Questions cover such a broad area that they cannot be as minute and detailed as school exam questions.

In the public service similar kinds of work, or positions, are grouped together in one "class." This process is known as *position-classification*. All the positions in a class are paid according to the salary range for that class. One class title covers all of these positions, and they are all tested by the same examination.

B. FOUR BASIC STEPS

1) Study the announcement

How, then, can you know what subjects to study? Our best answer is: "Learn as much as possible about the class of positions for which you've applied." The exam will test the knowledge, skills and abilities needed to do the work.

Your most valuable source of information about the position you want is the official exam announcement. This announcement lists the training and experience qualifications. Check these standards and apply only if you come reasonably close to meeting them.

The brief description of the position in the examination announcement offers some clues to the subjects which will be tested. Think about the job itself. Review the duties in your mind. Can you perform them, or are there some in which you are rusty? Fill in the blank spots in your preparation.

Many jurisdictions preview the written test in the exam announcement by including a section called "Knowledge and Abilities Required," "Scope of the Examination," or some similar heading. Here you will find out specifically what fields will be tested.

2) Review your own background

Once you learn in general what the position is all about, and what you need to know to do the work, ask yourself which subjects you already know fairly well and which need improvement. You may wonder whether to concentrate on improving your strong areas or on building some background in your fields of weakness. When the announcement has specified "some knowledge" or "considerable knowledge," or has used adjectives like "beginning principles of…" or "advanced … methods," you can get a clue as to the number and difficulty of questions to be asked in any given field. More questions, and hence broader coverage, would be included for those subjects which are more important in the work. Now weigh your strengths and weaknesses against the job requirements and prepare accordingly.

3) Determine the level of the position

Another way to tell how intensively you should prepare is to understand the level of the job for which you are applying. Is it the entering level? In other words, is this the position in which beginners in a field of work are hired? Or is it an intermediate or advanced level? Sometimes this is indicated by such words as "Junior" or "Senior" in the class title. Other jurisdictions use Roman numerals to designate the level – Clerk I, Clerk II, for example. The word "Supervisor" sometimes appears in the title. If the level is not indicated by the title, check the description of duties. Will you be working under very close supervision, or will you have responsibility for independent decisions in this work?

4) Choose appropriate study materials

Now that you know the subjects to be examined and the relative amount of each subject to be covered, you can choose suitable study materials. For beginning level jobs, or even advanced ones, if you have a pronounced weakness in some aspect of your training, read a modern, standard textbook in that field. Be sure it is up to date and has general coverage. Such books are normally available at your library, and the librarian will be glad to help you locate one. For entry-level positions, questions of appropriate difficulty are chosen – neither highly advanced questions, nor those too simple. Such questions require careful thought but not advanced training.

If the position for which you are applying is technical or advanced, you will read more advanced, specialized material. If you are already familiar with the basic principles of your field, elementary textbooks would waste your time. Concentrate on advanced textbooks and technical periodicals. Think through the concepts and review difficult problems in your field.

These are all general sources. You can get more ideas on your own initiative, following these leads. For example, training manuals and publications of the government agency which employs workers in your field can be useful, particularly for technical and professional positions. A letter or visit to the government department involved may result in more specific study suggestions, and certainly will provide you with a more definite idea of the exact nature of the position you are seeking.

III. KINDS OF TESTS

Tests are used for purposes other than measuring knowledge and ability to perform specified duties. For some positions, it is equally important to test ability to make adjustments to new situations or to profit from training. In others, basic mental abilities not dependent on information are essential. Questions which test these things may not appear as pertinent to the duties of the position as those which test for knowledge and information. Yet they are often highly important parts of a fair examination. For very general questions, it is almost impossible to help you direct your study efforts. What we can do is to point out some of the more common of these general abilities needed in public service positions and describe some typical questions.

1) General information

Broad, general information has been found useful for predicting job success in some kinds of work. This is tested in a variety of ways, from vocabulary lists to questions about current events. Basic background in some field of work, such as sociology or economics, may be sampled in a group of questions. Often these are principles which have become familiar to most persons through exposure rather than through formal training. It is difficult to advise you how to study for these questions; being alert to the world around you is our best suggestion.

2) Verbal ability

An example of an ability needed in many positions is verbal or language ability. Verbal ability is, in brief, the ability to use and understand words. Vocabulary and grammar tests are typical measures of this ability. Reading comprehension or paragraph interpretation questions are common in many kinds of civil service tests. You are given a paragraph of written material and asked to find its central meaning.

3) Numerical ability

Number skills can be tested by the familiar arithmetic problem, by checking paired lists of numbers to see which are alike and which are different, or by interpreting charts and graphs. In the latter test, a graph may be printed in the test booklet which you are asked to use as the basis for answering questions.

4) Observation

A popular test for law-enforcement positions is the observation test. A picture is shown to you for several minutes, then taken away. Questions about the picture test your ability to observe both details and larger elements.

5) Following directions

In many positions in the public service, the employee must be able to carry out written instructions dependably and accurately. You may be given a chart with several columns, each column listing a variety of information. The questions require you to carry out directions involving the information given in the chart.

6) Skills and aptitudes

Performance tests effectively measure some manual skills and aptitudes. When the skill is one in which you are trained, such as typing or shorthand, you can practice. These tests are often very much like those given in business school or high school courses. For many of the other skills and aptitudes, however, no short-time preparation can be made. Skills and abilities natural to you or that you have developed throughout your lifetime are being tested.

Many of the general questions just described provide all the data needed to answer the questions and ask you to use your reasoning ability to find the answers. Your best preparation for these tests, as well as for tests of facts and ideas, is to be at your physical and mental best. You, no doubt, have your own methods of getting into an exam-taking mood and keeping "in shape." The next section lists some ideas on this subject.

IV. KINDS OF QUESTIONS

Only rarely is the "essay" question, which you answer in narrative form, used in civil service tests. Civil service tests are usually of the short-answer type. Full instructions for answering these questions will be given to you at the examination. But in case this is your first experience with short-answer questions and separate answer sheets, here is what you need to know:

1) Multiple-choice Questions

Most popular of the short-answer questions is the "multiple choice" or "best answer" question. It can be used, for example, to test for factual knowledge, ability to solve problems or judgment in meeting situations found at work.

A multiple-choice question is normally one of three types—
- It can begin with an incomplete statement followed by several possible endings. You are to find the one ending which *best* completes the statement, although some of the others may not be entirely wrong.
- It can also be a complete statement in the form of a question which is answered by choosing one of the statements listed.

- It can be in the form of a problem – again you select the best answer.

Here is an example of a multiple-choice question with a discussion which should give you some clues as to the method for choosing the right answer:

When an employee has a complaint about his assignment, the action which will *best* help him overcome his difficulty is to
  A. discuss his difficulty with his coworkers
  B. take the problem to the head of the organization
  C. take the problem to the person who gave him the assignment
  D. say nothing to anyone about his complaint

In answering this question, you should study each of the choices to find which is best. Consider choice "A" – Certainly an employee may discuss his complaint with fellow employees, but no change or improvement can result, and the complaint remains unresolved. Choice "B" is a poor choice since the head of the organization probably does not know what assignment you have been given, and taking your problem to him is known as "going over the head" of the supervisor. The supervisor, or person who made the assignment, is the person who can clarify it or correct any injustice. Choice "C" is, therefore, correct. To say nothing, as in choice "D," is unwise. Supervisors have and interest in knowing the problems employees are facing, and the employee is seeking a solution to his problem.

2) True/False Questions

The "true/false" or "right/wrong" form of question is sometimes used. Here a complete statement is given. Your job is to decide whether the statement is right or wrong.

SAMPLE: A roaming cell-phone call to a nearby city costs less than a non-roaming call to a distant city.

This statement is wrong, or false, since roaming calls are more expensive.

This is not a complete list of all possible question forms, although most of the others are variations of these common types. You will always get complete directions for answering questions. Be sure you understand *how* to mark your answers – ask questions until you do.

V. RECORDING YOUR ANSWERS

Computer terminals are used more and more today for many different kinds of exams.
For an examination with very few applicants, you may be told to record your answers in the test booklet itself. Separate answer sheets are much more common. If this separate answer sheet is to be scored by machine – and this is often the case – it is highly important that you mark your answers correctly in order to get credit.
An electronic scoring machine is often used in civil service offices because of the speed with which papers can be scored. Machine-scored answer sheets must be marked with a pencil, which will be given to you. This pencil has a high graphite content which responds to the electronic scoring machine. As a matter of fact, stray dots may register as answers, so do not let your pencil rest on the answer sheet while you are pondering the correct answer. Also, if your pencil lead breaks or is otherwise defective, ask for another.

Since the answer sheet will be dropped in a slot in the scoring machine, be careful not to bend the corners or get the paper crumpled.

The answer sheet normally has five vertical columns of numbers, with 30 numbers to a column. These numbers correspond to the question numbers in your test booklet. After each number, going across the page are four or five pairs of dotted lines. These short dotted lines have small letters or numbers above them. The first two pairs may also have a "T" or "F" above the letters. This indicates that the first two pairs only are to be used if the questions are of the true-false type. If the questions are multiple choice, disregard the "T" and "F" and pay attention only to the small letters or numbers.

Answer your questions in the manner of the sample that follows:

32. The largest city in the United States is
    A. Washington, D.C.
    B. New York City
    C. Chicago
    D. Detroit
    E. San Francisco

1) Choose the answer you think is best. (New York City is the largest, so "B" is correct.)
2) Find the row of dotted lines numbered the same as the question you are answering. (Find row number 32)
3) Find the pair of dotted lines corresponding to the answer. (Find the pair of lines under the mark "B.")
4) Make a solid black mark between the dotted lines.

VI. BEFORE THE TEST

Common sense will help you find procedures to follow to get ready for an examination. Too many of us, however, overlook these sensible measures. Indeed, nervousness and fatigue have been found to be the most serious reasons why applicants fail to do their best on civil service tests. Here is a list of reminders:

- Begin your preparation early – Don't wait until the last minute to go scurrying around for books and materials or to find out what the position is all about.
- Prepare continuously – An hour a night for a week is better than an all-night cram session. This has been definitely established. What is more, a night a week for a month will return better dividends than crowding your study into a shorter period of time.
- Locate the place of the exam – You have been sent a notice telling you when and where to report for the examination. If the location is in a different town or otherwise unfamiliar to you, it would be well to inquire the best route and learn something about the building.
- Relax the night before the test – Allow your mind to rest. Do not study at all that night. Plan some mild recreation or diversion; then go to bed early and get a good night's sleep.
- Get up early enough to make a leisurely trip to the place for the test – This way unforeseen events, traffic snarls, unfamiliar buildings, etc. will not upset you.
- Dress comfortably – A written test is not a fashion show. You will be known by number and not by name, so wear something comfortable.

- Leave excess paraphernalia at home – Shopping bags and odd bundles will get in your way. You need bring only the items mentioned in the official notice you received; usually everything you need is provided. Do not bring reference books to the exam. They will only confuse those last minutes and be taken away from you when in the test room.
- Arrive somewhat ahead of time – If because of transportation schedules you must get there very early, bring a newspaper or magazine to take your mind off yourself while waiting.
- Locate the examination room – When you have found the proper room, you will be directed to the seat or part of the room where you will sit. Sometimes you are given a sheet of instructions to read while you are waiting. Do not fill out any forms until you are told to do so; just read them and be prepared.
- Relax and prepare to listen to the instructions
- If you have any physical problem that may keep you from doing your best, be sure to tell the test administrator. If you are sick or in poor health, you really cannot do your best on the exam. You can come back and take the test some other time.

VII. AT THE TEST

The day of the test is here and you have the test booklet in your hand. The temptation to get going is very strong. Caution! There is more to success than knowing the right answers. You must know how to identify your papers and understand variations in the type of short-answer question used in this particular examination. Follow these suggestions for maximum results from your efforts:

1) Cooperate with the monitor

The test administrator has a duty to create a situation in which you can be as much at ease as possible. He will give instructions, tell you when to begin, check to see that you are marking your answer sheet correctly, and so on. He is not there to guard you, although he will see that your competitors do not take unfair advantage. He wants to help you do your best.

2) Listen to all instructions

Don't jump the gun! Wait until you understand all directions. In most civil service tests you get more time than you need to answer the questions. So don't be in a hurry. Read each word of instructions until you clearly understand the meaning. Study the examples, listen to all announcements and follow directions. Ask questions if you do not understand what to do.

3) Identify your papers

Civil service exams are usually identified by number only. You will be assigned a number; you must not put your name on your test papers. Be sure to copy your number correctly. Since more than one exam may be given, copy your exact examination title.

4) Plan your time

Unless you are told that a test is a "speed" or "rate of work" test, speed itself is usually not important. Time enough to answer all the questions will be provided, but this does not mean that you have all day. An overall time limit has been set. Divide the total time (in minutes) by the number of questions to determine the approximate time you have for each question.

5) Do not linger over difficult questions

If you come across a difficult question, mark it with a paper clip (useful to have along) and come back to it when you have been through the booklet. One caution if you do this – be sure to skip a number on your answer sheet as well. Check often to be sure that you have not lost your place and that you are marking in the row numbered the same as the question you are answering.

6) Read the questions

Be sure you know what the question asks! Many capable people are unsuccessful because they failed to *read* the questions correctly.

7) Answer all questions

Unless you have been instructed that a penalty will be deducted for incorrect answers, it is better to guess than to omit a question.

8) Speed tests

It is often better NOT to guess on speed tests. It has been found that on timed tests people are tempted to spend the last few seconds before time is called in marking answers at random – without even reading them – in the hope of picking up a few extra points. To discourage this practice, the instructions may warn you that your score will be "corrected" for guessing. That is, a penalty will be applied. The incorrect answers will be deducted from the correct ones, or some other penalty formula will be used.

9) Review your answers

If you finish before time is called, go back to the questions you guessed or omitted to give them further thought. Review other answers if you have time.

10) Return your test materials

If you are ready to leave before others have finished or time is called, take ALL your materials to the monitor and leave quietly. Never take any test material with you. The monitor can discover whose papers are not complete, and taking a test booklet may be grounds for disqualification.

VIII. EXAMINATION TECHNIQUES

1) Read the general instructions carefully. These are usually printed on the first page of the exam booklet. As a rule, these instructions refer to the timing of the examination; the fact that you should not start work until the signal and must stop work at a signal, etc. If there are any *special* instructions, such as a choice of questions to be answered, make sure that you note this instruction carefully.

2) When you are ready to start work on the examination, that is as soon as the signal has been given, read the instructions to each question booklet, underline any key words or phrases, such as *least, best, outline, describe* and the like. In this way you will tend to answer as requested rather than discover on reviewing your paper that you *listed without describing*, that you selected the *worst* choice rather than the *best* choice, etc.

3) If the examination is of the objective or multiple-choice type – that is, each question will also give a series of possible answers: A, B, C or D, and you are called upon to select the best answer and write the letter next to that answer on your answer paper – it is advisable to start answering each question in turn. There may be anywhere from 50 to 100 such questions in the three or four hours allotted and you can see how much time would be taken if you read through all the questions before beginning to answer any. Furthermore, if you come across a question or group of questions which you know would be difficult to answer, it would undoubtedly affect your handling of all the other questions.

4) If the examination is of the essay type and contains but a few questions, it is a moot point as to whether you should read all the questions before starting to answer any one. Of course, if you are given a choice – say five out of seven and the like – then it is essential to read all the questions so you can eliminate the two that are most difficult. If, however, you are asked to answer all the questions, there may be danger in trying to answer the easiest one first because you may find that you will spend too much time on it. The best technique is to answer the first question, then proceed to the second, etc.

5) Time your answers. Before the exam begins, write down the time it started, then add the time allowed for the examination and write down the time it must be completed, then divide the time available somewhat as follows:
    - If 3-1/2 hours are allowed, that would be 210 minutes. If you have 80 objective-type questions, that would be an average of 2-1/2 minutes per question. Allow yourself no more than 2 minutes per question, or a total of 160 minutes, which will permit about 50 minutes to review.
    - If for the time allotment of 210 minutes there are 7 essay questions to answer, that would average about 30 minutes a question. Give yourself only 25 minutes per question so that you have about 35 minutes to review.

6) The most important instruction is to *read each question* and make sure you know what is wanted. The second most important instruction is to *time yourself properly* so that you answer every question. The third most important instruction is to *answer every question*. Guess if you have to but include something for each question. Remember that you will receive no credit for a blank and will probably receive some credit if you write something in answer to an essay question. If you guess a letter – say "B" for a multiple-choice question – you may have guessed right. If you leave a blank as an answer to a multiple-choice question, the examiners may respect your feelings but it will not add a point to your score. Some exams may penalize you for wrong answers, so in such cases *only*, you may not want to guess unless you have some basis for your answer.

7) Suggestions
    a. Objective-type questions
        1. Examine the question booklet for proper sequence of pages and questions
        2. Read all instructions carefully
        3. Skip any question which seems too difficult; return to it after all other questions have been answered
        4. Apportion your time properly; do not spend too much time on any single question or group of questions

5. Note and underline key words – *all, most, fewest, least, best, worst, same, opposite,* etc.
6. Pay particular attention to negatives
7. Note unusual option, e.g., unduly long, short, complex, different or similar in content to the body of the question
8. Observe the use of "hedging" words – *probably, may, most likely,* etc.
9. Make sure that your answer is put next to the same number as the question
10. Do not second-guess unless you have good reason to believe the second answer is definitely more correct
11. Cross out original answer if you decide another answer is more accurate; do not erase until you are ready to hand your paper in
12. Answer all questions; guess unless instructed otherwise
13. Leave time for review

  b. Essay questions
  1. Read each question carefully
  2. Determine exactly what is wanted. Underline key words or phrases.
  3. Decide on outline or paragraph answer
  4. Include many different points and elements unless asked to develop any one or two points or elements
  5. Show impartiality by giving pros and cons unless directed to select one side only
  6. Make and write down any assumptions you find necessary to answer the questions
  7. Watch your English, grammar, punctuation and choice of words
  8. Time your answers; don't crowd material

8) Answering the essay question

Most essay questions can be answered by framing the specific response around several key words or ideas. Here are a few such key words or ideas:

M's: manpower, materials, methods, money, management
P's: purpose, program, policy, plan, procedure, practice, problems, pitfalls, personnel, public relations

  a. Six basic steps in handling problems:
  1. Preliminary plan and background development
  2. Collect information, data and facts
  3. Analyze and interpret information, data and facts
  4. Analyze and develop solutions as well as make recommendations
  5. Prepare report and sell recommendations
  6. Install recommendations and follow up effectiveness

  b. Pitfalls to avoid
  1. *Taking things for granted* – A statement of the situation does not necessarily imply that each of the elements is necessarily true; for example, a complaint may be invalid and biased so that all that can be taken for granted is that a complaint has been registered

2. *Considering only one side of a situation* – Wherever possible, indicate several alternatives and then point out the reasons you selected the best one
3. *Failing to indicate follow up* – Whenever your answer indicates action on your part, make certain that you will take proper follow-up action to see how successful your recommendations, procedures or actions turn out to be
4. *Taking too long in answering any single question* – Remember to time your answers properly

IX. AFTER THE TEST

Scoring procedures differ in detail among civil service jurisdictions although the general principles are the same. Whether the papers are hand-scored or graded by machine we have described, they are nearly always graded by number. That is, the person who marks the paper knows only the number – never the name – of the applicant. Not until all the papers have been graded will they be matched with names. If other tests, such as training and experience or oral interview ratings have been given, scores will be combined. Different parts of the examination usually have different weights. For example, the written test might count 60 percent of the final grade, and a rating of training and experience 40 percent. In many jurisdictions, veterans will have a certain number of points added to their grades.

After the final grade has been determined, the names are placed in grade order and an eligible list is established. There are various methods for resolving ties between those who get the same final grade – probably the most common is to place first the name of the person whose application was received first. Job offers are made from the eligible list in the order the names appear on it. You will be notified of your grade and your rank as soon as all these computations have been made. This will be done as rapidly as possible.

People who are found to meet the requirements in the announcement are called "eligibles." Their names are put on a list of eligible candidates. An eligible's chances of getting a job depend on how high he stands on this list and how fast agencies are filling jobs from the list.

When a job is to be filled from a list of eligibles, the agency asks for the names of people on the list of eligibles for that job. When the civil service commission receives this request, it sends to the agency the names of the three people highest on this list. Or, if the job to be filled has specialized requirements, the office sends the agency the names of the top three persons who meet these requirements from the general list.

The appointing officer makes a choice from among the three people whose names were sent to him. If the selected person accepts the appointment, the names of the others are put back on the list to be considered for future openings.

That is the rule in hiring from all kinds of eligible lists, whether they are for typist, carpenter, chemist, or something else. For every vacancy, the appointing officer has his choice of any one of the top three eligibles on the list. This explains why the person whose name is on top of the list sometimes does not get an appointment when some of the persons lower on the list do. If the appointing officer chooses the second or third eligible, the No. 1 eligible does not get a job at once, but stays on the list until he is appointed or the list is terminated.

X. HOW TO PASS THE INTERVIEW TEST

The examination for which you applied requires an oral interview test. You have already taken the written test and you are now being called for the interview test – the final part of the formal examination.

You may think that it is not possible to prepare for an interview test and that there are no procedures to follow during an interview. Our purpose is to point out some things you can do in advance that will help you and some good rules to follow and pitfalls to avoid while you are being interviewed.

What is an interview supposed to test?

The written examination is designed to test the technical knowledge and competence of the candidate; the oral is designed to evaluate intangible qualities, not readily measured otherwise, and to establish a list showing the relative fitness of each candidate – as measured against his competitors – for the position sought. Scoring is not on the basis of "right" and "wrong," but on a sliding scale of values ranging from "not passable" to "outstanding." As a matter of fact, it is possible to achieve a relatively low score without a single "incorrect" answer because of evident weakness in the qualities being measured.

Occasionally, an examination may consist entirely of an oral test – either an individual or a group oral. In such cases, information is sought concerning the technical knowledges and abilities of the candidate, since there has been no written examination for this purpose. More commonly, however, an oral test is used to supplement a written examination.

Who conducts interviews?

The composition of oral boards varies among different jurisdictions. In nearly all, a representative of the personnel department serves as chairman. One of the members of the board may be a representative of the department in which the candidate would work. In some cases, "outside experts" are used, and, frequently, a businessman or some other representative of the general public is asked to serve. Labor and management or other special groups may be represented. The aim is to secure the services of experts in the appropriate field.

However the board is composed, it is a good idea (and not at all improper or unethical) to ascertain in advance of the interview who the members are and what groups they represent. When you are introduced to them, you will have some idea of their backgrounds and interests, and at least you will not stutter and stammer over their names.

What should be done before the interview?

While knowledge about the board members is useful and takes some of the surprise element out of the interview, there is other preparation which is more substantive. It *is* possible to prepare for an oral interview – in several ways:

1) Keep a copy of your application and review it carefully before the interview

This may be the only document before the oral board, and the starting point of the interview. Know what education and experience you have listed there, and the sequence and dates of all of it. Sometimes the board will ask you to review the highlights of your experience for them; you should not have to hem and haw doing it.

2) Study the class specification and the examination announcement

Usually, the oral board has one or both of these to guide them. The qualities, characteristics or knowledges required by the position sought are stated in these documents. They offer valuable clues as to the nature of the oral interview. For example, if the job involves supervisory responsibilities, the announcement will usually indicate that knowledge of modern supervisory methods and the qualifications of the candidate as a supervisor will be tested. If so, you can expect such questions, frequently in the form of a hypothetical situation which you are expected to solve. NEVER go into an oral without knowledge of the duties and responsibilities of the job you seek.

3) Think through each qualification required

Try to visualize the kind of questions you would ask if you were a board member. How well could you answer them? Try especially to appraise your own knowledge and background in each area, *measured against the job sought*, and identify any areas in which you are weak. Be critical and realistic – do not flatter yourself.

4) Do some general reading in areas in which you feel you may be weak

For example, if the job involves supervision and your past experience has NOT, some general reading in supervisory methods and practices, particularly in the field of human relations, might be useful. Do NOT study agency procedures or detailed manuals. The oral board will be testing your understanding and capacity, not your memory.

5) Get a good night's sleep and watch your general health and mental attitude

You will want a clear head at the interview. Take care of a cold or any other minor ailment, and of course, no hangovers.

What should be done on the day of the interview?

Now comes the day of the interview itself. Give yourself plenty of time to get there. Plan to arrive somewhat ahead of the scheduled time, particularly if your appointment is in the fore part of the day. If a previous candidate fails to appear, the board might be ready for you a bit early. By early afternoon an oral board is almost invariably behind schedule if there are many candidates, and you may have to wait. Take along a book or magazine to read, or your application to review, but leave any extraneous material in the waiting room when you go in for your interview. In any event, relax and compose yourself.

The matter of dress is important. The board is forming impressions about you – from your experience, your manners, your attitude, and your appearance. Give your personal appearance careful attention. Dress your best, but not your flashiest. Choose conservative, appropriate clothing, and be sure it is immaculate. This is a business interview, and your appearance should indicate that you regard it as such. Besides, being well groomed and properly dressed will help boost your confidence.

Sooner or later, someone will call your name and escort you into the interview room. *This is it.* From here on you are on your own. It is too late for any more preparation. But remember, you asked for this opportunity to prove your fitness, and you are here because your request was granted.

What happens when you go in?

The usual sequence of events will be as follows: The clerk (who is often the board stenographer) will introduce you to the chairman of the oral board, who will introduce you to the other members of the board. Acknowledge the introductions before you sit down. Do not be surprised if you find a microphone facing you or a stenotypist sitting by. Oral interviews are usually recorded in the event of an appeal or other review.

Usually the chairman of the board will open the interview by reviewing the highlights of your education and work experience from your application – primarily for the benefit of the other members of the board, as well as to get the material into the record. Do not interrupt or comment unless there is an error or significant misinterpretation; if that is the case, do not hesitate. But do not quibble about insignificant matters. Also, he will usually ask you some question about your education, experience or your present job – partly to get you to start talking and to establish the interviewing "rapport." He may start the actual questioning, or turn it over to one of the other members. Frequently, each member undertakes the questioning on a particular area, one in which he is perhaps most competent, so you can expect each member to participate in the examination. Because time is limited, you may also expect some rather abrupt switches in the direction the questioning takes, so do not be upset by it. Normally, a board member will not pursue a single line of questioning unless he discovers a particular strength or weakness.

After each member has participated, the chairman will usually ask whether any member has any further questions, then will ask you if you have anything you wish to add. Unless you are expecting this question, it may floor you. Worse, it may start you off on an extended, extemporaneous speech. The board is not usually seeking more information. The question is principally to offer you a last opportunity to present further qualifications or to indicate that you have nothing to add. So, if you feel that a significant qualification or characteristic has been overlooked, it is proper to point it out in a sentence or so. Do not compliment the board on the thoroughness of their examination – they have been sketchy, and you know it. If you wish, merely say, "No thank you, I have nothing further to add." This is a point where you can "talk yourself out" of a good impression or fail to present an important bit of information. Remember, *you close the interview yourself*.

The chairman will then say, "That is all, Mr. _____, thank you." Do not be startled; the interview is over, and quicker than you think. Thank him, gather your belongings and take your leave. Save your sigh of relief for the other side of the door.

How to put your best foot forward

Throughout this entire process, you may feel that the board individually and collectively is trying to pierce your defenses, seek out your hidden weaknesses and embarrass and confuse you. Actually, this is not true. They are obliged to make an appraisal of your qualifications for the job you are seeking, and they want to see you in your best light. Remember, they must interview all candidates and a non-cooperative candidate may become a failure in spite of their best efforts to bring out his qualifications. Here are 15 suggestions that will help you:

1) Be natural – Keep your attitude confident, not cocky

If you are not confident that you can do the job, do not expect the board to be. Do not apologize for your weaknesses, try to bring out your strong points. The board is interested in a positive, not negative, presentation. Cockiness will antagonize any board member and make him wonder if you are covering up a weakness by a false show of strength.

2) Get comfortable, but don't lounge or sprawl

Sit erectly but not stiffly. A careless posture may lead the board to conclude that you are careless in other things, or at least that you are not impressed by the importance of the occasion. Either conclusion is natural, even if incorrect. Do not fuss with your clothing, a pencil or an ashtray. Your hands may occasionally be useful to emphasize a point; do not let them become a point of distraction.

3) Do not wisecrack or make small talk

This is a serious situation, and your attitude should show that you consider it as such. Further, the time of the board is limited – they do not want to waste it, and neither should you.

4) Do not exaggerate your experience or abilities
In the first place, from information in the application or other interviews and sources, the board may know more about you than you think. Secondly, you probably will not get away with it. An experienced board is rather adept at spotting such a situation, so do not take the chance.

5) If you know a board member, do not make a point of it, yet do not hide it
Certainly you are not fooling him, and probably not the other members of the board. Do not try to take advantage of your acquaintanceship – it will probably do you little good.

6) Do not dominate the interview
Let the board do that. They will give you the clues – do not assume that you have to do all the talking. Realize that the board has a number of questions to ask you, and do not try to take up all the interview time by showing off your extensive knowledge of the answer to the first one.

7) Be attentive
You only have 20 minutes or so, and you should keep your attention at its sharpest throughout. When a member is addressing a problem or question to you, give him your undivided attention. Address your reply principally to him, but do not exclude the other board members.

8) Do not interrupt
A board member may be stating a problem for you to analyze. He will ask you a question when the time comes. Let him state the problem, and wait for the question.

9) Make sure you understand the question
Do not try to answer until you are sure what the question is. If it is not clear, restate it in your own words or ask the board member to clarify it for you. However, do not haggle about minor elements.

10) Reply promptly but not hastily
A common entry on oral board rating sheets is "candidate responded readily," or "candidate hesitated in replies." Respond as promptly and quickly as you can, but do not jump to a hasty, ill-considered answer.

11) Do not be peremptory in your answers
A brief answer is proper – but do not fire your answer back. That is a losing game from your point of view. The board member can probably ask questions much faster than you can answer them.

12) Do not try to create the answer you think the board member wants
He is interested in what kind of mind you have and how it works – not in playing games. Furthermore, he can usually spot this practice and will actually grade you down on it.

13) Do not switch sides in your reply merely to agree with a board member
Frequently, a member will take a contrary position merely to draw you out and to see if you are willing and able to defend your point of view. Do not start a debate, yet do not surrender a good position. If a position is worth taking, it is worth defending.

14) Do not be afraid to admit an error in judgment if you are shown to be wrong
The board knows that you are forced to reply without any opportunity for careful consideration. Your answer may be demonstrably wrong. If so, admit it and get on with the interview.

15) Do not dwell at length on your present job
The opening question may relate to your present assignment. Answer the question but do not go into an extended discussion. You are being examined for a *new* job, not your present one. As a matter of fact, try to phrase ALL your answers in terms of the job for which you are being examined.

Basis of Rating
Probably you will forget most of these "do's" and "don'ts" when you walk into the oral interview room. Even remembering them all will not ensure you a passing grade. Perhaps you did not have the qualifications in the first place. But remembering them will help you to put your best foot forward, without treading on the toes of the board members.

Rumor and popular opinion to the contrary notwithstanding, an oral board wants you to make the best appearance possible. They know you are under pressure – but they also want to see how you respond to it as a guide to what your reaction would be under the pressures of the job you seek. They will be influenced by the degree of poise you display, the personal traits you show and the manner in which you respond.

ABOUT THIS BOOK

This book contains tests divided into Examination Sections. Go through each test, answering every question in the margin. We have also attached a sample answer sheet at the back of the book that can be removed and used. At the end of each test look at the answer key and check your answers. On the ones you got wrong, look at the right answer choice and learn. Do not fill in the answers first. Do not memorize the questions and answers, but understand the answer and principles involved. On your test, the questions will likely be different from the samples. Questions are changed and new ones added. If you understand these past questions you should have success with any changes that arise. Tests may consist of several types of questions. We have additional books on each subject should more study be advisable or necessary for you. Finally, the more you study, the better prepared you will be. This book is intended to be the last thing you study before you walk into the examination room. Prior study of relevant texts is also recommended. NLC publishes some of these in our Fundamental Series. Knowledge and good sense are important factors in passing your exam. Good luck also helps. So now study this Passbook, absorb the material contained within and take that knowledge into the examination. Then do your best to pass that exam.

EXAMINATION SECTION

EXAMINATION SECTION
TEST 1

DIRECTIONS: Each question or incomplete statement is followed by several suggested answers or completions. Select the one that BEST answers the question or completes the statement. *PRINT THE LETTER OF THE CORRECT ANSWER IN THE SPACE AT THE RIGHT.*

Questions 1-6.

DIRECTIONS: Questions 1 through 6 are to be answered on the basis of the circuit diagram below. All switches are initially open.

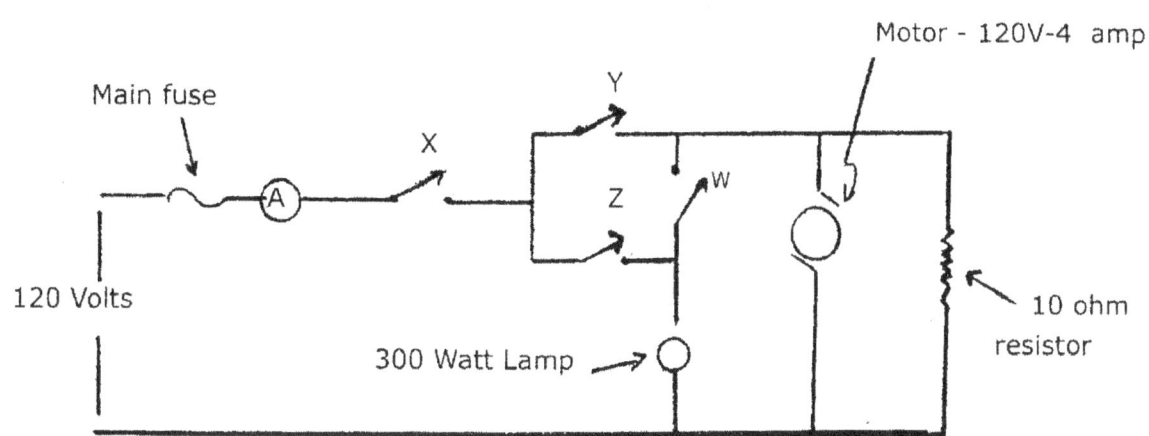

1. To light the 300 watt lamp, the following switches MUST be closed: 1.____

   A. X and Y   B. Y and Z   C. X and Z   D. X and W

2. If all of the switches W, X, Y, and Z are closed, the following will happen: 2.____

   A. The lamp will light and the motor will rotate
   B. The lamp will light and the motor will not rotate
   C. The lamp will not light and the motor will not rotate
   D. A short circuit will occur and the main fuse will blow

3. With 120 volts applied across the 10 ohm resistor, the current drawn by the resistor is _____ amp(s). 3.____

   A. 1/12   B. 1.2   C. 12   D. 1200

4. With 120 volts applied to the 10 ohm resistor, the power used by the resistor is _____ kw. 4.____

   A. 1.44   B. 1.2   C. .144   D. .12

5. The current drawn by the 300 watt lamp when lighted should be APPROXIMATELY _____ amps. 5.____

   A. 2.5   B. 3.6   C. 25   D. 36

1

6. In the circuit shown, the symbol A is used to indicate a (n)

   A. ammeter
   B. *and* circuit
   C. voltmeter
   D. wattmeter

7. Of the following materials, the BEST conductor of electricity is

   A. iron
   B. copper
   C. aluminum
   D. glass

8. The sum of 6'6", 5'9", and 2' 1 1/2" is

   A. 13'4 1/2"
   B. 13'6 1/2"
   C. 14'4 1/2"
   D. 14'6 1/2"

9.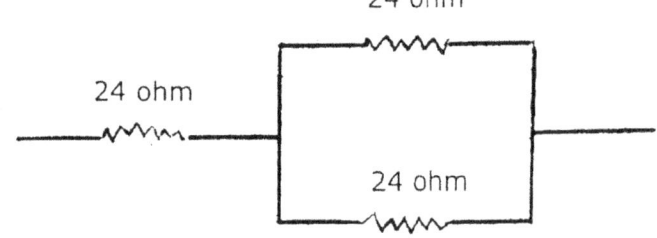

   The equivalent resistance of the three resistors shown in the sketch above is _____ ohms.

   A. 8
   B. 24
   C. 36
   D. 72

10.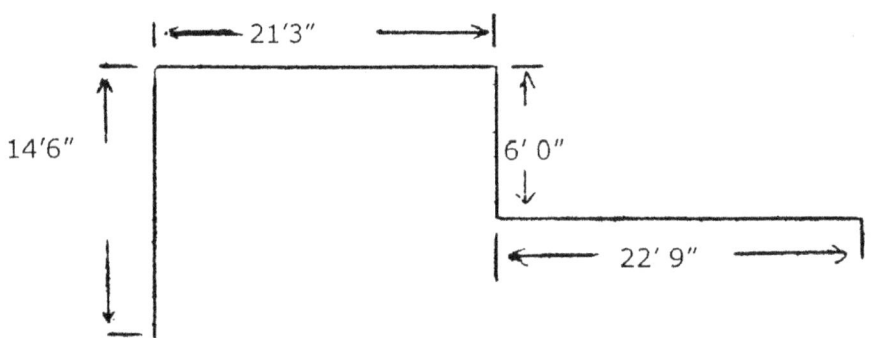

    The TOTAL length of electrical conduit that must be run along the path shown on the diagram above is

    A. 63'8"
    B. 64'6"
    C. 65'6"
    D. 66'8"

11. Of the following electrical devices, the one that is NOT normally used in direct current electrical circuits is a (n)

    A. circuit breaker
    B. double-pole switch
    C. transformer
    D. inverter

12. The number of 120-volt light bulbs that should NORMALLY be connected in series across a 600-volt electric line is

    A. 1
    B. 2
    C. 3
    D. 5

13. Of the following motors, the one that does NOT have any brushes is the _____ motor.   13._____

    A. d.c. shunt   B. d.c. series
    C. squirrel cage induction   D. compound

14. Of the following materials, the one that is COMMONLY used as an electric heating element in an electric heater is   14._____

    A. zinc   B. brass
    C. terne plate   D. nichrome

Questions 15-25.

DIRECTIONS: Questions 15 through 25 are to be answered on the basis of the instruments listed below. Each instrument is listed with an identifying number in front of it.

    1 - Hygrometer   9 - Vernier caliper
    2 - Ammeter   10 - Wire gage
    3 - Voltmeter   11 - 6-foot folding rule
    4 - Wattmeter   12 - Architect's scale
    5 - Megger   13 - Planimeter
    6 - Oscilloscope   14 - Engineer's scale
    7 - Frequency meter   15 - Ohmmeter
    8 - Micrometer

15. The instrument that should be used to accurately measure the resistance of a 4,700 ohm resistor is Number   15._____

    A. 3   B. 4   C. 7   D. 15

16. To measure the current in an electrical circuit, the instrument that should be used is Number   16._____

    A. 2   B. 7   C. 8   D. 15

17. To measure the insulation resistance of a rubber-covered electrical cable, the instrument that should be used is Number   17._____

    A. 4   B. 5   C. 8   D. 15

18. An AC motor is hooked up to a power distribution box.   18._____
    In order to check the voltage at the motor terminals, the instrument that should be used is Number

    A. 2   B. 3   C. 4   D. 7

19. To measure the shaft diameter of a motor accurately to one-thousandth of an inch, the instrument that should be used is Number   19._____

    A. 8   B. 10   C. 11   D. 14

20. The instrument that should be used to determine whether 25 Hz. or 60 Hz. is present in an electrical circuit is Number   20._____

    A. 4   B. 5   C. 7   D. 8

21. Of the following, the PROPER instrument to use to determine the diameter of the conductor of a piece of electrical hook-up wire is Number

    A. 10   B. 11   C. 12   D. 14

22. The amount of electrical power being used in a balanced three-phase circuit should be measured with Number

    A. 2   B. 3   C. 4   D. 5

23. The electrical wave form at a given point in an electronic circuit can be observed with Number

    A. 2   B. 3   C. 6   D. 7

24. The PROPER instrument to use for measuring the width of a door is Number

    A. 11   B. 12   C. 13   D. 14

25. A one-inch hole with a tolerance of plus or minus three-thousandths is reamed in a steel block.
    The PROPER instrument to use to accurately check the diameter of the hole is Number

    A. 8   B. 9   C. 11   D. 14

KEY (CORRECT ANSWERS)

1. C
2. A
3. C
4. A
5. A

6. A
7. B
8. C
9. C
10. B

11. C
12. D
13. C
14. D
15. D

16. A
17. B
18. B
19. A
20. C

21. A
22. C
23. C
24. A
25. B

TEST 2

DIRECTIONS: Each question or incomplete statement is followed by several suggested answers or completions. Select the one that BEST answers the question or completes the statement. *PRINT THE LETTER OF THE CORRECT ANSWER IN THE SPACE AT THE RIGHT.*

1. The number of conductors required to connect a 3-phase delta connected heater bank to an electric power panel board is

    A. 2 B. 3 C. 4 D. 5

    1._____

2. Of the following, the wire size that is MOST commonly used for branch lighting circuits in homes is _____ A.W.G.

    A. #12 B. #8 C. #6 D. #4

    2._____

3. When installing electrical circuits, the tool that should be used to pull wire through a conduit is a

    A. mandrel
    B. snake
    C. rod
    D. pulling iron

    3._____

4. Of the following AC voltages, the LOWEST voltage that a neon test lamp can detect is _____ volts.

    A. 6 B. 12 C. 80 D. 120

    4._____

5. Of the following, the BEST procedure to use when storing tools that are subject to rusting is to

    A. apply a thin coating of soap onto the tools
    B. apply a light coating of oil to the tools
    C. wrap the tools in clean cheesecloth
    D. place the tools in a covered container

    5._____

6. If a 3 1/2 inch long nail is required to nail wood framing members together, the nail size to use should be

    A. 2d B. 4d C. 16d D. 60d

    6._____

7. Of the four motors listed below, the one that can operate only on alternating current is a(n) _____ motor.

    A. series
    B. shunt
    C. compound
    D. induction

    7._____

8. The sum of 1/3 + 2/5 + 5/6 is

    A. 1 17/30 B. 1 3/5 C. 1 15/24 D. 1 5/6

    8._____

9. Of the following instruments, the one that should be used to measure the state of charge of a lead-acid storage battery is a(n)

    A. ammeter
    B. ohmmeter
    C. hydrometer
    D. thermometer

    9._____

5

10. If three 1 1/2 volt dry cell batteries are wired in series, the TOTAL voltage provided by the three batteries is _____ volts.

    A. 1.5 B. 3 C. 4.5 D. 6.0

11. Taking into account time and one-half payment for time over 40 hours of work, the gross pay of an employee who works 43 hours in a week at a rate of pay of $10.68 per hour is

    A. $427.20 B. $459.24 C. $475.26 D. $491.28

12. The sum of 0.365 + 3.941 + 10.676 + 0.784 is

    A. 13.766 B. 15.666 C. 15.756 D. 15.766

13. In order to transmit mechanical power between two rotating shafts at right angles to each other, two gears are used. Of the following, the type of gears that should be used are _____ gears.

    A. herringbone
    B. spur
    C. bevel
    D. rack and pinion

14. To properly ground the service electrical equipment in a building, a ground connection should be made to _____ the building.

    A. the waste or soil line leaving
    B. the vent line going to the exterior of
    C. any steel beam in
    D. the cold water line entering

15. The area of the triangle shown at the right is _____ square inches.
    A. 120
    B. 240
    C. 360
    D. 480

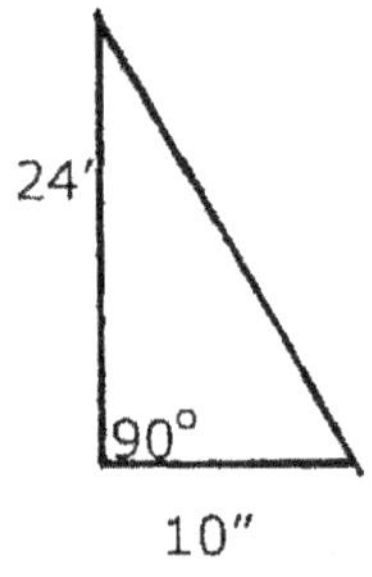

Questions 16-25.

DIRECTIONS: Questions 16 through 25 are to be answered on the basis of the tools shown on the next page. The tools are not shown to scale. Each tool is shown with an identifying number alongside it.

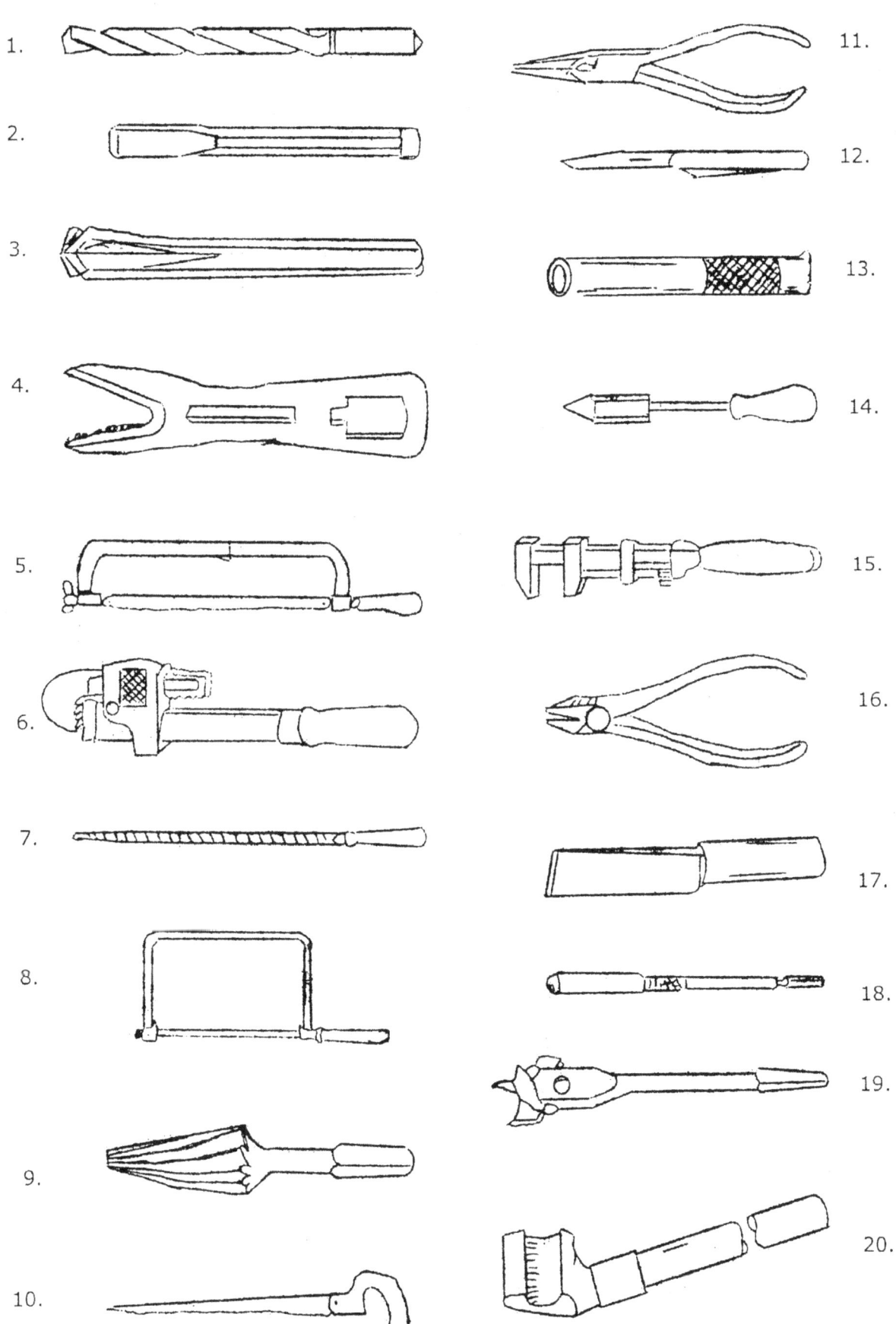

16. The tool that should be used for cutting thin wall steel conduit is Number 16._____
    A. 5   B. 8   C. 10   D. 16

17. The tool that should be used for cutting a 1 7/8 inch diameter hole in a wood joist is Number 17._____
    A. 3   B. 9   C. 14   D. 19

18. The tool that should be used for soldering splices in electrical wire is Number 18._____
    A. 3   B. 7   C. 13   D. 14

19. After cutting off a piece of 3/4 inch diameter electrical conduit, the tool that should be used for removing a burr from the inside of the conduit is Number 19._____
    A. 9   B. 11   C. 12   D. 14

20. The tool that should be used for turning a coupling onto a threaded conduit is Number 20._____
    A. 6   B. 11   C. 15   D. 16

21. The tool that should be used for cutting wood lathing in plaster walls is Number 21._____
    A. 5   B. 7   C. 10   D. 12

22. The tool that should be used for drilling a 3/8 inch diameter hole in a steel beam is Number 22._____
    A. 1   B. 2   C. 3   D. 9

23. Of the following, the BEST tool to use for stripping insulation from electrical hook-up wire is Number 23._____
    A. 11   B. 12   C. 15   D. 20

24. The tool that should be used for bending an electrical wire around a terminal post is Number 24._____
    A. 4   B. 11   C. 15   D. 16

25. The tool that should be used for cutting electrical hookup wire is Number 25._____
    A. 5   B. 12   C. 16   D. 17

KEY (CORRECT ANSWERS)

1. B
2. A
3. B
4. C
5. B

6. C
7. D
8. A
9. C
10. C

11. C
12. D
13. C
14. D
15. A

16. A
17. D
18. D
19. A
20. A

21. C
22. A
23. B
24. B
25. C

TEST 3

DIRECTIONS: Each question or incomplete statement is followed by several suggested answers or completions. Select the one that BEST answers the question or completes the statement. *PRINT THE LETTER OF THE CORRECT ANSWER IN THE SPACE AT THE RIGHT.*

1. An electric circuit has current flowing through it. The panel board switch feeding the circuit is opened, causing arcing across the switch contacts.
   Generally, this arcing is caused by

   A. a lack of energy storage in the circuit
   B. electrical energy stored by a capacitor
   C. electrical energy stored by a resistor
   D. magnetic energy induced by an inductance

   1.____

2. MOST filter capacitors in radios have a capacity rating given in

   A. microvolts   B. milliamps
   C. millihenries   D. microfarads

   2.____

3. Of the following, the electrical wire size that is COMMONLY used for telephone circuits is _____ A.W.G.

   A. #6   B. #10   C. #12   D. #22

   3.____

Questions 4-9.

DIRECTIONS: Questions 4 through 9 are to be answered on the basis of the electrical circuit diagram shown below, where letters are used to identify various circuit components.

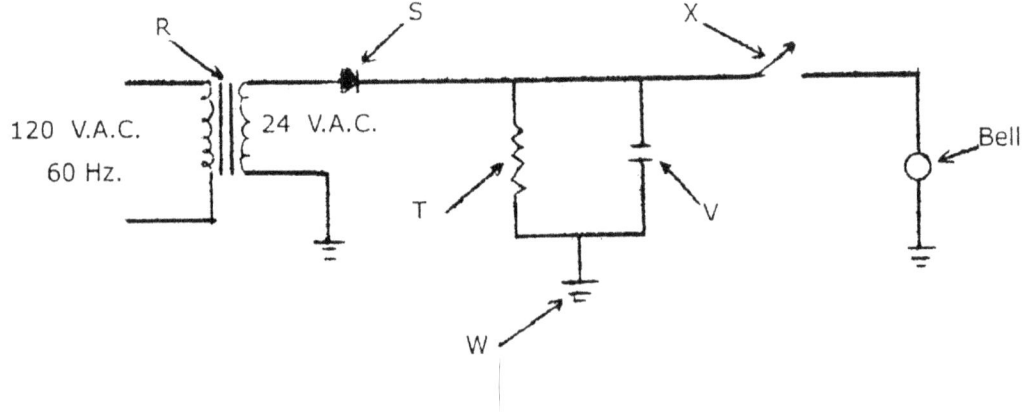

4. The device indicated by the letter R is a

   A. capacitor   B. converter
   C. resistor   D. transformer

   4.____

5. The device indicated by the letter S is a

   A. transistor   B. diode
   C. thermistor   D. directional relay

   5.____

6. The devices indicated by the letters T and V are used together to _____ components of the secondary current.

   A. reduce the AC
   B. reduce the DC
   C. transform the AC
   D. invert the AC

7. The letter W points to a standard electrical symbol for a

   A. wire
   B. ground
   C. terminal
   D. lightning arrestor

8. Closing switch X will apply the following type of voltage to the bell:

   A. 60 Hz. AC
   B. DC
   C. pulsating AC
   D. 120 Hz. AC

9. The circuit shown contains a _____ rectifier.

   A. mercury-arc
   B. full-wave
   C. bridge
   D. half-wave

10. A bolt specified as 1/4-28 means the following:
    The

    A. bolt is 1/4 inch in diameter and has 28 threads per inch
    B. bolt is 1/4 inch in diameter and is 2.8 inches long
    C. bolt is 1/4 inch long and has 28 threads
    D. threaded portion of the bolt is 1/4 inch long and has 28 threads per inch

11. When cutting 0.045-inch thickness sheet metal, it is BEST to use a hacksaw blade that has _____ teeth per inch.

    A. 7
    B. 12
    C. 18
    D. 32

12. To accurately tighten a bolt to 28 foot-pounds, it is BEST to use a(n) _____ wrench.

    A. pipe
    B. open end
    C. box
    D. torque

13. When bending a 2-inch diameter conduit, the CORRECT tool to use is a

    A. hickey
    B. pipe wrench
    C. hydraulic bender
    D. stock and die

14. When soldering two #20 A.W.G. copper wires together to form a splice, the solder that SHOULD be used is _____ solder.

    A. acid-core
    B. solid-core
    C. rosin-core
    D. liquid

15. A bathroom heating unit draws 10 amperes at 115 volts.
    The hot resistance of the heating unit should be _____ ohms.

    A. .08
    B. 8
    C. 11.5
    D. 1150

16. Of the following materials, the one that is NOT suitable as an electrical insulator is

    A. glass
    B. mica
    C. rubber
    D. platinum

17. An air conditioning unit is rated at 1000 watts. The unit is run for 10 hours per day, five days per week.
If the cost for electrical energy is 5 cents per kilowatt-hour, the weekly cost for electricity should be

    A. 25¢ B. 50¢ C. $2.50 D. $25.00

18. If a fuse is protecting the circuit of a 15 ohm electric heater and it is designed to blow out at a current exceeding 10 amperes, the MAXIMUM voltage from among the following that should be applied across the terminals of the heater is _____ volts.

    A. 110 B. 120 C. 160 D. 600

19. Before opening a pneumatic hose connection, it is important to remove pressure from the hose line PRIMARILY to avoid

    A. losing air
    B. personal injury
    C. damage to the hose connection
    D. a build-up of pressure in the air compressor

20. If the scale on a shop drawing is 1/4 inch to the foot, then a part which measures 3 3/8 inches long on the drawing has an ACTUAL length of _____ feet _____ inches.

    A. 12; 6 B. 13; 6 C. 13; 9 D. 14; 9

21. The function that is USUALLY performed by a motor controller is to

    A. start and stop a motor
    B. protect a motor from a short circuit
    C. prevent bearing failure of a motor
    D. control the brush wear in a motor

22. Of the following galvanized sheet metal electrical outlet boxes, the one that is NOT a commonly used size is the _____ box.

    A. 4" square
    B. 4" octagonal
    C. 4" x 2 1/8"
    D. 4" x 1"

23. When soldering a transistor into a circuit, it is MOST important to protect the transistor from

    A. the application of an excess of rosin flux
    B. excessive heat
    C. the application of an excess of solder
    D. too much pressure

24. When installing BX type cable, it is important to protect the wires in the cable from the cut ends of the armored sheath.
The APPROVED method of providing this protection is to

    A. use a fiber or plastic insulating bushing
    B. file the cut ends of the sheath smooth
    C. use a connector where the cable enters a junction box
    D. tie the wires into an Underwriter's knot

25. While lifting a heavy piece of equipment off the floor, a person should NOT

    A. twist his body
    B. grasp it firmly
    C. maintain a solid footing on the ground
    D. bend his knees

26. It is important that metal cabinets and panels that house electrical equipment should be grounded PRIMARILY in order to

    A. prevent short circuits from occurring
    B. keep all circuits at ground potential
    C. minimize shock hazards
    D. reduce the effects of electrolytic corrosion

27. A foreman explains a technical procedure to a new employee. If the employee does not understand the instructions he has received, it would be BEST if he were to

    A. follow the procedure as best he could
    B. ask the foreman to explain it to him again
    C. avoid following the procedure
    D. ask the foreman to give him other work

28. Of the following, the BEST connectors to use when mounting an electrical panel box directly onto a concrete wall are

    A. threaded studs   B. machine screws
    C. lag screws   D. expansion bolts

29. Of the following, the BEST instrument to use to measure the small gap between relay contacts is

    A. a micrometer   B. a feeler gage
    C. inside calipers   D. a plug gage

30. A POSSIBLE result of mounting a 40 ampere fuse in a fuse box for a circuit requiring a 20 ampere fuse is that the 40 ampere fuse may

    A. provide twice as much protection to the circuit from overloads
    B. blow more easily than the smaller fuse due to an overload
    C. cause serious damage to the circuit from an overload
    D. reduce power consumption in the circuit

KEY (CORRECT ANSWERS)

1.	D	16.	D
2.	D	17.	C
3.	D	18.	B
4.	D	19.	B
5.	B	20.	B
6.	A	21.	A
7.	B	22.	D
8.	B	23.	B
9.	D	24.	A
10.	A	25.	A
11.	D	26.	C
12.	D	27.	B
13.	C	28.	D
14.	C	29.	B
15.	C	30.	C

EXAMINATION SECTION
TEST 1

DIRECTIONS: Each question or incomplete statement is followed by several suggested answers or completions. Select the one that BEST answers the question or completes the statement. *PRINT THE LETTER OF THE CORRECT ANSWER IN THE SPACE AT THE RIGHT.*

1. A piece of equipment listed as drawing 100 watts is plugged into a 24 volt DC circuit. The MINIMUM size fuse which would handle this load is _____ amps.

   A. 2   B. 3   C. 4   D. 5

2. A resistor of 1000 ohms has 3 milliamperes passing through it. The voltage drop across the resistor is _____ volts.

   A. 3   B. 6   C. 15   D. 300

3. A certain resistor has three colored bands around it. The one nearest the end is green, the next one is orange, and the next one is red.
   The value of this register is _____ ohms.

   A. 74   B. 270   C. 5300   D. 64,000

4. An alternating voltage is applied to a capacitor.
   As the frequency of this voltage is increased, the impedance of the capacitor

   A. increases
   B. decreases
   C. remains the same
   D. increases or decreases depending on its construction

5. The one of the following that is NOT a part of a transistor is the

   A. emitter   B. collector   C. base   D. grid

6. A 0.2 ufd capacitor is connected in series with a 0.1 ufd capacitor.
   The resultant capacity is _____ ufd.

   A. 0.067   B. 0.67   C. 0.15   D. 0.3

7. The term *Hertz* means the same as

   A. degrees Centigrade   B. degrees Fahrenheit
   C. revolutions per minute   D. cycles per second

8. In an electrolytic condenser, the dielectric material is

   A. mylar   B. aluminum oxide
   C. paper   D. sodium chloride

9. The amount by which a transformer will step up or step down a voltage is determined by its

   A. inductance   B. resistance
   C. magnetic flux   D. turns ratio

15

10. The electrolyte in a lead plate storage battery (such as that used in cars) is   10.____

    A. aluminum hydroxide   B. sulfuric acid
    C. hydrochloric acid   D. sodium chloride

11. A diode in an electronic circuit is used to   11.____

    A. amplify   B. oscillate   C. attenuate   D. rectify

12. The MAIN function of a filter in a power supply is to   12.____

    A. increase the voltage
    B. decrease the load
    C. smooth out the peaks of the ripple frequency
    D. protect the power transformer

13. The expression *pH* as applied to a liquid refers to its   13.____

    A. salinity   B. specific gravity
    C. viscosity   D. acidity/alkalinity

14. The speed of a synchronous motor is controlled by   14.____

    A. the voltage applied to it
    B. the frequency of the alternating current applied to it
    C. a mechanical governor
    D. the current it draws

15. The capacitance of a condenser is measured in   15.____

    A. oersteds   B. ohms   C. henrys   D. farads

16. The power lost in a 20-ohm resistor, with 0.25 amperes passing through it, is _____   16.____
    watts.

    A. 0.04   B. 0.4   C. 1.25   D. 5

17. When soldering a transistor into a circuit, it is good practice to clamp a pair of long-nosed   17.____
    pliers on the lead between the transistor and the end being soldered.
    This is done to

    A. prevent the lead from moving
    B. prevent burning the fingers
    C. ground the transistor
    D. prevent the soldering iron's heat from reaching the transistor

18. The commutator of a motor should   18.____

    A. not be lubricated
    B. be lubricated with light oil
    C. be lubricated with heavy grease
    D. be lubricated with hypoid oil

19. The band of wavelengths of visible light covers   19.____

    A. 20-50 centimeters   B. 10-50 meters
    C. 400-700 millimicrons   D. 400-700 millimeters

20. The heat reaching the earth from the sun is transmitted by   20.____

    A. ions   B. convection
    C. radiation   D. cosmic rays

21. A *thermistor* is a   21.____

    A. type of thermometer
    B. high power transistor
    C. water heating device
    D. resistor with a negative temperature coefficient

22. In an AC circuit, the term *power factor* refers to the   22.____

    A. horsepower
    B. BTU per watt
    C. ratio of the resistance to the impedance
    D. kilowatts per horsepower

23.   23.____

    In the above circuit, the TOTAL resistance between points A and B is _____ ohms.

    A. 5   B. 14   C. 20   D. 45

24. Of the four gases listed below, the one that is NOT an air pollutant is   24.____

    A. carbon dioxide   B. carbon monoxide
    C. sulfur dioxide   D. hydrogen sulfide

25. The term *milli-roentgen* refers to a unit of   25.____

    A. x-ray radiation   B. ultraviolet radiation
    C. reluctance   D. inductance

26. An AC motor drawing 12 amps is plugged into a 15-amp circuit. The starting surge of the motor, however, is 18 amps.   26.____
    The PROPER type of fuse to be used in this situation is

    A. varistor   B. thermistor
    C. fast-blow   D. slow-blow

27. Degrees Kelvin is numerically equal to degrees   27.____

    A. Fahrenheit - 15   B. Centigrade + 27
    C. Fahrenheit + 135   D. Centigrade + 273

28. In the term *micromicrofarads*, the prefix *micromicro* means multiply by

   A. 10^6 B. 10^3 C. 10^{-12} D. 10^{-6}

29. One horsepower is equivalent to

   A. 276 joules
   B. 746 kilowatts
   C. 746 watts
   D. 291 calories

30. Laminated iron or steel is generally used instead of solid metal in the construction of the field and armature cores in motors and generators.
   The reason for this is to

   A. reduce eddy current losses
   B. increase the voltage
   C. decrease the flux
   D. reduce the cost

31. The instrument used to measure current flow is called a(n)

   A. wattmeter
   B. voltmeter
   C. ammeter
   D. wavemeter

32. Reversing the polarity of the voltage applied to a mica condenser will

   A. destroy it
   B. increase its capacity
   C. decrease its capacity
   D. have no effect on it

33. The *decibel* is the unit used for expressing

   A. light levels
   B. DC voltage
   C. AC current
   D. the ratio between two quantities of either electrical or sound energy

34. In a three-phase Y-connected AC power system, the voltage from leg to ground is 120 volts.
   The voltage between each pair of hot legs is _____ volts.

   A. 160   B. 180   C. 208   D. 240

35. An hygrometer is an instrument which measures

   A. humidity
   B. temperature
   C. specific gravity
   D. luminosity

36. The impedance ratio of a transformer varies _____ the turns ratio.

   A. directly with
   B. as the square of
   C. as the square root of
   D. inversely with

37. Two resistors are connected in series. The current through these resistors is 3 amperes. Resistance #1 has a value of fifty ohms; resistance #2 has a voltage drop of fifty volts across its terminals.
   The TOTAL impressed voltage (across both resistors) is _____ volts.

   A. 100   B. 150   C. 200   D. 250

38. The piece of equipment that should be used to obtain more than one voltage from a fixed voltage direct current source is a(n)

    A. multitap transformer
    B. resistance-type voltage divider
    C. autotransformer
    D. copper oxide rectifier

38.____

39. The ratio of peak to effective (rms) voltage value of a sine wave is

    A. 2 to 1   B. 1 to 2   C. .707 to 1   D. 1.414 to 1

39.____

40. Two coils are connected in series.
    If there is no mutual inductance between the coils, the TOTAL inductance of the two coils is the _____ inductances.

    A. sum of the individual
    B. product of the individual
    C. product of the square roots of the two
    D. sum of the squares of the individual

40.____

41. The impedance of a coil with zero resistance is called the

    A. reluctance   B. conductance
    C. inductive reactance   D. flux

41.____

42. The ratio of the energy stored to the energy lost in a coil over a period of one cycle is called its

    A. efficiency   B. Q
    C. reactance   D. resistance

42.____

43. In a vacuum tube, the current is carried by

    A. ions   B. neutrons   C. electrons   D. molecules

43.____

44. The device used to vary the intensity of an incandescent light on a 120V AC circuit is a

    A. variable capacitor
    B. silicon controlled rectifier
    C. copper oxide rectifier
    D. rf amplifier

44.____

45. High power transistors must be mounted on *heat sinks*. The purpose of the heat sinks is to

    A. improve voltage regulation
    B. increase the transistors' output
    C. keep the transistors warm
    D. keep the transistors cool

45.____

46. The one of the following materials that has the HIGHEST conductivity is

    A. iron   B. zinc   C. copper   D. silver

46.____

47. The unit used to express the alternating current impedance of a circuit is the   47.____
    A. mho   B. farad   C. ohm   D. rel

48. A certain resistor has four colored bands on it. The fourth band is gold.   48.____
    This means that the resistor
    A. is wirewound   B. is non-inductive
    C. has a ± 20% tolerance   D. has a ± 5% tolerance

49. An amplifier has an output voltage waveform that does not exactly follow that of the input   49.____
    voltage.
    This type of distortion is called _____ distortion.
    A. modular   B. frequency
    C. resonance   D. amplitude

50. A parallel circuit, resonant at 1000 khz, has its value of capacity doubled and its value of   50.____
    inductance halved.
    Its resonant frequency now is _____ khz.
    A. 500   B. 1000   C. 1500   D. 2000

KEY (CORRECT ANSWERS)

1. D	11. D	21. D	31. C	41. C
2. A	12. C	22. C	32. D	42. B
3. C	13. D	23. B	33. D	43. C
4. B	14. B	24. A	34. C	44. B
5. D	15. D	25. A	35. A	45. D
6. A	16. C	26. D	36. B	46. D
7. D	17. D	27. D	37. C	47. C
8. B	18. A	28. C	38. B	48. D
9. D	19. C	29. C	39. D	49. D
10. B	20. C	30. A	40. A	50. B

TEST 2

DIRECTIONS: Each question or incomplete statement is followed by several suggested answers or completions. Select the one that BEST answers the question or completes the statement. *PRINT THE LETTER OF THE CORRECT ANSWER IN THE SPACE AT THE RIGHT.*

1. A voltmeter which reads 100V full scale has a specified accuracy of 3%. It is hooked across a circuit and reads 97 volts.
   The TRUE voltage can be assumed to be somewhere between

   A. 96.7 and 97.3
   B. 94 and 100
   C. 96.07 and 97.03
   D. 95.5 and 98.5

   1.____

2. The product of 127.2 and .0037 is

   A. 4706.4   B. 470.64   C. .47064   D. .0047064

   2.____

3. The wind velocity at a certain location was measured four times in a 24-hour period. The readings were 32 mph, 10 mph, 16 mph, and 2 mph.
   The AVERAGE wind velocity for that day was _____ mph.

   A. 24   B. 20   C. 15   D. 13

   3.____

4. When 280 is divided by .014, the answer is

   A. .002   B. 20   C. 200   D. 20,000

   4.____

5. The square root of 289 is

   A. 1.7   B. 9.7   C. 17   D. 144.5

   5.____

6. The watts drawn by a resistive load is to be determined. To do this, a voltmeter (10V full scale) is connected across the load, and an ammeter (10 amps full scale) is connected in series with the load. Both instruments are specified as having 1% (full scale) accuracy. The voltmeter reads 9.2V; the ammeter reads 8.3 amps.
   The MOST valid value for the watts drawn is _____ watts.

   A. 76   B. 76.36   C. 76.4   D. 80

   6.____

7. The formula for converting degrees Centigrade to degrees Fahrenheit is: $°F = (9/5) \cdot (°C) + 32$.
   A temperature of 25° C is equal to

   A. 102.6° F   B. 85° F   C. 77° F   D. 43° F

   7.____

8. The prefix *kilo* means

   A. multiply by one million
   B. divide by one million
   C. multiply by one thousand
   D. divide by one hundred

   8.____

9. 2^8 is equal to

   A. 512   B. 256   C. 124   D. 82

   9.____

10. The prefix *milli* means

    A. multiply by 100
    B. divide by one thousand
    C. divide by one million
    D. multiply by one million

11. If 1/X = 1/20 + 1/20 + 1/40, the value of X is

    A. .125   B. 8   C. 16   D. 20

12. 2×10^6 multiplied by 4×10^{-6} equals

    A. 8   B. 8×10^{-12} C. 8×10^{12} D. 8×10^3

13. 1 inch equals _____ cm.

    A. 0.62   B. 2.54   C. 3.94   D. 16.2

14. 1 kg equals

    A. 2.2 lbs.   B. 17.3 oz.   C. 0.52 lbs.   D. 12 oz.

15. 1 liter equals

    A. 3.78 quarts
    B. 1.057 quarts
    C. 1.39 pints
    D. .067 gallons

16. A circle has a radius of 10 inches.
    Its circumference is _____ inches.

    A. 72.3   B. 62.8   C. 31.4   D. 25

17. A right angle triangle has sides measuring 3 inches and 4 inches; its hypotenuse is 5 inches.
    The area of this triangle is _____ square inches.

    A. 6   B. 20   C. 15   D. 60

18. A square has an area of 81 square inches.
    The length of each side is _____ inches.

    A. 7.9   B. 9   C. 11   D. 17

19. A bottle contains 11 pints of liquid. To this bottle 1.32 pints is then added.
    This is an increase of

    A. 6%   B. 9%   C. 12%   D. 16%

20. A week ago a storage battery read 12.4V. Today its voltage is 8.1% less.
    Its voltage is now

    A. 11.4   B. 10.8   C. 9.3   D. 10.2

21. The advantage of a vacuum tube voltmeter over a regular voltmeter is that it

    A. operates on batteries
    B. operates on 120V AC
    C. has a low input impedance
    D. has a high input impedance

22. A g$_m$ tube tester measures a vacuum tube's   22._____

    A. capacitance   B. resistance
    C. emission   D. transconductance

23. A cathode ray tube is used in a(n)   23._____

    A. audio amplifier   B. radio frequency amplifier
    C. oscilloscope   D. volt-ohm-milliammeter

24. A voltmeter is described as having *1000 ohms per volt*. The current required to produce   24._____
    full scale deflection is

    A. 1 milliampere   B. 1 ampere
    C. 20 milliamperes   D. 0.05 milliamperes

25. The PRIMARY use of a test oscilloscope is to   25._____

    A. analyze complex waveforms
    B. measure resistance
    C. measure capacitance
    D. measure DC voltages

26. A spectrophotometer is an instrument that measures   26._____

    A. photographic film density
    B. the amount of light of a particular wavelength
    C. the amount of airborne dust
    D. x-ray radiation

27. The test instrument generally known as a *multitester* will measure, among other things,   27._____

    A. temperature   B. beta radiation
    C. AC watts   D. DC milliamperes

28. A lightmeter used in measuring incident light gives readings in   28._____

    A. footcandles   B. candlepower
    C. lumens   D. foot-lamberts

29. A selenium photocell is a type known as photo-   29._____

    A. emissive   B. resistive
    C. voltaic   D. transistive

30. In wiring electronic circuits, the solder GENERALLY used is _____ solder.   30._____

    A. silver   B. acid core
    C. aluminum   D. rosin core

31. An unconscious victim of electric shock should be orally administered   31._____

    A. nothing
    B. coffee
    C. alcohol
    D. aromatic apirits of ammonia

32. Persons operating x-ray equipment should wear

   A. safety goggles
   B. insulating gloves
   C. a lead-coated apron and gloves
   D. a surgical mask

33. Harmful radiation is emitted by the element

   A. neon   B. lithium   C. platinum   D. radium

34. When a victim of electrical shock or near drowning is given artificial respiration and he does not appear to respond, the treatment should continue for at least

   A. four hours   B. fifteen minutes
   C. five minutes   D. fifteen hours

35. A person maintaining high voltage equipment should avoid wearing

   A. long hair
   B. sneakers
   C. rings and metallic watchbands
   D. eyeglasses

36. Portable AC equipment is often equipped with a three-wire cable and a three-prong male plug.
    The reason for this is to prevent

   A. radiation   B. electric shock
   C. oscillation   D. ground currents

37. Smoke is seen issuing from a piece of electronic equipment. The FIRST thing that should be done is to

   A. call the fire department
   B. pour water on it
   C. look for a fire extinguisher
   D. shut off the power

38. A match should not be used when inspecting the electrolyte level in a lead-acid battery because the cells emit

   A. nitrogen   B. hydrogen
   C. carbon dioxide   D. sulfur dioxide

39. A person feels nauseated, his mental capacity has been lowered, and he has a severe throbbing headache. It is suspected that he has been poisoned by gas, but there is no apparent odor.
    The poisonous gas is MOST likely to be

   A. sulfur dioxide   B. hydrogen cyanide
   C. carbon monoxide   D. chlorine

40. The purpose of an interlock on a piece of electronic equipment is to   40._____

    A. prevent theft of the vacuum tubes
    B. prevent electrical shock to maintenance personnel
    C. prevent rf radiation
    D. keep the equipment cool

41. An alternating voltage is applied to an inductance.   41._____
    As the frequency of the voltage is decreased, the impedance of the inductance

    A. decreases
    B. increases
    C. follows the alternating voltage
    D. remains the same

42. A 0.25 ufd condenser is connected in parallel with a 0.50 ufd condenser.   42._____
    The resultant capacity is _____ ufd.

    A. 0.167   B. 0.37   C. 0.75   D. 2.5

43. The electrolyte in a carbon-zinc dry cell is   43._____

    A. sulfuric acid   B. ammonium chloride
    C. lithium chloride   D. sodium chloride

44. A 5000-ohm resistor has a voltage of 25 volts applied to it.   44._____
    The current drawn by the resistor is

    A. 5 milliamperes   B. 5 amperes
    C. 75 milliamperes   D. 1.25 milliamperes

45. A certain resistor has three colored bands around it.   45._____
    The one nearest the end is red, the next one is gray, and the next one is yellow.
    The value of the resistor is

    A. 2.7 megaohms   B. 280,000 ohms
    C. 3270 ohms   D. 449 ohms

Questions 46-50.

DIRECTIONS: Questions 46 through 50 are to be answered on the basis of the following paragraph.

The second half of the twin triode acts as a phase modulator. The rf output of the crystal oscillator is impressed on the phase-modulator grid by means of a blocking condenser. The cathode circuit is provided with a large amount of degeneration by an un-bypassed cathode resistor. Because of this degenerative feedback, the transconductance of the triode is abnormally low, so low that the plate current is affected as much by the direct grid-plate capacitance as by the transconductance. The two effects result in plate current vectors almost 180° apart, and the total plate current is the resultant of the two components. In phase, it will be about 90° removed from the phase of the voltage impressed on the grid.

46. As used in the above paragraph, the word *impressed* means MOST NEARLY 46.___
    A. applied B. blocked C. changed D. detached

47. As used in the above paragraph, the word *components* refers to the 47.___
    A. blocking condenser and cathode resistor
    B. twin triode
    C. plate current vectors
    D. grid-plate capacitance

48. According to the above paragraph, degenerative feedback is obtained by means of 48.___
    A. a crystal oscillator
    B. the plate voltage
    C. an un-bypassed cathode resistor
    D. a blocking condenser

49. According to the above paragraph, the cathode resistor is 49.___
    A. very large
    B. not bypassed
    C. in series with an inductance
    D. shunted by a blocking condenser

50. According to the above paragraph, the phase angle between the grid voltage and the total plate current is APPROXIMATELY 50.___
    A. 180° B. 90° C. 270° D. zero

KEY (CORRECT ANSWERS)

1. B	11. B	21. D	31. A	41. A
2. C	12. C	22. D	32. C	42. C
3. C	13. B	23. C	33. D	43. B
4. D	14. A	24. A	34. A	44. A
5. C	15. B	25. A	35. C	45. B
6. A	16. B	26. B	36. B	46. A
7. C	17. A	27. D	37. D	47. C
8. C	18. B	28. A	38. B	48. C
9. B	19. C	29. C	39. C	49. B
10. B	20. A	30. D	40. B	50. B

EXAMINATION SECTION

TEST 1

DIRECTIONS: Each question or incomplete statement is followed by several suggested answers or completions. Select the one that BEST answers the question or completes the statement. *PRINT THE LETTER OF THE CORRECT ANSWER IN THE SPACE AT THE RIGHT.*

Questions 1-17:
Use the following diagrams of tools to answer questions 1 through 17. (Tools are NOT drawn to scale.)

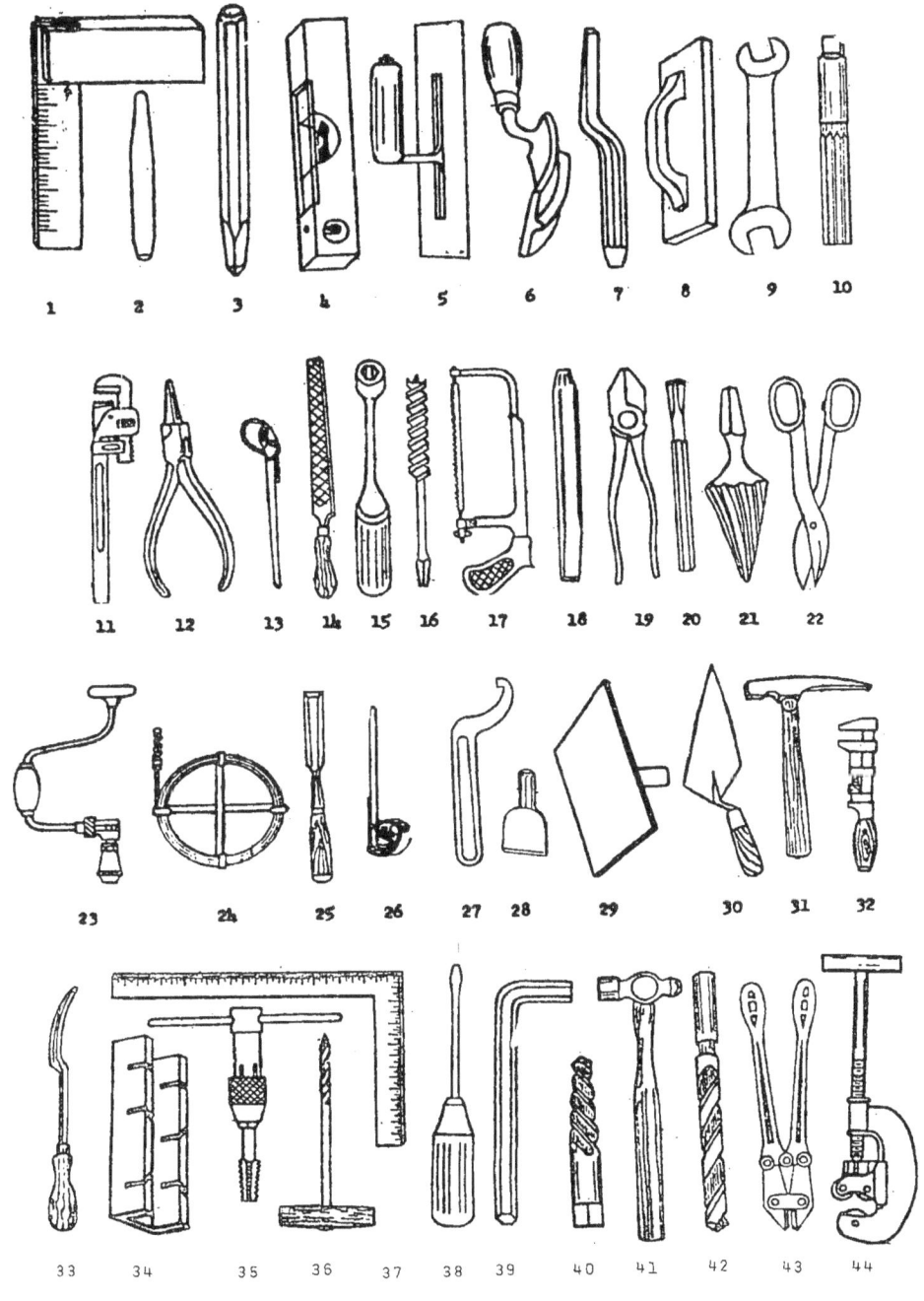

2 (#1)

1. To tighten an elbow on a threaded pipe, a mechanic should use tool number
    A. 9   B. 11   C. 26   D. 32

    1._____

2. To cut grooves in a newly poured cement floor, a mechanic should use tool number
    A. 5   B. 6   C. 28   D. 29

    2._____

3. To "caulk" a lead joint, a mechanic should use tool number
    A. 7   B. 10   C. 25   D. 33

    3._____

4. The term "snips" should be applied by a mechanic to tool number
    A. 12   B. 22   C. 36   D. 43

    4._____

5. To slightly enlarge an existing 17/32" diameter hole in a metal plate, a mechanic should use tool number
    A. 3   B. 10   C. 14   D. 35

    5._____

6. The term "snake" should be applied by a mechanic to tool number
    A. 21   B. 23   C. 24   D. 40

    6._____

7. If the threaded portion of a 1/2" brass pipe breaks off inside a gate valve, the piece should be removed with tool number
    A. 15   B. 35   C. 39   D. 40

    7._____

8. To cut a face brick into a bat, a mechanic should use tool number
    A. 3   B. 18   C. 25   D. 28

    8._____

9. A mechanic should cut a 3" x 2" x 3/16" angle iron with tool number
    A. 3   B. 17   C. 22   D. 43

    9._____

10. A mechanic should tighten a chrome-plated water supply pipe by using tool number
    A. 11   B. 19   C. 26   D. 32

    10._____

11. The term "hawk" should be applied by a mechanic to tool number
    A. 28   B. 29   C. 30   D. 33

    11._____

12. If your coworker asks you to pass him the "star" drill, you should hand him tool number
    A. 16   B. 20   C. 40   D. 42

    12._____

13. After threading a 1" diameter piece of pipe, a mechanic should debur the inside by using tool number
    A. 14   B. 21   C. 36   D. 40

    13._____

14. A mechanic should apply the term "float" to tool number 14.____
    A. 4   B. 6   C. 8   D. 28

15. If a mechanic has to cut a dozen 15-inch lengths of 3/4" steel pipe for 15.____
    spacers, he should use tool number
    A. 18   B. 26   C. 43   D. 44

16. If a mechanic is erecting two structural steel plates and needs to line up 16.____
    the bolt holes, he should use tool number
    A. 2   B. 3   C. 33   D. 42

17. To cut reinforcing wire mesh to be used in a concrete floor, you should 17.____
    use tool number
    A. 7   B. 17   C. 18   D. 43

18. The MAIN reason for overhauling a power tool on a regular basis is to 18.____
    A. make the men more familiar with the tool
    B. keep the men busy during slack times
    C. insure that the tool is used occasionally
    D. minimize breakdowns

19. A mechanic should NOT press too heavily on a hacksaw while using it to 19.____
    cut through a steel rod because this may
    A. create flying steel particles
    B. bend the frame
    C. break the blade
    D. overheat the rod

20. Creosote is COMMONLY used with wood to 20.____
    A. speed up the seasoning   B. make the wood fireproof
    C. make painting easier   D. preserve the wood

21. A mitre box should be used to 21.____
    A. hold a saw while sharpening it
    B. store expensive tools
    C. hold a saw at a fixed angle
    D. encase steel beams for protection

22. Wood scaffold planks should be inspected 22.____
    A. at regular intervals   B. once a week
    C. before they are stored away   D. each time before use

23. Continuous sheeting should be used when excavating deep trenches in 23.____
    A. rock   B. stiff clay
    C. firm earth   D. unstable soil

24. The MAIN reason for requiring that certain special tools be returned to the tool room after a job has been completed is that
    A. missing tools can be replaced
    B. the men will not need to care for the tools
    C. more tools will be available for use
    D. this permits easier inspection and maintenance of tools

24._____

25. The BEST material to use to extinguish an oil fire is
    A. sand   B. water   C. sawdust   D. gravel

25._____

26. A "Lally" column is
    A. fabricated from angles and plates
    B. fabricated by tying two channels together with lattice bars
    C. a steel member that has unequal sections
    D. a pipe fitted with a base plate at each end

26._____

27. The BEST action for you to take if you discover a small puddle of oil on the shop floor is to first
    A. have it cleaned up
    B. find out who spilled it
    C. discover the source of the leak
    D. cover it with newspaper

27._____

28. You should listen to your foreman even when he insists on explaining the procedure for a job you have done many times before because
    A. you can do the job the way you want when he leaves
    B. he may make an error and you can show that you know your job
    C. it is wise to humor him even if he is wrong
    D. you are required to do the job the way the foreman wants it

28._____

Questions 29-34:
Answer questions 29 through 34 by referring to the sketches that follow.

29. The indicated pressure is, MOST NEARLY, _____ psi.   29._____
    A. 132   B. 137   C. 143   D. 148

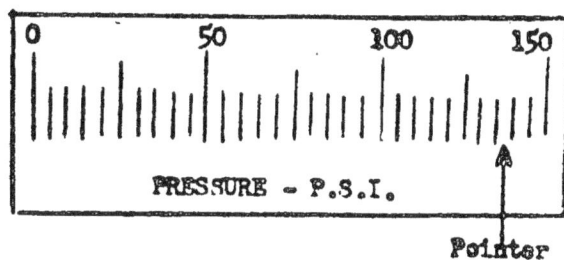

30. The LEAST number of shims, of any combination of thickness, required to   30._____
    exactly fill the 1/4" gap shown is
    A. 7   B. 8   C. 9   D. 10

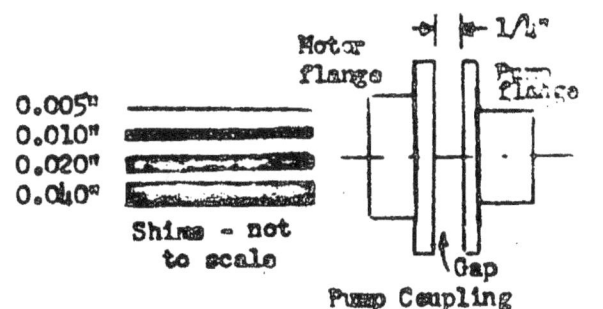

31. The dimension "X" on the keyway shown is   31._____
    A. 3-3/8"   B. 3-9/16"   C. 3-3/4"   D. 4"

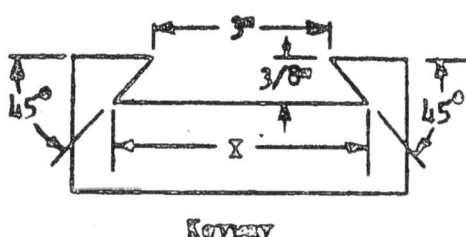

32. If the tank gauge reads 120 psi, then the pipe gauge should read ___ psi.   32._____
    A. 80   B. 120   C. 180   D. 240

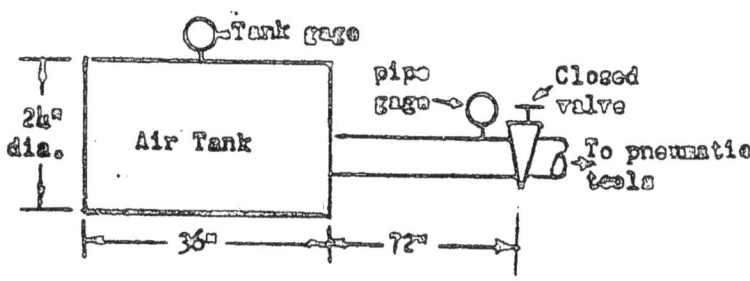

33. The MINIMUM number of feet of chainlink fence needed to completely enclose the storage yard shown is
    A. 278   B. 286   C. 295   D. 304

34. The distance "X" between the holes is
    A. 1-7/8"   B. 2-1/16"   C. 2-3/8"   D. 2-9/16"

35. A rule requires all employees to report defective equipment to their superiors, even when the maintenance of the particular pieces of equipment is handled by someone else. The MAIN purpose of this rule is to
    A. determine who is doing the job improperly
    B. have repairs made before trouble occurs
    C. encourage all employees to be alert at all times
    D. reduce the cost of equipment

36. Some equipment is fitted with wing nuts. Such nuts are ESPECIALLY useful when
    A. the nut is to be wired closed
    B. space is limited
    C. the equipment is subject to vibration
    D. the nuts must be removed frequently

37. It is considered BAD practice to use water to put out electrical fires MAINLY because the water may
    A. rust the equipment
    B. short circuit the lines
    C. cause a serious shock
    D. damage the electrical insulation

38. The BEST instrument to use to make certain that two points, separated by a vertical distance of nine feet, are in perfect vertical alignment is a
    A. square   B. level   C. plumb bob   D. protractor

39. While you are being trained, you will be assigned to work with an experienced mechanic. It would be BEST for you to
    A. remind the mechanic that he is responsible for your training
    B. tell him frequently how much you know about the work
    C. let him do all the work while you observe closely
    D. be as cooperative and helpful a you can

40. If a measurement scaled from a drawing is one inch, and the scale of the drawing is 1/8 inch to the foot, then the one-inch measurement would represent an ACTUAL length of
    A. 8 feet   B. 2 feet   C. 1/8 of a foot   D. 8 inches

KEY (CORRECT ANSWERS)

1. B	11. B	21. C	31. C
2. B	12. B	22. D	32. B
3. A	13. B	23. D	33. D
4. B	14. C	24. D	34. A
5. B	15. D	25. A	35. B
6. C	16. A	26. D	36. D
7. D	17. D	27. A	37. C
8. D	18. D	28. D	38. C
9. B	19. C	29. B	39. D
10. C	20. D	30. A	40. A

TEST 2

DIRECTIONS: Each question or incomplete statement is followed by several suggested answers or completions. Select the one that BEST answers the question or completes the statement. *PRINT THE LETTER OF THE CORRECT ANSWER IN THE SPACE AT THE RIGHT.*

1. Cloth tapes should NOT be used when accurate measurements must be obtained because
   A. the numbers soon become worn and thus difficult to read
   B. there are not enough subdivisions of each inch on the tape
   C. the ink runs when wet, thus making the tape difficult to read
   D. small changes in the pull on the tape will make considerable differences in tape readings

   1._____

2. It is considered GOOD practice to release the pressure from an air hose before uncoupling the hose connection because this avoids
   A. wasting air
   B. possible personal injury
   C. damage to the air tool
   D. damage to the air compressor

   2._____

3. In brick construction, a structural steel member is used to support the wall above door and window openings. This member is called a
   A. purlin   B. sill   C. truss   D. lintel

   3._____

4. The BEST procedure to use to properly ignite an oxyacetylene cutting torch is to
   A. crack the acetylene valve, apply the spark, and open the oxygen valve
   B. crack the acetylene valve, then the oxygen valve, and apply the spark
   C. crack the oxygen valve, then the acetylene valve, and apply the spark
   D. crack the oxygen valve, apply the spark, open the acetylene valve

   4._____

5. The information in an accident report which may be MOST useful in helping to prevent similar-type accidents from happening is the
   A. cause of the accident   B. time of day it happened
   C. type of injuries suffered   D. number of people injured

   5._____

6. The MAIN reason why each coat of paint should be of a different color when two coats of paint are specified is that
   A. cheaper paint can be used as the undercoat
   B. less care need be taken in applying the coats
   C. any missed areas will be easier to spot
   D. the colors do not have to be exact

   6._____

7. To prevent manila hoisting ropes from raveling, the ends are
   A. moused B. whipped C. spliced D. eyed

8. The MAIN advantage of aluminum ladders over wooden ladders is that they are
   A. much stronger
   B. lighter
   C. cheaper
   D. more stable

9. The splices in columns in steel construction are USUALLY made
   A. two feet above floor level
   B. two feet below floor level
   C. at floor level
   D. midway between floors

10. Open-end wrenches with small openings are generally made shorter in overall length than open-end wrenches with larger openings. The MOST important reason for this is to
    A. save material
    B. provide compactness
    C. prevent overstressing the wrench
    D. provide correct leverage

11. Galvanized steel wire is wire that has been coated with
    A. zinc B. copper C. tin D. lead

12. "Camber" in a steel roof truss refers to the
    A. grade of steel used
    B. stress in the steel
    C. finish applied to the steel
    D. upward curve of the lower chord

13. A structural member is marked 8WF18. The 18 in this designation is the
    A. depth of the web
    B. width of the flange
    C. length of the member
    D. weight per foot

14. A strictly enforced safety rule in a rigging gang is that only one man gives the signals to the crane operator. However the ONE signal that anyone in the gang is allowed to give is the
    A. hoist-up signal
    B. boom-down signal
    C. swing signal
    D. stop signal

15. "Turnbuckles" are GENERALLY used to
    A. raise heavy loads
    B. splice two cables
    C. tie a cable to a column
    D. tighten a cable

16. If a mechanic opens the strands of a piece of manila rope and finds sawdust-like material inside the rope, it means the rope

    A. has dried out and must be re-oiled before use
    B. is relatively new
    C. has been damaged and should be discarded
    D. is to be used only for light loads until the sawdust has been cleaned out

16._____

Questions 17-21:
Refer to the passage below to answer questions 17 through 21.

REGULATIONS FOR SMALL GROUPS WHO MOVE FROM POINT TO POINT ON THE TRACKS

Employees who perform duties on the tracks in small groups and who move from point to point along the trainway, must be on the alert at all times and prepared to clear the track when a train approaches without unnecessarily slowing it down. Underground at all times, and out-of-doors between sunset and sunrise, such employees must not enter upon the tracks unless each of them is equipped with an approved light. Flashlights must not be used for protection by such groups. Upon clearing the track to permit a train to pass, each member of the group must give a proceed signal, by hand or light, to the motorman of the train. Whenever such small groups are working in an area protected by caution lights or flags, but are not members of the gang for whom the flagging protection was established, they must not give proceed signals to motormen. The purpose of this rule is to avoid a motorman's confusing such signal with that of the flagman who is protecting a gang. Whenever a small group is engaged in work of an engrossing nature or at any time when the view of approaching trains is limited by reason of curves or otherwise, one man of the group, equipped with a whistle, must be assigned properly to warn and protect the man or men at work and must not perform any other duties while so assigned.

17. If a small group of men are traveling along the tracks toward their work location and a train approaches, they should

    A. stop the train
    B. signal the motorman to go slowly
    C. clear the track
    D. stop immediately

17._____

18. Small groups may enter upon the tracks

    A. only between sunset and sunrise
    B. provided each has an approved light
    C. provided their foreman has a good flashlight
    D. provided each man has an approved flashlight

18._____

4 (#2)

19. After a small group has cleared the tracks in an area unprotected by caution lights or flags,
    A. each member must give the proceed signal to the motorman
    B. the foreman signals the motorman to proceed
    C. the motorman can proceed provided he goes slowly
    D. the last member off the tracks gives the signal to the motorman

19._____

20. If a small group is working in an area protected by the signals of a track gang, the members of the small group
    A. need not be concerned with train movement
    B. must give the proceed signal together with the track gang
    C. can delegate one of their members to give the proceed signal
    D. must not give the proceed signal

20._____

21. If the view of approaching trains is blocked, the small group should
    A. move to where they can see the trains
    B. delegate one of the group to warn and protect them
    C. keep their ears alert for approaching trains
    D. refuse to work at such locations

21._____

Questions 22-28:
Refer to the sketched below to answer questions 22 through 28.

22. The distance "Y" is
    A. 5/8"   B. 7/8"   C. 1-1/8"   D. 1-3/8"

22._____

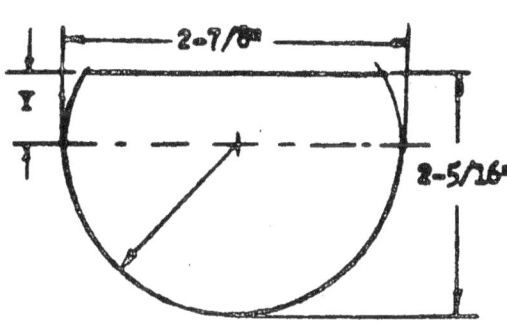

23. The sketch shows the float-operated trippers for operating a sump pump. If you want the pump to start sooner, you should
    A. lower the upper tripper   B. lower the lower tripper
    C. raise the upper tripper   D. raise the lower tripper

23._____

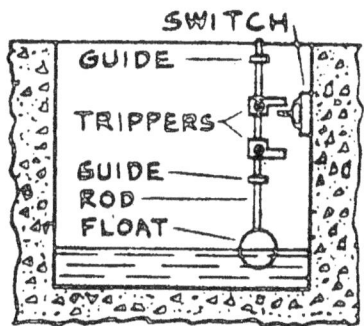

24. The width of the wood stud shown is 24._____
    A. 1-1/8" B. 1-5/16" C. 1-5/8" D. 3-5/8"

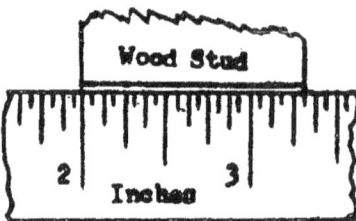

25. The right angle shown has been divided into four unequal parts. The number of degrees in angle "X" is 25._____
    A. 31° B. 33° C. 38° D. 45°

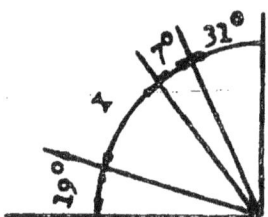

26. The reading on the meter shown is MOST NEARLY 26._____
    A. 0465 B. 0475 C. 0566 D. 1566

27. The length "X" of the slot shown is 27._____
    A. 2-3/8" B. 2-7/16" C. 2-1/2" D. 2-9/16"

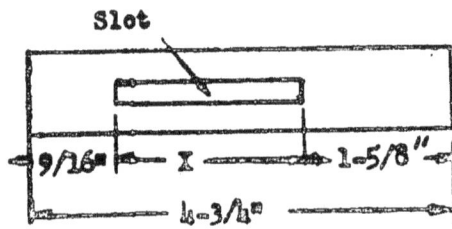

28. The volume of the bar shown is _____ cubic inches. 28._____
    A. 132 B. 356 C. 420 D. 516

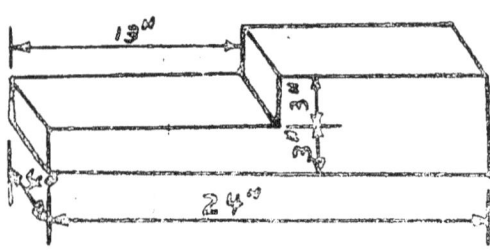

Questions 29-34:
Use the sketch below to answer questions 29 through 34.

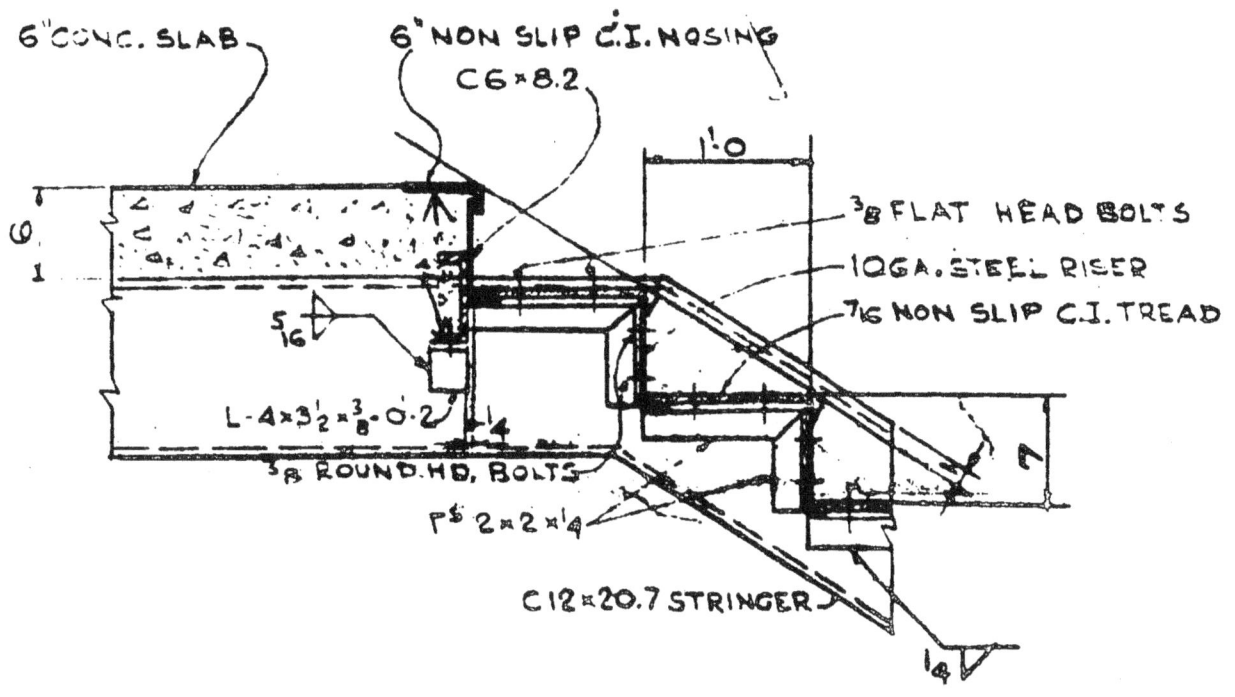

29. The stringer for this stair is a(n)
    A. I-beam   B. angle   C. H-beam   D. channel

30. The riser is made of
    A. concrete   B. sheet metal
    C. cast iron   D. wood

31. The 2 x 2 x 1/4 angles are secured to the stringer by
    A. 5/16" welds   B. 1/4" welds
    C. 3/8" flat head bolts   D. 3/8" round head bolts

32. The treads are made of
    A. concrete   B. sheet metal
    C. cast iron   D. wood

33. The height of the riser is
    A. 6"   B. 7"   C. 8"   D. 12"

34. The width of the tread is
    A. 6"   B. 7"   C. 8"   D. 12"

Questions 35-40:

DIRECTIONS: Questions 35 through 40 show the top view of an object in the first column, the front view of the same object in the second column, and four drawings in the third column, one of which correctly represents the RIGHT side view of the object. Select the CORRECT right side view. As a guide, the first one is an illustrative example, the correct answer of which is C.

	TOP VIEW	FRONT VIEW	RIGHT SIDE VIEW			
SAMPLE			A	B	C	D
35.			A	B	C	D
36.			A	B	C	D
37.			A	B	C	D
38.			A	B	C	D
39.			A	B	C	D
40.			A	B	C	D

KEY (CORRECT ANSWERS)

1. D	11. A	21. B	31. B
2. B	12. D	22. B	32. C
3. D	13. D	23. D	33. B
4. A	14. D	24. B	34. D
5. A	15. D	25. B	35. C
6. C	16. C	26. A	36. A
7. B	17. C	27. D	37. C
8. B	18. B	28. C	38. B
9. A	19. A	29. D	39. B
10. D	20. D	30. B	40. C

EXAMINATION SECTION
TEST 1

DIRECTIONS: Each question or incomplete statement is followed by several suggested answers or completions. Select the one that *BEST* answers the question or completes the statement. *PRINT THE LETTER OF THE CORRECT ANSWER IN THE SPACE AT THE RIGHT.*

1. A circular mil is a measure of

    A. area   B. length   C. volume   D. weight

2. In electrical tests, a megger is calibrated to read

    A. amperes   B. ohms   C. volts   D. watts

3. Metal cabinets for lighting circuits are grounded in order to

    A. save insulating material
    B. provide a return for the neutral current
    C. eliminate short circuits
    D. minimize the possibility of shock

4. In an a.c. circuit containing only resistance, the power factor will be

    A. zero
    C. 50% leading
    B. 50% lagging
    D. 100%

5. The size of fuse for a two-wire lighting circuit using No. 14 wire should not exceed

    A. 15 amperes
    C. 25 amperes
    B. 20 amperes
    D. 30 amperes

6. When working near acid storage batteries, extreme care should be taken to guard against sparks mainly because a spark may

    A. cause an explosion
    B. set fire to the electrolyte
    C. short circuit a cell
    D. ignite the battery case

7. If a blown fuse in an existing lighting circuit is replaced by another of the same rating which also blows, the proper maintenance procedure is to

    A. use a higher rating fuse
    B. cut out some of the outlets in the circuit
    C. check the circuit for grounds or shorts
    D. install a renewable fuse

8. The number of fuses required in a three-phase four-wire branch circuit with grounded neutral is

    A. one   B. two   C. three   D. four

9. The electrodes of the common dry cell are carbon and

    A. zinc   B. lead   C. steel   D. tin

10. An electrician's hickey is used to

    A. strip insulation off wire
    B. pull cable through conduits
    C. thread metallic conduit
    D. bend metallic conduit

11. A group of wire sizes that is correctly arranged in order of *INCREASING* current-carrying capacity is

    A. 6; 12; 3/0
    B. 12; 6; 3/0
    C. 3/0; 12; 6
    D. 3/0; 6; 12

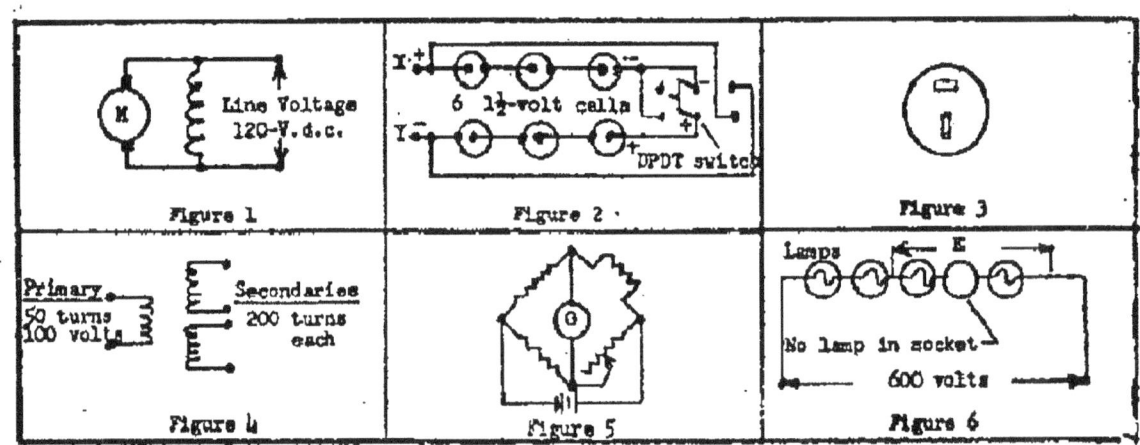

Questions 12 - 19.
Questions 12 through 19 refer to the figures above. Each question gives the proper figure to use with that question.

12. Figure 1 shows the standard diagram for

    A. a synchronous motor
    B. a shunt motor
    C. a series motor
    D. an induction motor

13. In Figure 1, if the line current is 5 amperes, the energy consumed by the motor if in continuous operation for 3 hours is

    A. 200 watthours
    B. 600 watthours
    C. 1800 watthours
    D. 9000 watthours

14. In Figure 2, with the DPDT switch closed to the right, the voltage between X and Y is

    A. 0   B. 1 1/2   C. 4 1/2   D. 9

15. In Figure 2, with the DPDT closed to the left, the voltage between X and Y is

    A. 9   B. 4 1/2   C. 1 1/2   D. 0

16. The convenience outlet shown in Figure 3 is used particularly for a device which

    A. is polarized
    B. is often disconnected
    C. takes a heavy current
    D. vibrates

17. In Figure 4, the *MAXIMUM* secondary voltage possible by interconnecting the secondaries is   17._____

    A. 50 volts   B. 200 volts
    C. 400 volts   D. 800 volts

18. Figure 5 shows a Wheatstone bridge which is used to measure   18._____

    A. voltage   B. resistance
    C. current   D. power

19. In Figure 6, with one of the five good lamps removed from its socket as indicated, the voltage is nearest to   19._____

    A. 240   B. 0   C. 600   D. 360

20. The metal which is the best conductor of electricity is   20._____

    A. silver   B. copper
    C. aluminum   D. nickel

21. If the two supply wires to a d.c. series motor are reversed, the motor will   21._____

    A. run in the opposite direction
    B. not run
    C. run in the same direction
    D. become a generator

22. Before doing work on a motor, to prevent accidental starting you should   22._____

    A. short circuit the motor leads
    B. remove the fuses
    C. block the rotor
    D. ground the frame

23. The material commonly used for brushes on d.c. motors is   23._____

    A. copper   B. carbon
    C. brass   D. aluminum

24. The conductors of a two-wire No. 12 armored cable used in an ordinary lighting circuit are   24._____

    A. stranded and rubber insulated
    B. solid and rubber insulated
    C. stranded and cotton insulated
    D. solid and cotton insulated

25. The rating, 125 V.-10A., 250 V.-5A., commonly applies to a   25._____

    A. snap switch   B. lamp
    C. conductor   D. fuse

26. Commutators are found on   26._____

    A. alternators   B. d.c. motors
    C. transformers   D. circuit breakers

27. A proper use for an electrician's knife is to

    A. cut wires
    B. pry out a small cartridge fuse
    C. mark the placd where a conduit is to be cut
    D. skin wires

28. A d.c. device taking one milliampere at one kilovolt takes a total power of

    A. one milliwatt
    B. one watt
    C. one kilowatt
    D. one megawatt

29. In connection with electrical work, it is good practice to

    A. scrape the silvery coating from a wire before soldering
    B. nick a wire in several places before bending it around a terminal
    C. assume that a circuit is alive
    D. open a switch to check the load

30. Mica is commonly used as an insulation

    A. for cartridge fuse cases
    B. between commutator bars
    C. between lead acid battery plates
    D. between transformer steel laminations

31. The function of a step-down transformer is to decrease the

    A. voltage
    B. current
    C. power
    D. frequency

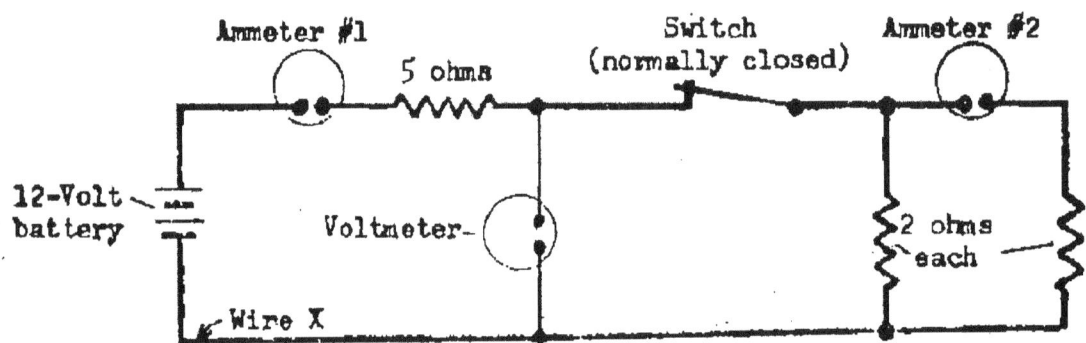

Questions 32-39.
Questions 32 through 39 refer to the circuit above. Neglect the effects of the various meters on the circuit.

32. The three resistors connected as shown have an equivalent resistance of

    A. 9 ohms   B. 7 ohms   C. 6 ohms   D. 4 ohms

33. When ammeter #1 indicates 2 amperes, ammeter #2 will indicate

    A. 1 ampere
    B. 2 amperes
    C. 3 amperes
    D. 4 amperes

34. If the two wires to ammeter #1 are reversed the

    A. ammeter needle will move backwards
    B. ammeter needle will indicate zero
    C. ammeter will burn out
    D. current in the rest of the circuit will be reversed

35. With the switch either open or closed, the current in wire X is

    A. greater than in ammeter #1
    B. less than in ammeter #1
    C. the same as in ammeter #2
    D. the same as in ammeter #1

36. When ammeter #1 indicates 2 amperes, the power consumed by the 5-ohm resistor is

    A. 2.5 watts			B. 10 watts
    C. 20 watts			D. 50 watts

37. The highest voltage measured anywhere in the circuit is across the

    A. 5-ohm resistor		B. No. 1 ammeter
    C. battery			D. closed switch

38. If the normally-closed switch is opened, the meter that would still show an appreciable reading is

    A. the voltmeter		B. ammeter #1
    C. ammeter #2		D. none

39. The device in the circuit which undoubtedly has the highest resistance is the

    A. battery			B. 5-ohm resistor
    C. No. 1 ammeter		D. voltmeter

40. A conduit run is most often terminated in

    A. a coupling			B. an elbow
    C. a bushing			D. an outlet box

41. In long conduit runs, pull boxes are sometimes installed at intermediate points to

    A. avoid using couplings
    B. support the conduit
    C. make use of short lengths of conduit
    D. facilitate pulling wire

42. A rheostat would *LEAST* likely be used in connection with the operation of

    A. transformers		B. motors
    C. generators			D. battery charging M.G. sets

43. The fiber bushing inserted at the end of a piece of flexible metallic conduit prevents

    A. moisture from entering the cable
    B. the rough edges from cutting the insulation
    C. the wires from touching each other
    D. the wires from slipping back into the armor

44. Portable lamp cord is most likely to have

    A. paper insulation
    B. solid wire
    C. armored wire
    D. stranded wire

45. Thermal relays are used in motor circuits to protect against

    A. reverse current
    B. overspeed
    C. overvoltage
    D. overload

46. It is good practice to connect the ground wire for a building electrical system to a

    A. vent pipe
    B. steam pipe
    C. cold water pipe
    D. gas pipe

47. A good magnetic material is

    A. brass B. copper C. silver D. iron

48. The most practical way to determine in the field the approximate length of insulated wire in a large coil is to

    A. unreel the wire and measure it with a 6-foot rule
    B. find another coil with the length marked on it and compare
    C. count the turns and multiply by the average circumference
    D. weigh the coil and compare it with a 1000-ft. coil

49. When the connections for a d.c. voltmeter are moved from one test point to another, the needle moves backwards. This means that the

    A. second test point is a.c.
    B. meter is defective
    C. meter is magnetized
    D. meter leads are reversed

50. A good insulating material that can be machined readily to a required shape is

    A. mica
    B. porcelain
    C. bakelite
    D. varnished cambric

KEY (CORRECT ANSWERS)

1. A	11. B	21. C	31. A	41. D
2. B	12. B	22. B	32. C	42. A
3. D	13. C	23. B	33. A	43. B
4. D	14. C	24. B	34. A	44. D
5. A	15. A	25. A	35. D	45. D
6. A	16. A	26. B	36. C	46. C
7. C	17. D	27. D	37. C	47. D
8. C	18. B	28. B	38. A	48. C
9. A	19. C	29. C	39. D	49. D
10. D	20. A	30. B	40. D	50. C

TEST 2

DIRECTIONS: Each question or incomplete statement is followed by several suggested answers or completions. Select the one that *BEST* answers the question or completes the statement. *PRINT THE LETTER OF THE CORRECT ANSWER IN THE SPACE AT THE RIGHT.*

1. In most cases, the logical and proper source from which you should first seek explanation of one of the transit rules you do not understand would be the

   A. Transit Authority
   B. head of your department
   C. maintainer with whom you are assigned to work
   D. helper who has an assignment similar to your own

   1.____

2. Employees of the transit system whose work requires them to enter upon the tracks in the subway are cautioned not to wear loose fitting clothing. The *MOST* important reason for this caution is that loose fitting clothing may

   A. interfere when men are using heavy tools
   B. catch on some projection of a passing train
   C. tear more easily than snug fitting clothing
   D. give insufficient protection against subway dust

   2.____

3. Your work will probably be *MOST* appreciated by your superior if you show that

   A. you like your work by asking all the questions you can about it
   B. you're on the job by keeping him informed whenever you think someone has violated a rule
   C. you're interested in improving the job by continually coming to him with suggestions
   D. you're willing to do your share by completing assigned tasks properly and on time

   3.____

4. On the rapid transit system, it would be *MOST* logical to expect to find floodlights located in

   A. subway storage rooms
   B. maintenance headquarters
   C. outdoor train storage yards
   D. under-river tunnels

   4.____

5. The most important reason for insisting on neatness in maintenance quarters is that it

   A. keeps the men busy in slack periods
   B. prevents tools from becoming rusty
   C. makes a good impression on visitors and officials
   D. decreases the chances of accidents to employees

   5.____

6. Maintenance workers whose duties require them to work on the tracks in the subway generally work in pairs. The *LEAST* likely of the following possible reasons for this practice is that

   A. some of the work requires two men
   B. the men can help each other in case of accident

   6.____

C. there is too much equipment for one man to carry
D. it protects against vandalism

7. A foreman reprimands a helper for walking across the subway tracks unnecessarily in violation of the rules and regulations. The BEST reaction of the helper in this situation is to

   A. tell the foreman that he was careful and that he did not take any chances
   B. explain that he took this action to save time
   C. keep quiet and accept the criticism
   D. demand that the foreman show him the rule he violated

8. The type of screwdriver which will develop the greatest turning force is a

   A. screwdriver-bit and brace
   B. spiral push-type
   C. standard straight handle
   D. straight handle with ratchet

9. The book of rules and regulations states that employees must give notice in person or by telephone of their intention to be absent from work at least one hour before they are scheduled to report for duty. The MOST logical reason for having this rule is so that

   A. the employee's excuse can be checked
   B. the employee's pay can be stopped for that day
   C. a substitute can be provided
   D. absences will be limited to necessary ones

10. In a shop, it would be most necessary to provide a fitted cover on the metal container for

    A. old paint brushes
    B. oily rags and waste
    C. sand
    D. broken glass

11. A vertical cylindrical tank 4 feet in diameter and 5 feet high has a capacity of 470 gallons. The number of gallons in the tank when filled to a depth of 1'6" is nearest to

    A. 45   B. 95   C. 140   D. 180

12. A crate contains 3 pieces of equipment weighing 43, 59, and 66 pounds respectively. If the crate is lifted by 4 men each lifting one corner of the crate, the average number of pounds lifted by each of the men is

    A. 56   B. 51   C. 42   D. 36

13. The principal objection to using water from a hose to put out a fire involving electrical equipment is that

    A. serious shock may result
    B. metal parts may rust
    C. fuses may blow out
    D. it may spread the fire

14. Maintainers of the transit system are required to report defective equipment to their superiors, even when the maintenance of the particular equipment is handled by another bureau. The purpose of this rule is to

A. punish employees who don't do their jobs
   B. have repairs made before serious trouble occurs
   C. keep employees on their toes
   D. reward those who keep their eyes open

15. When summoning an ambulance for an injured person, it is most important to give the   15.____

    A. name of the injured person
    B. nature of the injuries
    C. cause of the accident
    D. location of the injured person

16. Employees using supplies from one of the first aid kits available throughout the subway   16.____
    are required to submit an immediate report of the occurrence. Logical reasoning shows
    that the most important purpose for this report is so that the

    A. supplies used will be sure to be replaced
    B. first aid kit can be properly sealed again
    C. employee will be credited for his action
    D. record of first aid supplies will be up to date

17. The tool shown at the right is used to   17.____

    A. set nails
    B. set lead anchors
    C. drill holes in concrete
    D. centerpunch for holes

18. The tool shown at the right is a   18.____
    A. punch
    B. Phillips-type screwdriver
    C. drill holder
    D. socket wrench

19. The tool shown at the right is   19.____
    A. an Allen-head wrench
    B. an offset screwdriver
    C. a double scraper
    D. a nail puller

20. The tool shown at the right is   20.____
    A. an offset wrench
    B. a spanner wrench
    C. a box wrench
    D. an open end wrench

21. The tool shown at the right is used to   21.____
    A. ream holes in wood
    B. countersink holes in soft metals
    C. turn Phillips-head screws
    D. drill holes in concrete

22. If the head of a hammer has become loose on the handle, it should properly be tightened by

   A. driving the handle further into the head
   B. using a slightly larger wedge
   C. driving a nail alongside the present wedge
   D. soaking the handle in water

22.____

23. The right angle shown has been divided into three parts. The number of degrees in the unmarked part is
   A. 46
   B. 36
   C. 21
   D. 6

23.____

24. Assume that you have burned your hand accidentally while on the job. The POOREST first aid remedy for the burn would be

   A. tannic acid   B. iodine
   C. vaseline   D. baking soda

24.____

25. The decimal which is nearest 33/64 is

   A. 0.516   B. 0.500   C. 34/64   D. 1.939

25.____

26. A rule of the transit system is that the telephone must not be used for personal calls. The most important reason for this rule is that the added personal calls

   A. require additional operators
   B. waste company time
   C. tie up telephones which may be urgently needed for company business
   D. increase telephone maintenance

26.____

27. The main purpose of period inspections made by the maintainers on transit system equipment is probably to

   A. encourage the men to take better care of the equipment
   B. discover minor faults before they develop into serious breakdowns
   C. make the men familiar with the equipment
   D. keep the maintenance men busy during otherwise slack periods

27.____

28. A maintainer puts in the following order, "standard stranded, No. 1 gage, bare, galvanized, high strength, steel wire." The required missing information is the

   A. length   B. diameter   C. type   D. material

28.____

29. A coil-spring one foot long has a mark 3 inches from the left end. If this spring is stretched from one end to the other of a yardstick, the mark will be at

   A. 1" on yardstick   B. 3" on yardstick
   C. 9" on yardstick   D. 12" on yardstick

29.____

30. There is a series of holes along a straight line in a piece. The first hole is 1", the second hole is 3/4", the 3rd is 1/2" and the 4th is 1/4". "If this pattern repeats continuously, the 10th hole is

    A. 1" B. 3/4" C. 1/2" D. 1/4"

31. A rule of the transit system states that, "In walking on the track, walk opposite to the direction of traffic on that track if possible." By logical reasoning, the principal safety idea behind this rule is that the man on the track

    A. is more likely to see an approaching train
    B. will be seen more readily by the motorman
    C. need not be as careful
    D. is better able to judge the speed of the train

32. From your observation and knowledge of the subway, the logical reason that certain employees who work on the tracks carry small parts in fiber pails rather than steel pails is that fiber pails

    A. are stronger
    B. can't rust
    C. can't be dented by rough usage
    D. do not conduct electricity

33. When you are newly assigned as a helper to an experienced maintainer, he is most likely to give you good training if your attitude is that

    A. you need the benefit of his experience
    B. he is responsible for your progress
    C. you have the basic knowledge but lack the details
    D. he should do the job where little is to be learned

34. An employee will most likely avoid accidental injury if he

    A. stops to rest frequently
    B. works alone
    C. keeps mentally alert
    D. works very slowly

35. When making a piping or conduit installation, small steel pipe is best turned by using a

    A. monkey wrench   B. stillson wrench
    C. spanner wrench   D. chain wrench

36. A box contains an equal number of iron and brass castings. Each iron casting weighs 2 pounds and each brass casting one pound. If the box contents weigh 240 lbs., the number of brass pieces in the box is

    A. 40 B. 80 C. 120 D. 160

37. The sum of 5 feet 2-3/4 inches, 8 feet 1/2 inch, and 12-1/2 inches is

    A. 25 feet 3-3/4 inches   B. 14 feet 3-3/4 inches
    C. 13 feet 5-3/4 inches   D. 13 feet 3-3/4 inches

38. It ordinarily requires 5 days for 2 men to complete a certain job. If the management wants to have this work done in two days, the number of men required would be

    A. 10	B. 7	C. 6	D. 5

39. If your maintainer makes contact with a 600-volt conductor and remains in contact, your first action should be to

    A. search for the disconnecting switch
    B. ground the conductor with a bare wire
    C. pull him loose by his clothing
    D. cut the conductor

40. Before using an electric drill to make a hole in a piece of scrap iron, it is best to mark the location of the hole with a center punch in order to

    A. make the location easier to see
    B. keep the drill from wandering
    C. C . eliminate the need for a marking device
    D. keep the fuse from blowing

41. Small cuts or injuries should be

    A. taken care of immediately to avoid infection
    B. ignored because they are seldom important
    C. ignored unless they are painful
    D. taken care of at the end of the day

42. If you feel that one of your co-workers is not doing his share of the work, your best procedure is to

    A. increase your own output as a good example
    B. reduce your work output to bring this matter to a head
    C. point this out to the foreman
    D. take no action and continue to do your job properly

43. In case of accident, employees who witnessed the accident are required by the rules to make *INDIVIDUAL* written reports on prescribed forms as soon as possible. The most logical reason for requiring such individual reports rather than a single joint report signed by all witnesses is because the individual reports are

    A. more likely to result in decreasing the number of accidents
    B. less likely to be lost at the same time
    C. less likely to contain unnecessary information
    D. more likely to give the complete picture

44. If a helper finds two orders on his headquarters bulletin board giving conflicting instructions with regard to his work, his most helpful action would be to

    A. call it to the attention of his superior
    B. comply with the order which is easier to follow
    C. follow the order which is best in his judgment
    D. defer that part of the work until a clarifying order is posted

45. The purpose of giving certain transit employees training in first aid is to

    A. provide temporary emergency aid
    B. eliminate the need for calling doctors in accident cases
    C. save money
    D. decrease the number of accidents

46. When you are first appointed as a helper and are assigned to work with a maintainer, he will probably expect you to

    A. make plenty of mistakes
    B. do very little work
    C. do all of the unpleasant work
    D. pay close attention to instructions

47. According to a safety report, a frequent cause of accidents to workers is the improper use of tools. The most helpful conclusion that you can draw from this statement is that

    A. most tools are difficult to use properly
    B. most tools are dangerous to use
    C. many accidents from tools are unavoidable
    D. many accidents from tools occur because of poor working habits

48. The best way to locate a point on the floor directly below the center of a hole in the ceiling is to use a

    A. plumb bob
    B. measuring tape
    C. folding rule
    D. center punch

49. It is generally known that the voltage of the third rail on the New York City subway system is about

    A. 120   B. 600   C. 1000   D. 3000

50. Roadside equipment associated with rapid transit railroad operation is generally housed in a cast iron case. The case is so designed that a gasket is compressed between the door edges and the door frame when the door is locked. By logical reasoning, it is clear that the principal purpose of the gasket is to

    A. act as a cushion to prevent cracking of the cast iron
    B. seal the case so dust and water cannot enter
    C. protect the equipment in the case against vibration
    D. prevent the door from becoming sealed tight by rust

KEY (CORRECT ANSWERS)

1. C	11. C	21. C	31. A	41. A
2. B	12. C	22. B	32. D	42. D
3. D	13. A	23. B	33. A	43. D
4. C	14. B	24. B	34. C	44. A
5. D	15. D	25. A	35. B	45. A
6. D	16. A	26. C	36. B	46. D
7. C	17. C	27. B	37. B	47. D
8. A	18. D	28. A	38. D	48. A
9. C	19. B	29. C	39. C	49. B
10. B	20. D	30. B	40. B	50. B

EXAMINATION SECTION
TEST 1

DIRECTIONS: Each question or incomplete statement is followed by several suggested answers or completions. Select the one that BEST answers the question or completes the statement. *PRINT THE LETTER OF THE CORRECT ANSWER IN THE SPACE AT THE RIGHT.*

1. The one of the following which could NOT be correctly used in describing a toggle switch is   1.____

    A. single-hole mounting B. slow-acting
    C. three-way D. double-pole

2. The flexible power cord connected to a portable tool is sure to have   2.____

    A. steel armor B. stranded wires
    C. aluminum D. asbestos insulation

3. The conductors in a large lead-covered telephone cable are usually   3.____

    A. stranded and rubber insulated
    B. solid and rubber insulated
    C. stranded and paper insulated
    D. solid and paper insulated

4. The rating-terms "240 volts, 10 H.P." would be properly used as part of the specifications for   4.____

    A. transformers B. motors
    C. storage batteries D. heaters

5. To measure the power taken by a d.c. electric motor with only a single instrument you should use   5.____

    A. a voltmeter B. an ammeter
    C. a wattmeter D. a power factor meter

6. Wire splices in modern home and business building wiring systems are made both mechanically firm and of low resistance by means of   6.____

    A. mechanical connectors B. spot welding
    C. brazing D. plastic tape

7. From your knowledge of electrical equipment you know that the part of a transformer which is most subject to damage from high temperature is the   7.____

    A. iron core B. copper winding
    C. winding insulation D. frame or case

8. The power factor of an a.c. circuit containing both a resistor and a condenser is   8.____

    A. 0 B. between 0 and 1.0
    C. 1.0 D. between 1.0 and 2.0

9. The material NOT likely to be found in use as insulation on electrical wires and cables is   9.____

    A. varnished cambric B. paper
    C. glazed porcelain D. asbestos

10. Lighting of many of the subway stations is provided by groups of 5 lamps. Each group of 5 lamps is connected in series and each lamp is rated at 130 volts.
    For full voltage burning of the lamps, the voltage of the supply which feeds these circuits must be

    A. 650 volts
    B. 260 volts
    C. 130 volts
    D. 26 volts

11. Recent safety reports indicate that a principal cause of injury to transit employees is "falls" while on the job. Such reports tend to emphasize that safety on the job is best assured by

    A. following every rule
    B. keeping alert
    C. never working alone
    D. working very slowly

12. The one of the following statements about a plug fuse that is most valid is that it should

    A. always be screwed in lightly to assure easy removal
    B. never be used to hold a coin in the fuse socket
    C. never be replaced by someone unfamiliar with the circuit
    D. always be replaced by a larger size if it burns out frequently

13. The circumference of a circle is given by the formula $C = \pi D$, where C is the circumference, D is the diameter and π is about 3 1/7. If a coil of 20 turns of wire has an average diameter of 16 inches, the total length of wire on the coil is nearest to

    A. 45 feet
    B. 65 feet
    C. 75 feet
    D. 85 feet

14. When the level of the liquid in a storage battery cell is too low, the proper liquid to add to bring the level up to normal is

    A. alkaline solution
    B. distilled water
    C. acid solution
    D. alcohol

15. Mercury toggle switches are sometimes used instead of regular toggle switches because they

    A. cost less
    B. are lighter
    C. are easier to install
    D. do not wear out as quickly

16. When a 100-watt, 120-volt lamp burns continuously for 8 hours at rated voltage the energy used is

    A. 800 watt-hours
    B. 960 watt-hours
    C. 12,000 watt-hours
    D. 96,000 watt-hours

17. Lead is the metal commonly used for

    A. transformer cores
    B. storage battery plates
    C. knife-switch blades
    D. power station panel boards

18. The term "60-watt" is most commonly used in identifying a

    A. fuse
    B. lamp
    C. cable
    D. switch

19. If the input to a 10 to 1 step-down transformer is 25 amperes at 12,000 volts, the secondary output would be nearest to

   A. 2.5 amperes at 12,000 volts
   B. 250 amperes at 120 volts
   C. 2.5 amperes at 120 volts
   D. 250 amperes at 12,000 volts

20. The plug fuse protecting a 120-volt circuit blows because of a dead short-circuit. If, while the short-circuit remains, a 120-volt lamp is screwed into the fuse socket in place of the burned out fuse, the lamp will

   A. burn dimly
   B. remain dark
   C. burn out
   D. burn normally

21. The number of 1 1/2-volt dry cells that must be connected in series to obtain 9 volts is

   A. 3   B. 4   C. 6   D. 9

22. Artificial respiration after a severe electric shock is always necessary when the shock results in

   A. unconsciousness
   B. a burn
   C. stoppage of breathing
   D. bleeding

23. When wire splices are soldered, a flux is used before the solder is applied. The purpose of the flux is to

   A. make the solder adhere readily to the wire
   B. reduce the amount of heat required to melt the solder
   C. save solder
   D. make it unnecessary to clean the wires after skinning

24. A 600-volt cartridge fuse is most easily distinguished from a 250-volt cartridge fuse of the same current rating by its

   A. brass ferrules
   B. smaller diameter
   C. greater length
   D. oval shape

25. The best way for you, as a maintainer's helper, to cooperate with your maintainer is by

   A. doing the work assigned to you to the best of your ability
   B. continually suggesting new ideas
   C. using your best judgment on a job even if in doubt as to a procedure
   D. constantly asking questions about the various phases of the work

26. An electrical helper notices that a certain relay does not pick up promptly when its control circuit is closed. Of the following faults, the only one that could be the cause of this delayed operation is a

   A. control wire broken off one of the relay terminals
   B. burned out fuse
   C. burned out relay coil
   D. fuse making poor contact

27. The principal objection to using water from a hose to put out a fire involving live electrical equipment is that

    A. insulation may be damaged
    B. cast iron parts may rust
    C. serious electric shock may result
    D. a short-circuit will result

27.____

28. If a standard incandescent electric lamp is operated at slightly more than its rated voltage the results will be

    A. shorter life and less light
    B. longer life but less light
    C. shorter life but more light
    D. longer life and more light

28.____

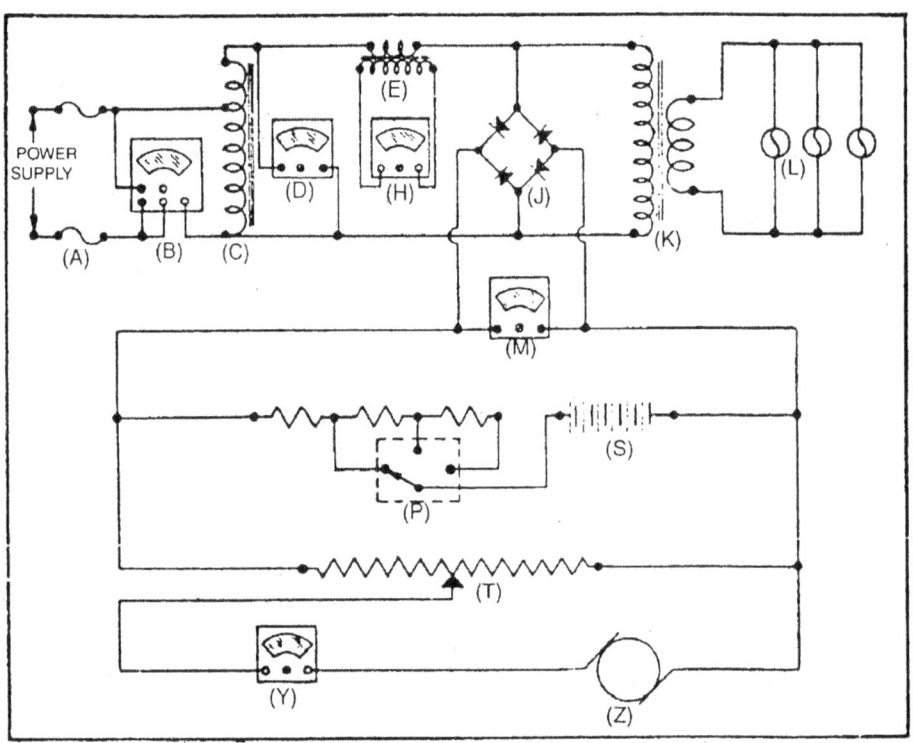

Questions 29 - 40.
Questions 29 through 40 are the names of various electrical devices and measuring instruments each of which is represented by one of the symbols in the above diagram. For each item below, select the appropriate symbol from the diagram. *PRINT,* in the correspondingly numbered item space at the right, the letter given below your selected symbol.

29. lamps   29.____

30. tap switch   30.____

31. battery   31.____

32. d.c. ammeter   32.____

33. d.c. voltmeter   33.____

34. potentiometer   34.____

35. auto-transformer   35.____

36. wattmeter   36.____

37. rectifier   37.____

38. a.c. voltmeter   38.____

39. fuse   39.____

40. a.c. ammeter   40.____

Questions 41 - 50.
Questions 4l through 50 refer to the use of tools shown in the diagram on the next page. Read the item, and for the operation given, select the proper tool to be used from those shown. *PRINT,* in the correspondingly numbered item space at the right, the letter given below your selected tool.

41. Tightening a coupling on the end of a piece of conduit   41.____

42. Making a hole in a concrete wall for a lead anchor   42.____

43. Cutting a one-inch conduit   43.____

44. Loosening the wire connection on the terminal of a standard electric light socket   44.____

45. Cutting 3/0 insulated copper cable   45.____

46. Measuring the total length of several coupled pieces of straight conduit behind a live switchboard without an assistant   46.____

47. Cutting a piece of #10 bare copper wire   47.____

48. Cleaning the burrs from the end of a piece of conduit after cutting   48.____

49. Tightening the drill in the chuck of an electric drill   49.____

50. Tightening the nut on a small stud terminal   50.____

6 (#1)

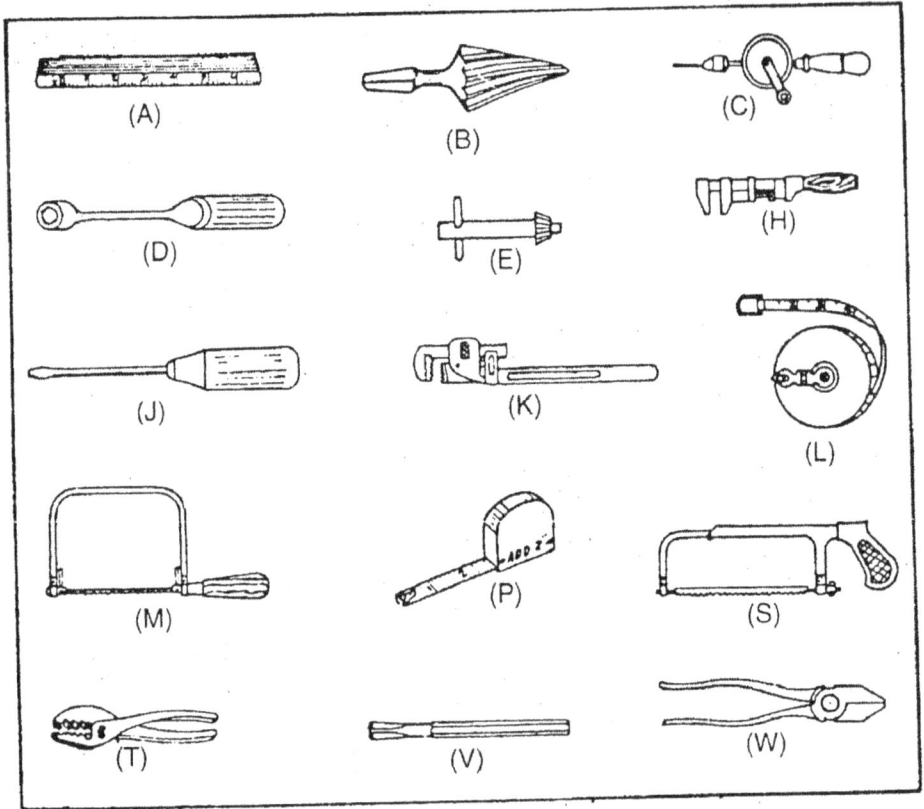

KEY (CORRECT ANSWERS)

1. B	11. B	21. C	31. S	41. K
2. B	12. B	22. C	32. Y	42. V
3. D	13. D	23. A	33. M	43. S
4. B	14. B	24. C	34. T	44. J
5. C	15. D	25. A	35. C	45. S
6. A	16. A	26. D	36. B	46. A
7. C	17. B	27. C	37. J	47. W
8. B	18. B	28. C	38. D	48. B
9. C	19. B	29. L	39. A	49. E
10. A	20. D	30. P	40. H	50. D

TEST 2

DIRECTIONS: Each question or incomplete statement is followed by several suggested answers or completions. Select the one that *BEST* answers the question or completes the statement. *PRINT THE LETTER OF THE CORRECT ANSWER IN THE SPACE AT THE RIGHT.*

1. When a long thread is used on one of two pieces of conduit joined by a coupling secured with a lock nut as indicated in the sketch, the probable reason for the use of this long thread is that
   A. one piece of conduit has been cut too short
   B. expansion or contraction of conduit due to temperature changes has to be compensated for
   C. neither conduit was free to turn when the coupling was made
   D. the joint has to be firmly anchored in a concrete wall

   1._____

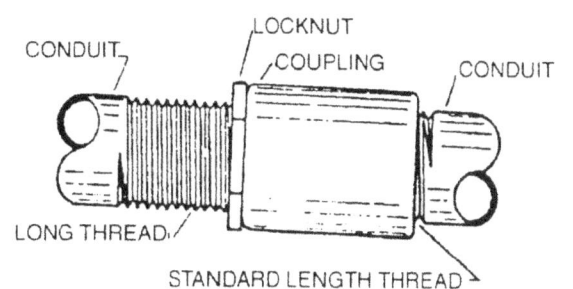

2. The flat-head screw is No.
   A. 1
   B. 2
   C. 3
   D. 4

   2._____

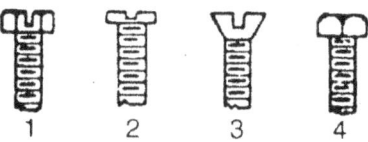

3. The "Phillips" head is No.
   A. 1
   B. 2
   C. 3
   D. 4

   3._____

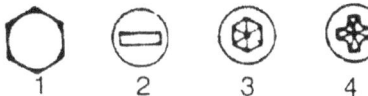

4. If the upper fuse is good and the lower fuse is burned out, the test lamp that will be lighted is No.
   A. 1
   B. 2
   C. 3
   D. 4

   4._____

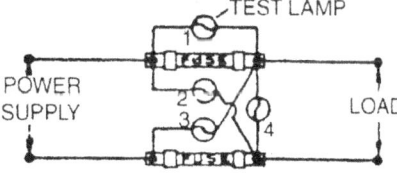

5. Assume you have decided to test a sealed box having two terminals by using the hookup shown. When you hold the test prods on the terminals, the voltmeter needle swings upscale and then quickly returns to zero. As an initial conclusion you would be correct in assuming that the box contained a

   5._____

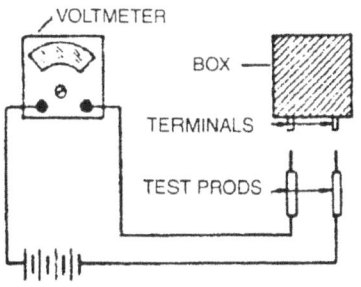

   A. condenser   B. choke   C. rectifier   D. resistor

65

6. Each of the four resistors shown has a resistance of 50 ohms. If the second resistor from the left becomes open-circuited, the reading of the voltmeter will
   A. increase slightly
   B. decrease slightly
   C. fall to zero
   D. become 240 volts

6._____

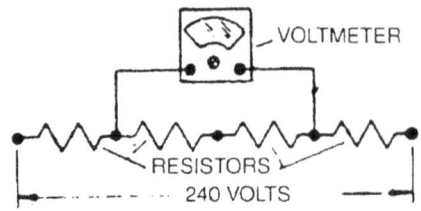

7. The reading of the ammeter should be
   A. 4.0
   B. 2.0
   C. 1.0
   D. 0.5

7._____

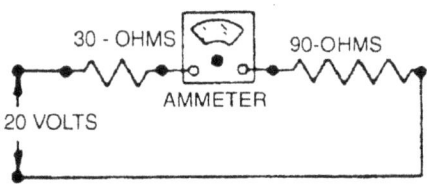

8. The reading of the voltmeter should be nearest to
   A. 30
   B. 90
   C. 120
   D. 240

8._____

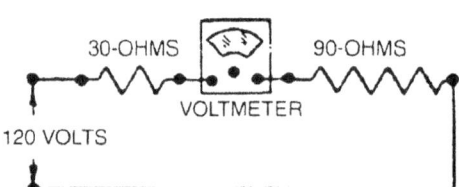

9. The resistor that carries the most current is the one whose resistance, in ohms, is
   A. 4
   B. 3
   C. 2
   D. 1

9._____

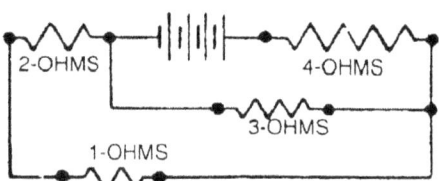

10. The reading of the voltmeter will be highest when the test prods are held on points
    A. 1 and 4
    B. 2 and 5
    C. 3 and 6
    D. 4 and 7

10._____

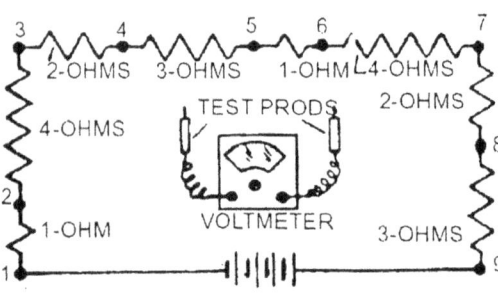

11. The two small a.c. motors are identical, but pinion #2 has twice the diameter of pinion #1. The motors are connected to the same power supply and are wired so that they normally tend to turn in *OPPOSITE* directions. When the power is first turned on

11._____

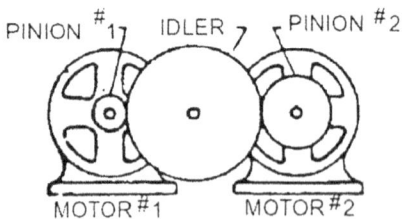

   A. the motors will stall
   B. both motors will turn at near normal speed in the same direction
   C. motor #2 will turn in its normal direction driving motor #1 backwards
   D. motor #1 will turn in its normal direction driving motor #2 backwards

12. Applying your knowledge of electrical measuring instruments, it is most likely that the scale shown is for

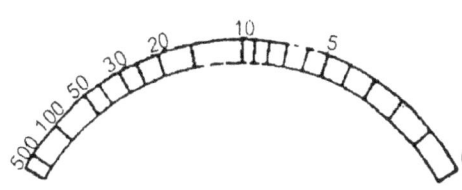

A. an ohmmeter
B. a voltmeter
C. an ammeter
D. a wattmeter

12.____

13. The diameter of the cable, compared to the diameter of a single conductor, is between
A. two and three times
B. three and four times
C. four and five times
D. five and six times

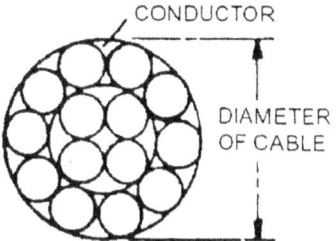

13.____

14. Compared to the total resistance of the variable resistor, the resistance between terminals 1 and 2 is
A. 90/330
B. 120/330
C. 120/360
D. 90/360

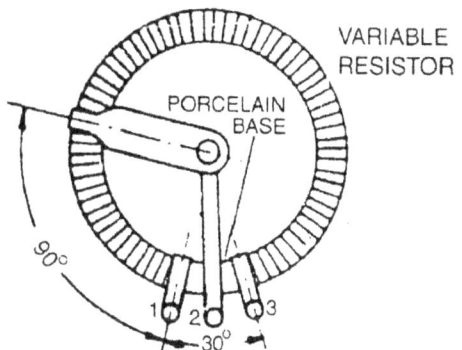

14.____

15. The instrument shown is properly connected to measure
A. a.c. amperes
B. d.c. amperes
C. a.c. volts
D. d.c. volts

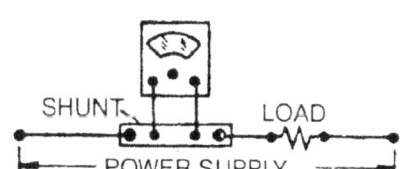

15.____

16. The reading of the voltmeter should be
A. 50
B. 10
C. 5
D. 0

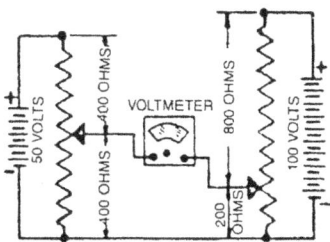

16.____

17. If each of the four 90 conduit elbows has the dimensions shown, the distance S is
    A. 20"
    B. 22"
    C. 24"
    D. 26"

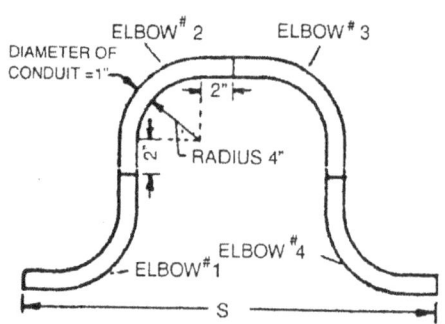

18. The range of both voltmeters shown is 0-300 volts. In this case, the a.c. meter will indicate the correct voltage and the d.c. meter will indicate
    A. zero
    B. a few volts too high
    C. a few volts too low
    D. the correct voltage

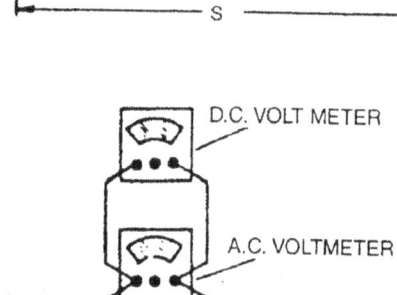

19. The reading on the meter scale shown is
    A. 46
    B. 52
    C. 64
    D. 72

20. The width of the pole piece, in inches, is
    A. 1 7/6
    B. 1 5/16
    C. 11/8
    D. 5 5/16

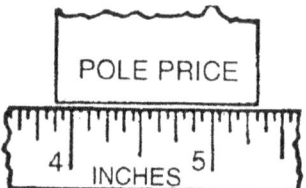

21. The wires in the right-hand junction box are to be spliced so that the switch will control both lighting fixtures and the fixtures will be connected in parallel. The wires to be spliced, in accordance with good wiring practice, are

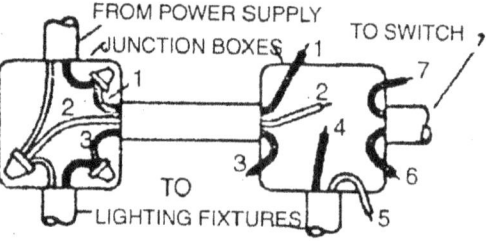

   A. 1 to 4, 2 to 6
      3 to both 5 and 7
   B. 1 to 6, 2 to 5,
      3 to both 4 and 7
   C. 1 to 7, 2 to both
      5 and 6, 3 to 4
   D. 1 to 5, 2 to both
      6 and 7, 3 to 4

22. The sketch shows four standard rigid electrical conduit sizes in cross-section. The one which is nominal 1/2-inch conduit is No.
    A. 1
    B. 2
    C. 3
    D. 4

22.____

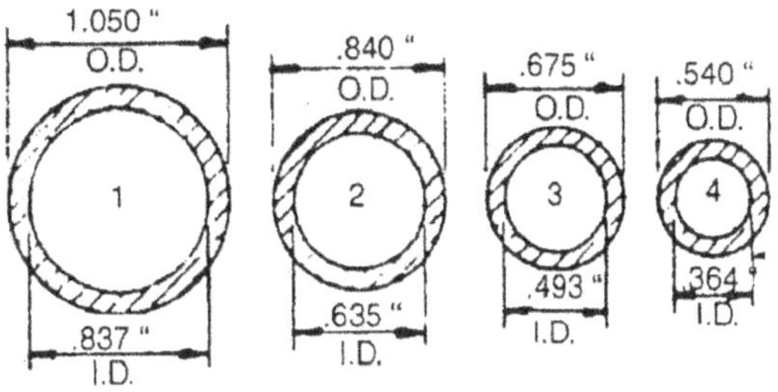

23. The device shown is one element of an iron grid-resistor. Such a large resistor would logically be used when the
    A. resistance required is very high
    B. voltage across it is very high
    C. resistor is to be used outdoors
    D. resistor must carry large currents

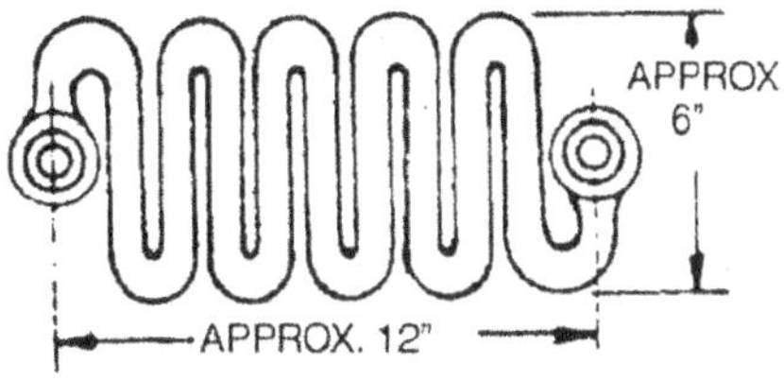

23.____

24. The purpose of the auxiliary blade on the knife switch shown is to
    A. delay the opening of the circuit when the handle is pulled open
    B. cut down arcing by opening the circuit quickly
    C. retain the blades in place
    D. increase the capacity of the switch

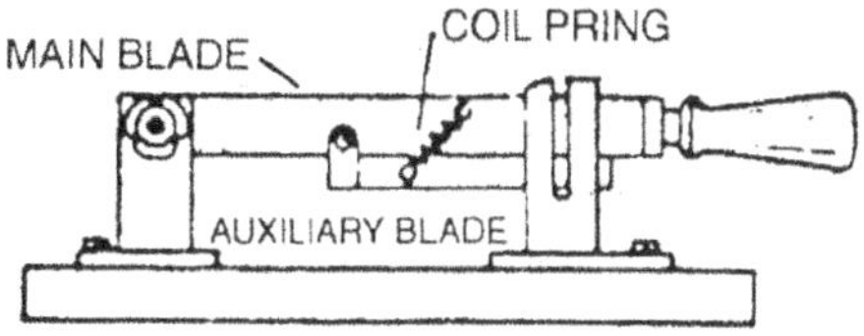

24.____

25. The sketch shows a head-on view of a three-pronged plug intended for use with portable electrical tools. Considering the danger of shock when using such tools, it is evident that the function of the U-shaped prong is to

25.____

   A. insure that the other two prongs enter the outlet with the proper polarity
   B. provide a half-voltage connection when doing light work
   C. prevent accidental pulling of the plug from the outlet
   D. connect the metallic shell of the tool motor to ground

26. Of the following, the poorest conductor of electricity is

26.____

   A. carbon
   C. copper
   B. aluminum
   D. silver

27. Condensers are sometimes connected across relay contacts that make and break frequently. The purpose of using a condenser in this manner is to

27.____

   A. store a charge for the next operation
   B. reduce arcing at the relay contacts
   C. reduce the energy required for relay operation
   D. make the relay quick acting

28. Certain vacuum tubes have four elements inside the glass envelope; namely, a heater, a cathode, a grid, and a plate. In most vacuum tube circuits, the highest "plus" d.c. voltage is applied to the

    A. plate   B. grid   C. cathode   D. heater

28.____

29. A fuse puller is used in replacing

    A. plug fuses   B. link fuses
    C. ribbon fuses   D. cartridge fuses

29.____

30. The National Electrical Code requires that conduit must be continuous from outlet to outlet, must be mechanically and electrically connected to all fittings, and must be suitably grounded. The reason for having the conduit electrically continuous and grounded is to

    A. provide a metallic return conductor
    B. shield the wires inside the conduit from external magnetic fields
    C. make it easy to test wiring connections
    D. prevent electrical shock which might otherwise result from contact with the conduit

30.____

31. If a fellow helper has frequent accidents, it is most likely that he is

    A. not physically strong enough to do the job
    B. simply one of those persons who is unlucky
    C. not paying enough attention to safe work habits
    D. trying too hard

31.____

32. When a certain motor is started up, the incandescent lights fed from the same circuit dim down somewhat and then return to approximately normal brightness as the motor comes up to speed. This definitely shows that the

    A. starting current of the motor is larger than the running current
    B. insulation of the circuit wiring is worn
    C. circuit fuse is not making good contact
    D. incandescent lamps are too large for the circuit

32.____

33. One type of electric motor tends to "run away" if it is not always connected to its load. This motor is the

    A. d.c. series   B. d.c. shunt
    C. a.c. induction   D. a.c. synchronous

33.____

34. The resistance of 1000 feet of #10 A.W.G. wire is approximately 1 ohm. If the resistance of a coil of #10 A.W.G. wire is 1.19 ohms, the length of wire in the coil is nearest to ____ feet.

    A. 1109   B. 1119   C. 1190   D. 1199

34.____

35. The proper tool with which to make a 3/4" diameter hole in a wooden cable cleat is the

    A. reamer   B. countersink   C. auger   D. keyhole saw

35.____

36. If three resistors of 175 ohms, 75 ohms, and 17 ohms respectively, are connected in parallel, the combined resistance will be

    A. greater than 175 ohms   B. between 175 ohms and 75 ohms
    C. between 75 ohms and 17 ohms   D. less than 17 ohms

36.____

37. To determine which wire of a two-wire 120-volt a.c. line is the grounded wire, one correct procedure is to

    A. connect a center-zero voltmeter across the line and note the direction of movement of the pointer
    B. quickly touch each line wire in turn to a cold-water pipe
    C. connect one lead of a test lamp to the conduit, and test each side of the line with the other lead
    D. thrust the two line wires about an inch apart into a slice of raw potato and watch for discoloration

38. While working on a certain track between stations in the subway, a helper notices a man standing on an adjacent track and suspects from the man's actions that he may have no business being there. The most reasonable procedure would be to

    A. continue working and ignore the man
    B. order the man to get off the tracks immediately
    C. ask the man what business he has being there
    D. hold the man for questioning by police

39. With respect to safety of personnel, it is probably *LEAST* important to

    A. have a place for each tool and put each tool in its place at the end of each day
    B. place each tool where it cannot fall down and hurt anyone when working on a job
    C. coat each tool with grease at the end of each day to prevent rust
    D. inspect carefully all tools to be used before beginning the day's work

40. The incoming power supply is usually wired to the "break" jaws rather than to the blades of an exposed knife switch. This practice is followed so that the

    A. blades will be dead when the switch is open
    B. arc will break quickly when the switch is opened
    C. fuses can be replaced without opening the switch
    D. switch can be closed with a minimum of arcing

41. The speed of a d.c. shunt motor is generally regulated by means of a

    A. switch for reversal of the armature supply
    B. source of variable supply voltage
    C. variable resistance in the armature circuit
    D. rheostat in the field circuit

42. With respect to fluorescent lamps it is correct to say that

    A. the filaments seldom burn out
    B. they are considerably easier to handle than incandescent lamps
    C. their efficiency is less than the efficiency of incandescent lamps
    D. the starters and the lamps must be replaced at the same time

43. If your maintainer asked you to bring the tools needed to install a metal first-aid cabinet on a concrete wall, you would need, besides a hammer and a screw driver, a

    A. hack saw   B. star drill
    C. cold chisel   D. socket wrench

44. A 6-32 machine screw necessarily differs from an 8-32 screw in

    A. length
    B. number of threads per inch
    C. shape of head
    D. diameter

45. A conduit coupling is sometimes tightened by using a strap wrench rather than by using a Stillson wrench.
    The strap wrench is used when it is important to avoid

    A. crushing the conduit
    B. stripping the pipe threads
    C. bending the conduit
    D. damaging the outside finish

46. As you are coming up the subway steps leading to the street, an incoming passenger asks you for traveling directions to a particular destination. If you are not sure of the exact directions, your best course is to

    A. give him the best directions you know
    B. tell him to ask a conductor when he is on the train
    C. tell him to ask the man in the change booth
    D. suggest that he should ask another passenger

47. An electrician's knife should NOT be used to

    A. cut copper wires
    B. remove rubber insulation
    C. cut friction tape
    D. sharpen pencils

48. A test lamp using an ordinary lamp bulb is commonly used to test

    A. for polarity of a d.c. power supply
    B. whether a power supply is a.c. or d.c.
    C. whether a circuit is overloaded
    D. for grounds on 120-volt circuits

49. The filament of a regular incandescent electric lamp is usually made of

    A. tungsten   B. carbon   C. nickel   D. iron

50. After No. 2 A.W.G., the next smaller copper wire or cable size is No.

    A. 0   B. 1   C. 3   D. 4

KEY (CORRECT ANSWERS)

1. C	11. D	21. B	31. C	41. D
2. C	12. A	22. B	32. A	42. A
3. D	13. C	23. D	33. A	43. B
4. C	14. A	24. B	34. C	44. D
5. A	15. B	25. D	35. C	45. D
6. D	16. C	26. A	36. D	46. C
7. C	17. D	27. B	37. C	47. A
8. C	18. A	28. A	38. C	48. D
9. A	19. C	29. D	39. C	49. A
10. B	20. A	30. D	40. A	50. C

EXAMINATION SECTION
TEST 1

DIRECTIONS: Each question or incomplete statement is followed by several suggested answers or completions. Select the one that *BEST* answers the question or completes the statement. *PRINT THE LETTER OF THE CORRECT ANSWER IN THE SPACE AT THE RIGHT.*

1. The letters S.P.S.T. frequently found on wiring plans refer to a type of   1._____

    A. cable   B. switch   C. fuse   D. motor

2. Renewable fuses differ from ordinary fuses in that   2._____

    A. they can carry higher overloads
    B. burned out fuses can be located more easily
    C. burned out fuse elements can be readily replaced
    D. they can be used on higher voltages

3. When a maintainer reports a minor trouble orally to his foreman, the most important information the foreman would require from the maintainer would be the   3._____

    A. type of trouble and its exact location
    B. names of all men with him when he discovered the trouble
    C. exact time the trouble was discovered
    D. work he was doing when he noted the trouble

4. A helper can most quickly make himself useful on the job if he   4._____

    A. asks questions of his foreman at every opportunity
    B. continually suggests changes in work procedures to the maintainer
    C. listens carefully to instructions and carries them out
    D. insists on doing all heavy lifting himself

5. After No. 10 A.W.G., the next smaller copper wire size in common use is No.   5._____

    A. 8   B. 9   C. 11   D. 12

6. The best of the following tools to use for cutting off a piece of single-conductor #6 rubber insulated lead covered cable is a   6._____

    A. pair of electrician's pliers
    B. hacksaw
    C. hammer and cold chisel
    D. lead knife

7. Transit employees whose work requires them to enter upon the tracks in the subway are cautioned not to wear loose fitting clothing. The most important reason for this caution is that loose fitting clothing may   7._____

    A. interfere when they are using heavy tools
    B. catch on some projection of a passing train
    C. give insufficient protection against dust
    D. tear more easily than snug fitting clothing

8. It would *NOT* be good practice to tighten a one-inch hexagon nut with   8.___

   A. a monkey wrench
   B. a one-inch fixed open end wrench
   C. an adjustable open-end wrench
   D. a Stillson wrench

9. Lock washers are used principally with   9.___

   A. machine screws   B. wood screws
   C. self-tapping screws   D. lag screws

10. Toggle bolts are most appropriate for use to fasten conduit clamps to a   10.___

    A. steel column   B. concrete wall
    C. hollow tile wall   D. brick wall

11. If a 10-24 by 3/4" machine screw is not available, the screw which could be most easily modified to use in an emergency is a   11.___

    A. 10-24 by 1/2"   B. 12-24 by 3/4"
    C. 10-24 by 1 1/2"   D. 8-24 by 3/4"

12. Lighting in many of the subway cars is provided by 22 lamps all connected in a single series circuit which is fed from the third rail at 600 volts. The voltage rating of each individual lamp in the series must be approximately   12.___

    A. 600 volts   B. 120 volts
    C. 30 volts   D. 22 volts

13. In attempting to revive a person who has stopped breathing after receiving an electric shock, it is most important to   13.___

    A. start artificial respiration immediately
    B. wrap the victim in a blanket
    C. massage the ankles and wrists
    D. force the victim to swallow a stimulant

14. After pulling the fuse of a 600-volt circuit, and before starting the work of connecting additional equipment to the circuit, the most important safety precaution to take is to   14.___

    A. examine the condition of the fuse
    B. disconnect all load from the circuit
    C. check that all tools have insulated handles
    D. test to make sure the circuit is dead

15. The most practical way to determine in the field if a large coil of #14 wire has the required length for a given job is to   15.___

    A. weigh the coil and compare with a new 1000-foot coil
    B. measure the electrical resistance and compare with a 1000-foot coil
    C. measure the length of one turn and multiply by the number of turns
    D. unwind the coil and lay the wire alongside the conduit before pulling it in

16. Maintainers of the transit system are required to report defective equipment to their superiors, even when the maintenance of the particular equipment is handled entirely by another bureau. The purpose of this rule is to

    A. fix responsibility
    B. discourage slackers
    C. encourage alertness
    D. prevent accidents

17. A standard pipe thread differs from a standard screw thread in that the pipe thread

    A. is tapered
    B. is deeper
    C. requires no lubrication when cutting
    D. has the same pitch for any diameter of pipe

18. The material which is LEAST likely to be found in use as the outer covering of rubber insulated wires or cables is

    A. cotton
    B. varnished cambric
    C. lead
    D. neoprene

19. In measuring to determine the size of a stranded insulated conductor, the proper place to use the wire gauge is on

    A. the insulation
    B. the outer covering
    C. the stranded conductor
    D. one strand of the conductor

20. Rubber insulation on an electrical conductor would most quickly be damaged by continuous contact with

    A. acid   B. water   C. oil   D. alkali

21. If a fuse clip becomes hot under normal circuit load, the most probable cause is that the

    A. clip makes poor contact with the fuse ferrule
    B. circuit wires are too small
    C. current rating of the fuse is too high
    D. voltage rating of the fuse is too low

22. If the input to a 10 to 1 step-down transformer is 15 amperes at 2400 volts, the secondary output would be nearest to

    A. 1.5 amperes at 24,000 volts
    B. 150 amperes at 240 volts
    C. 1.5 amperes at 240 volts
    D. 150 amperes at 24,000 volts

23. The resistance of a copper wire to the flow of electricity

    A. increases as the diameter of the wire increases
    B. decreases as the diameter of the wire decreases
    C. decreases as the length of the wire increases
    D. increases as the length of the wire increases

24. Where galvanized steel conduit is used, the primary purpose of the galvanizing is to   24.___

    A. increase mechanical strength
    B. retard rusting
    C. provide a good surface for painting
    D. provide good electrical contact for grounding

25. The lamps used for station and tunnel lighting in the subways are generally operated at   25.___
    slightly less than their rated voltage. The logical reason for this is to

    A. prevent overloading of circuits
    B. increase the life of the lamps
    C. decrease glare
    D. obtain a more even distribution of light

26. The correct method of measuring the power taken by an a.c. electric motor is to use a   26.___

    A. wattmeter
    B. voltmeter and an ammeter
    C. power factor meter
    D. tachometer

27. Assume that you have been asked to get the tools for a maintainer to use in taking down   27.___
    a run of exposed conduit (including outlet boxes) from its installed location on the surface
    of a concrete wall. The combination of tools which would probably prove most useful
    would be a

    A. Stillson wrench, a box wrench, and a hack saw
    B. hack saw, a screw driver, and an adjustable open-end wrench
    C. screw driver, an adjustable open-end wrench, and a Stillson wrench
    D. screw driver, a hammer, and a box wrench

Questions 28 - 37.
Questions 28 through 37 refer to the use of the tools shown on the next page. Read the item and, for the operation given, select the proper tool to be used from those shown. *PRINT,* in the correspondingly numbered item space at the right, the letter given below your selected tool.

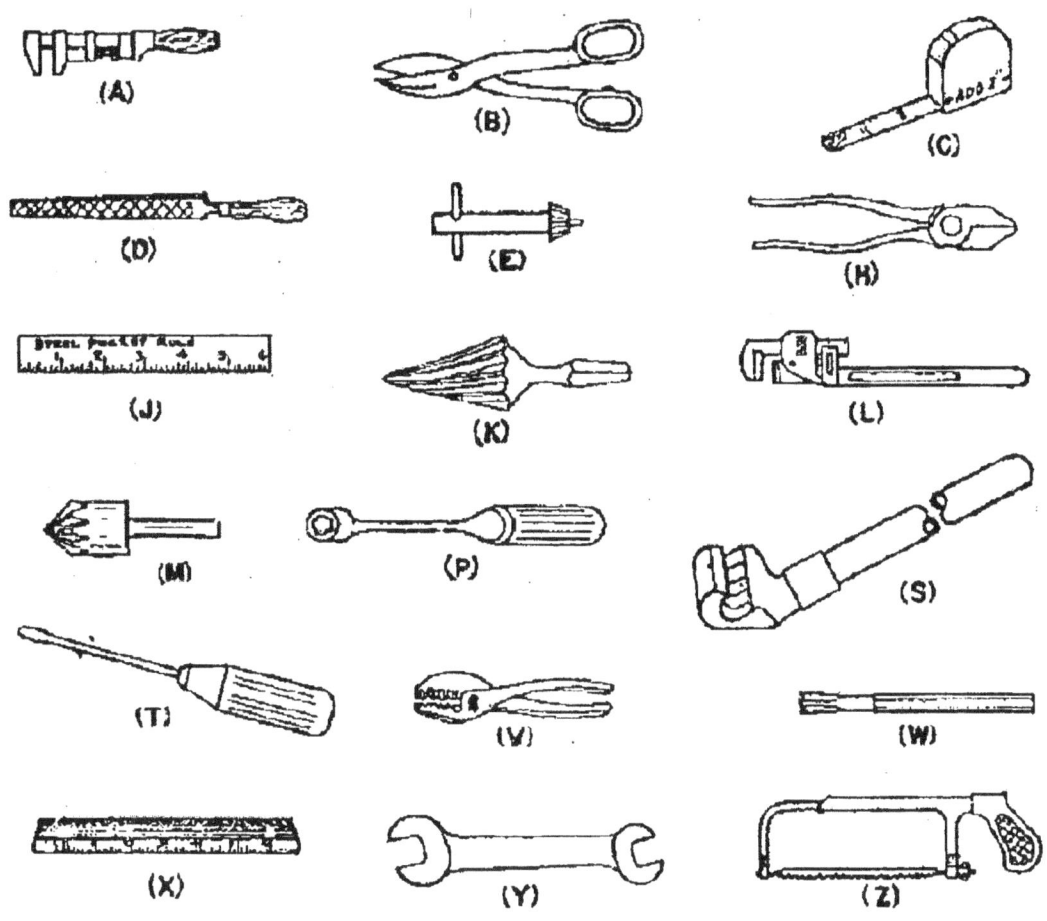

28. Loosening the nut holding a wire on a stud terminal. 28.____

29. Removing burrs from the inner edge of conduit after cutting it. 29.____

30. Measuring the distance between exposed terminals on a low-voltage switchboard which is alive. 30.____

31. Loosening a coupling which is tight on the end of a piece of conduit. 31.____

32. Tightening the chuck on an electric drill. 32.____

33. Tightening a 3/4 inch conduit bushing inside an outlet box. 33.____

34. Skinning a no. 14 A.W.G. rubber insulated wire. 34.____

35. Cutting off part of a brass machine screw which is too long. 35.____

36. Prying off a rubber gasket that is stuck to the inside of the cover that has been taken off a watertight pull box. 36.____

37. Making a hole for a lead anchor in a concrete wall. 37.____

38. The sketch which correctly represents the cross-section of a standard stranded copper conductor is

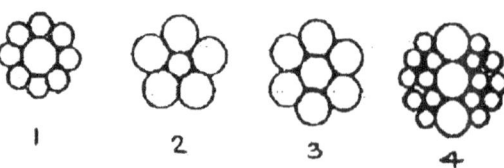

   A. 1   B. 2   C. 3   D. 4

39. The reading of the voltmeter should be

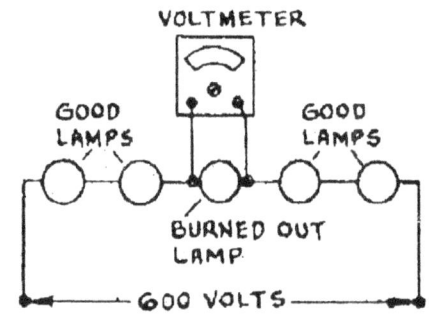

   A. 600   B. 300   C. 120   D. zero

40. If the voltage of each of the dry cells shown is 1.5 volts, the voltage between X and Y is
   A. 3
   B. 6
   C. 9
   D. 12

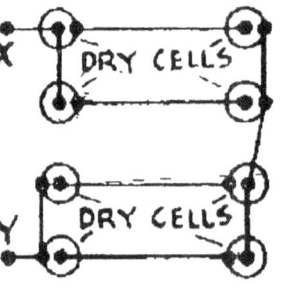

41. In accordance with the voltages shown, the power supply must be
   A. three-wire d.c.
   B. three-phase a.c.
   C. two-phase a.c.
   D. single-phase a.c.

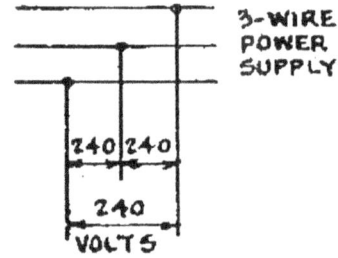

42. Meter 1 is
   A. an ammeter
   B. a frequency meter
   C. a wattmeter
   D. a voltmeter

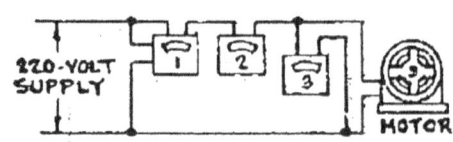

43. The insulator shown is a
    A. pin type insulator
    B. strain insulator
    C. suspension type insulator
    D. insulating bushing

43.____

44. The two coils are wound in the directions indicated and both coils have exactly the same number of turns. When the switch is closed, the north pole of the permanent magnet will be
    A. repelled by both the left-hand and right-hand cores
    B. attracted by both the left-hand and right-hand cores
    C. attracted by the left-hand core and repelled by the right-hand core
    D. repelled by the left-hand core and attracted by the right-hand core

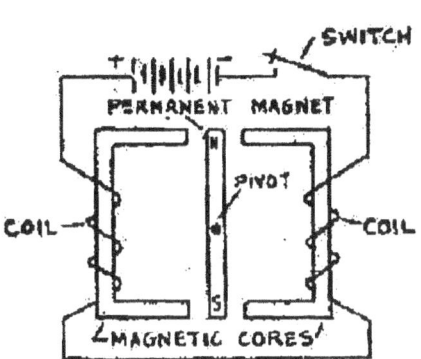

44.____

45. Regardless of the battery voltage, it is clear that the smallest current is in the resistor having a resistance of
    A. 200 ohms
    B. 300 ohms
    C. 400 ohms
    D. 500 ohms

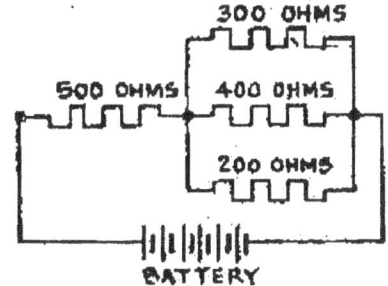

45.____

46. The five lamps shown are each rated at 120-volts 60-watts. If all are good lamps, lamp no. 5 will be
    A. much brighter than normal
    B. about its normal brightness
    C. much dimmer than normal
    D. completely dark

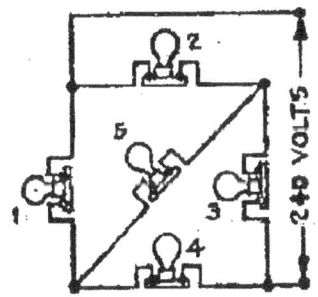

46.____

47. If the voltmeter reads 34 volts, the circuit voltage is about
    A. 68
    B. 85
    C. 102
    D. 119

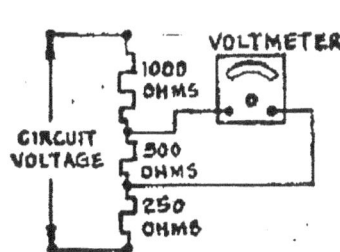

47.____

48. If the voltage of the supply is 120 volts, the readings of the voltmeter should be
    A. 60 volts on each meter
    B. 120 volts on each meter
    C. 80 volts on meter #1 and 40 volts on meter #2
    D. 80 volts on meter #2 and 40 volts on meter #1

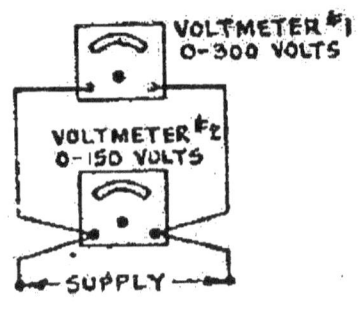

48.___

49. The sketch shows the four resistance dials and the multiplying dial of a resistance bridge. The four resistance dials can be set to any value of resistance up to 10,000 ohms, and the multiplier can be set at any of the nine points shown. In their present positions, the five pointers indicate a reading of
    A. 13.60
    B. 136,000
    C. 130,600
    D. 13.06

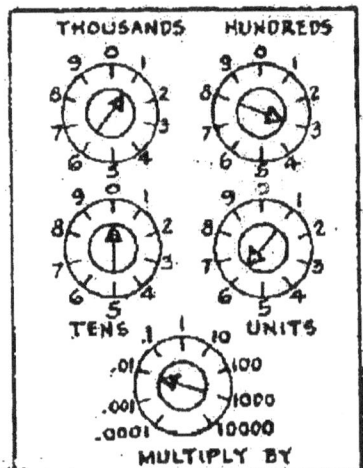

49.___

50. The indication on the meter scale is
    A. 266
    B. 258
    C. 253
    D. 251.5

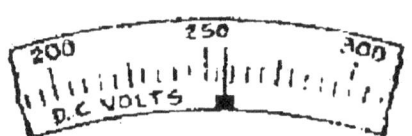

50.___

KEY (CORRECT ANSWERS)

1. B	11. C	21. A	31. L	41. B
2. C	12. C	22. B	32. E	42. C
3. A	13. A	23. D	33. V	43. A
4. C	14. D	24. B	34. H	44. A
5. D	15. C	25. B	35. H	45. C
6. B	16. D	26. A	36. T	46. D
7. B	17. A	27. C	37. W	47. D
8. D	18. B	28. P	38. C	48. B
9. A	19. D	29. K	39. A	49. D
10. C	20. C	30. X	40. B	50. B

TEST 2

DIRECTIONS: Each question or incomplete statement is followed by several suggested answers or completions. Select the one that BEST answers the question or completes the statement. *PRINT THE LETTER OF THE CORRECT ANSWER IN THE SPACE AT THE RIGHT.*

1. The reading of the kilowatt-hour meter is
    A. 7972
    B. 2786
    C. 1786
    D. 6872

    1.___

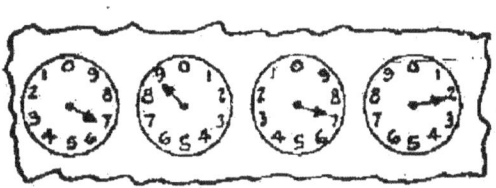

2. The reading shown on the micrometer is
    A. 0.203
    B. 0.222
    C. 0.228
    D. 0.247

    2.___

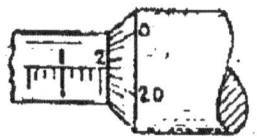

3. The center to center distance between the two poles is

    A. $\dfrac{11"}{16}$

    B. $1\dfrac{1"}{16}$

    C. $1\dfrac{11"}{16}$

    D. $1\dfrac{13"}{16}$

    3.___

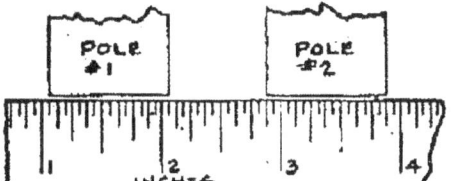

4. The outlet which will accept the plug is
    A. 1
    B. 2
    C. 3
    D. 4

    4.___

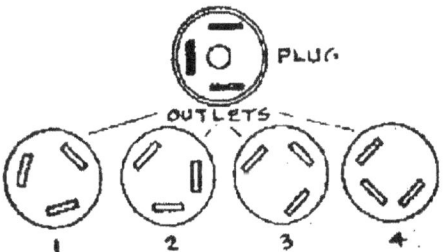

5. The double-pole double-throw switch which is properly connected as a reversing switch is
    A. 1
    B. 2
    C. 3
    D. 4

    5.___

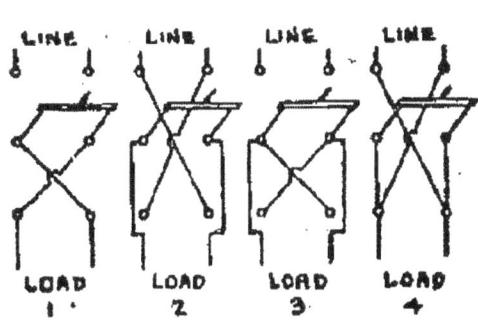

6. The standard coupling for rigid electrical conduit is
   A. 1
   B. 2
   C. 3
   D. 4

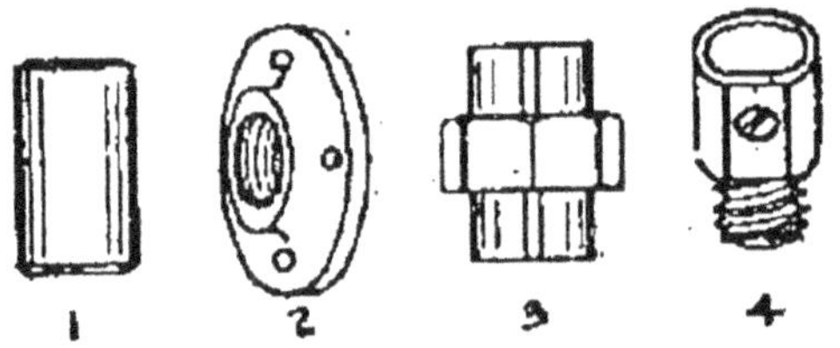

7. The shape of nut most commonly used on electrical terminals is
   A. 1
   B. 2
   C. 3
   D. 4

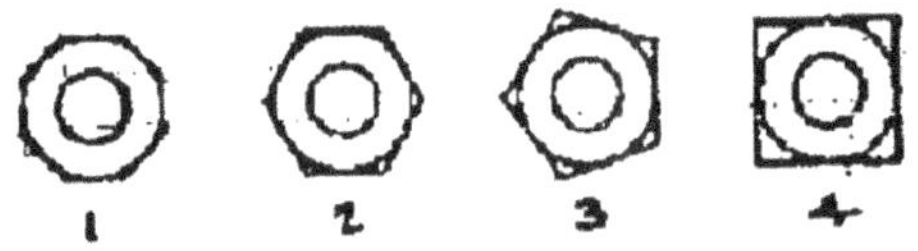

8. The stove bolt is
   A. 1
   B. 2
   C. 3
   D. 4

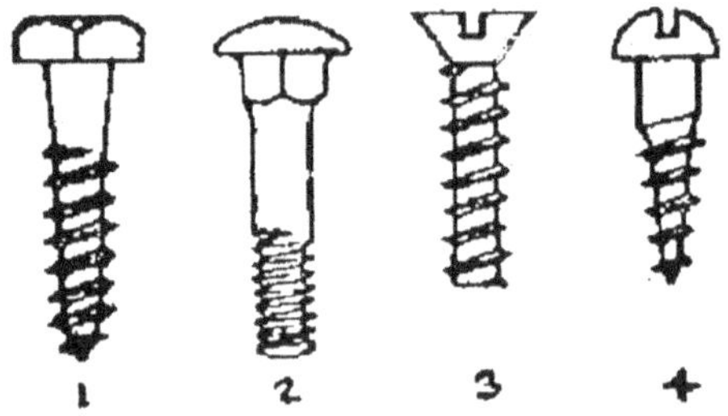

Questions 9 - 14.
Questions 9 through 14 refer to the figures on the following page.
Each item gives the proper figure to use with that item.

9. Referring to Figure 1, if the 500-ohm resistor becomes open circuited, the reading of the ammeter will probably
   A. remain unchanged   B. decrease
   C. increase   D. drop to zero

10. The total equivalent resistance in ohms between points X and Y in Figure 2 is
    A. 3   B. 5   C. 15   D. 45

11. The reading of the voltmeter in Figure 3 should be
    A. 150   B. 100   C. 50   D. zero

12. In Figure 4, if switch 1 only is closed the reading of the voltmeter will
    A. increase   B. decrease, but not to zero
    C. remain unchanged   D. become zero

13. In Figure 4, if switch 2 only is closed the reading of the voltmeter will
    A. increase   B. decrease, but not to zero
    C. remain unchanged   D. become zero

14. In Figure 4, if switch 3 only is closed the reading of the voltmeter will
    A. increase   B. decrease, but not to zero
    C. remain unchanged   D. become zero

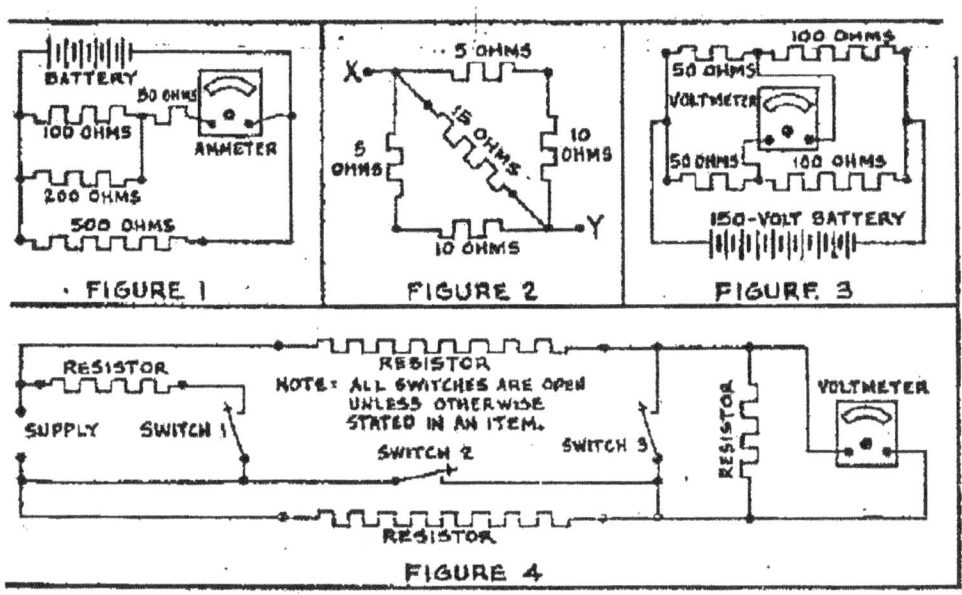

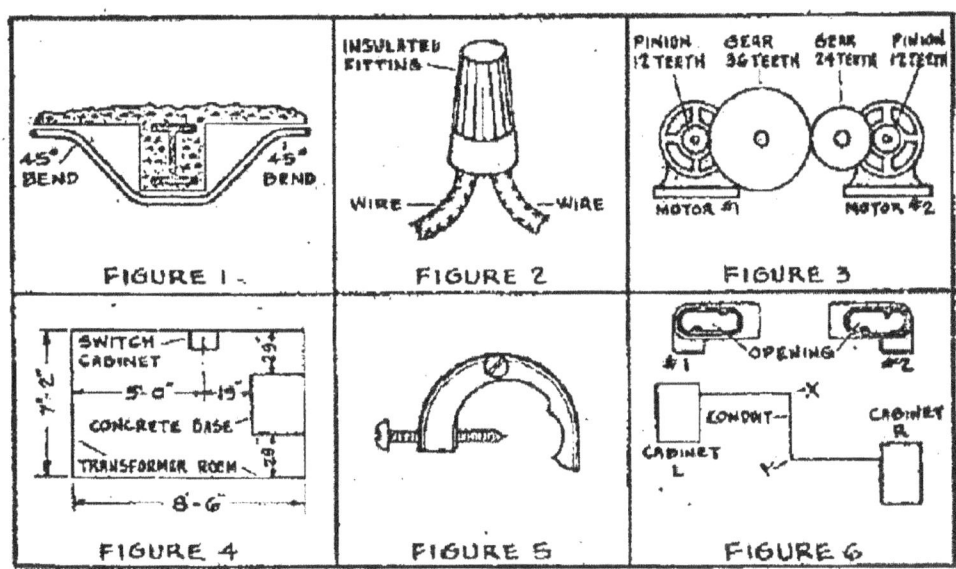

Questions 15 - 20.
Questions 15 through 20 refer to the figures above. Each item gives the proper figure to use with that item.

15. When a wire is pulled into the conduit in Figure 1, it must go around bends amounting to a total of

   A. 0° B. 90° C. 180° D. 360°

16. Wires are often spliced by the use of a fitting like the one shown in Figure 2. The use of this fitting does away with the need for

   A. skinning B. cleaning
   C. twisting D. soldering

17. The two identical motors in Figure 3 are connected to the same power supply and are wired so that they normally tend to turn in the same direction. When the power is turned on

   A. the motors will stall
   B. both motors will turn at normal speed in the same direction
   C. motor #1 will turn in its normal direction driving motor #2 backwards
   D. motor #2 will turn in its normal direction driving motor #1 backwards

17.___

18. The dimensions of the concrete base shown in Figure 4 are

   A. 14" x 28"   B. 23" x 28"
   C. 23" x 29"   D. 14" x 29"

18.___

19. The device shown in Figure 5 is a

   A. C-clamp   B. test clip
   C. battery connector D. ground clamp

19.___

20. Figure 6 shows two types of conduit fitting (#1 and #2) used as pull boxes at sharp bends in conduit runs. The figure also shows the layout of a conduit run on the wall between cabinets L and R. If wire is to be pulled into the conduit starting at cabinet L, and the wire is to be continuous without a splice from cabinet L to cabinet R, the best choice of fittings is to have a

   A. #1 at corner X and a #2 at corner Y
   B. #2 at both corners X and Y
   C. #1 at both corners X and Y
   D. #2 at corner X and a #1 at corner Y

20.___

21. Checking a piece of rigid electrical conduit with a steel scale, you measure the inside diameter as 1 1/16" and the outside diameter as 1 5/16". The nominal size of this conduit is

   A. 3/4"   B. 1"   C. C 1 1/4"   D. D 1 1/2"

21.___

22. Of the following, it would be most difficult to solder a copper wire to a metal plate made of

   A. copper   B. brass   C. iron   D. tin

22.___

23. After a piece of rigid conduit has been cut to length, it is most important to

   A. ream the inside edge to prevent injury to wires
   B. file the end flat to make an accurate fit
   C. coat the cut surface with red lead to prevent rust
   D. file the outside edge to a taper for ease in threading

23.___

24. When lamps on the transit system are installed at less than 7 ft. 6 in. from the floor, they are provided with lamp guards. The purpose of guards in such cases is most likely to

   A. reduce glare
   B. prevent accidental burning of passengers
   C. minimize lamp breakage
   D. discourage lamp thefts

24.___

25. Rigid conduit is generally secured to sheet metal outlet boxes by means of

    A. threadless couplings
    B. box connectors
    C. locknuts and bushings
    D. conduit clamps

26. According to generally recommended practice, helper Richard Roe answering the telephone at the Undercliff Ave. signal section headquarters would do best to say

    A. "Hello, this is Undercliff Ave., Roe speaking."
    B. "This is Roe, -Signal Section."
    C. "Roe, Signal Section, -Who's calling?"
    D. "Signal Section, Undercliff Ave., Roe speaking."

27. While a certain d.c. shunt motor is driving a light load, part of the field winding becomes short circuited. The motor will most likely

    A. increase its speed
    B. decrease its speed
    C. remain at the same speed
    D. come to a stop

28. The circumference of a circle is given by the formula $C = 2\pi R$, where C is the circumference, R is the radius, and π is approximately 3 1/7. The circumference of an oil drum having a diameter of one foot and nine inches is therefore about

    A. 132 inches
    B. 66 inches
    C. 33 inches
    D. 17 inches

29. Each time a certain electric heater is turned on, the incandescent lights connected to the same branch circuit become dimmer and when the heater is turned off the lamps become brighter. The factor which probably contributes most to this effect is the

    A. voltage of the circuit
    B. size of the circuit fuse
    C. current taken by the lamps
    D. size of the circuit conductors

30. Comparing the shunt field winding with the series field winding of a compound d.c. motor, it would be correct to say that the shunt field winding has

    A. more turns but the lower resistance
    B. more turns and the higher resistance
    C. fewer turns and the lower resistance
    D. fewer turns but the higher resistance

Questions 31 - 37.
Questions 31 through 37 are based on the motor inspection instructions given below. Read these instructions carefully before answering these questions.

GENERAL INSTRUCTIONS FOR WEEKLY MOTOR INSPECTION

Inspect each motor to see if there is any unusual amount of dust or chips on or near it, and to see if there is anything left lying about which might interfere with the free running or ventilation of the motor. Check lubrication in accordance with standard instructions for the type of motor. At the same time, take notice of any unusual noise or odor for evidence of excessive wear or overloading; feel bearing housings for heat and vibration. Inspect the commutator of each d.c. motor for discoloration, dirt, and uneven wear; look for sparking at the brushes while the motor is running.

Any minor defect should be corrected on the spot as soon as it is discovered, and the proper report made to your superior of the action taken. Any major defect that is found should be reported promptly to your superior so that it can be corrected before the damage becomes too great to be repaired.

31. One sure sign that there has been sparking at the brushes of a stopped d.c. motor would be

    A. the odor of hot rubber insulation
    B. hot bearings
    C. grooves worn around the commutator
    D. pits on the commutator surface

32. A common way of reducing the chances of uneven commutator wear is to

    A. use brushes of different hardness
    B. allow some end play in the motor bearings
    C. anneal the commutator after assembly
    D. turn the commutator down frequently

33. Upon entering a pump room in which a motor-driven pump is running, the maintainer detects the odor of hot insulating varnish. This odor indicates that the

    A. varnish has been freshly applied
    B. bearings are poorly lubricated
    C. room is insufficiently ventilated
    D. motor is being overloaded

34. If an unusual amount of dust is found around the base of a motor which is being inspected, the proper procedure to follow is to

    A. take no action but report the motor for further inspection
    B. remove the dust and note the action in your daily report
    C. inspect the bearings for signs of excessive wear
    D. lubricate the motor in accordance with standard instructions

35. If one bearing housing of a running motor feels exceptionally hot but there is no unusual vibration, the most logical conclusion is that the

    A. motor is being overloaded
    B. bearing needs lubrication
    C. shaft has become worn
    D. motor has been running a long time

36. During a weekly inspection, the motor driving a certain drainage pump is found to be unusually noisy when it runs. The starting and stopping of this motor is automatically controlled by a float switch. In order to comply with the above general instructions, the

    A. cause should be investigated and the condition reported promptly to your superior for corrective action
    B. float switch should be adjusted so that the motor will run less frequently
    C. motor should be shut down immediately
    D. bearings should be lubricated in accordance with standard instructions

37. When making a weekly motor inspection you would be LEAST likely to need a

    A. grease gun   B. dust brush
    C. thermometer   D. flashlight

38. The most important reason for using a fuse-puller when removing a cartridge fuse from the fuse clips is to

    A. prevent blowing of the fuse
    B. prevent injury to the fuse element
    C. reduce the chances of personal injury
    D. reduce arcing at the fuse clips

39. A coil of wire wound on an iron core draws exactly 5 amperes when connected across the terminals of a ten-volt storage battery. If this coil is now connected across the ten-volt secondary terminals of an ordinary power transformer, the current drawn will be

    A. less than 5 amperes
    B. more than 5 amperes
    C. exactly 5 amperes
    D. more or less than 5 amperes depending on the frequency

40. Standard iron conduit comes in 10-foot lengths. The number of such lengths required for a run of 23 yards is

    A. 3   B. 4   C. 6   D. 7

41. A revolution counter applied to the end of a rotating shaft reads 100 when a stop-watch is started. It reads 850 when the stop-watch indicates 90 seconds. The average RPM of the shaft is

    A. 8.4   B. 9.4   C. 500   D. 567

42. Motor speeds are generally measured directly in RPM by the use of a

    A. potentiometer   B. manometer
    C. dynamometer   D. tachometer

43. A rule of the transit system is that the system telephones must not be used for personal calls. The most important reason for this rule is that such personal calls

    A. increase telephone maintenance
    B. tie up telephones which may be urgently needed for company business
    C. waste company time
    D. require additional operators

44. To reverse the direction of rotation of a 3-phase motor, it is necessary to

   A. increase the resistance of the rotor circuit
   B. interchange any two of the three line connections
   C. interchange all three line connections
   D. reverse the polarity of the rotor circuit

45. Mica is commonly used in electrical construction for

   A. commutator bar separators
   B. switchboard panels
   C. strain insulators
   D. heater cord insulation

46. The rating term "1000 ohms, 10 watts" would generally be applied to a

   A. heater   B. relay   C. resistor   D. transformer

47. According to the National Electrical Code, the identified (or grounded) conductor of the branch circuit supplying an incandescent lamp socket must be connected to the screw shell. The most likely reason for this requirement is that

   A. longer lamp life results
   B. the wiring will be kept more nearly uniform
   C. persons are more likely to come in contact with the shell
   D. the shell can carry heavier currents

48. In an installation used to charge a storage battery from a motor-generator you would LEAST expect to find

   A. a rectifier   B. a rheostat
   C. a voltmeter   D. an ammeter

49. The letters R.I.L.C. are used in identifying

   A. transformers   B. motors
   C. cables   D. storage batteries

50. Two separate adjacent lamp bulbs are placed behind each colored lens of the train signals alongside the tracks in the subway. The logical reason why two bulbs are used instead of one bulb is to

   A. permit lower line voltage
   B. increase the light intensity
   C. permit the use of smaller bulbs
   D. keep the signal lighted in case one bulb fails

KEY (CORRECT ANSWERS)

1. D	11. D	21. B	31. D	41. C
2. B	12. C	22. C	32. B	42. D
3. D	13. A	23. A	33. D	43. B
4. C	14. D	24. D	34. B	44. B
5. B	15. C	25. C	35. B	45. A
6. A	16. D	26. D	36. A	46. C
7. B	17. A	27. A	37. C	47. C
8. C	18. B	28. B	38. C	48. A
9. C	19. D	29. D	39. A	49. C
10. B	20. D	30. B	40. D	50. D

EXAMINATION SECTION
TEST 1

DIRECTIONS: Each question or incomplete statement is followed by several suggested answers or completions. Select the one that BEST answers the question or completes the statement. PRINT THE LETTER OF THE CORRECT ANSWER IN THE SPACE AT THE RIGHT.

1. The core of an electro-magnet is usually

   A. aluminum   B. lead   C. brass   D. iron

2. The purpose of applying artificial respiration to the victim of an electric shock is to

   A. restore blood circulation
   B. avoid excessive loss of blood
   C. keep the victim warm
   D. supply oxygen to the lungs

3. Electrical maintenance workers whose duties require them to be on the tracks in the subway generally work In pairs. Of the following possible reasons for having the two men work together, the LEAST likely is that

   A. the tools and equipment are too much for one man to carry
   B. it provides better protection against vandalism
   C. some of the tests and maintenance work require two men
   D. the men can help each other in case of accident

4. A stranded wire is given the same size designation as a solid wire if it has the same

   A. cross-sectional area   B. weight per foot
   C. overall diameter   D. strength

5. Safety regulations prohibit testing even a 20-volt light socket with the fingers to see whether the socket is alive. The main reason for this prohibition is that

   A. such action can become a bad working habit
   B. a 20-volt shock is often fatal
   C. sockets usually have sharp edges
   D. the skin will become less sensitive to higher voltages

6. One advantage of cutting 1" rigid conduit with a hacksaw rather than with a 3-wheel pipe cutter is that

   A. the cut can be made with less exertion
   B. the pipe is not squeezed out of round
   C. less reaming is required after the cut
   D. no vise is needed

7. Rigid conduit used in the subway is galvanized inside and outside. The purpose of the galvanizing is to

   A. protect the wiring by covering rough spots
   B. improve the appearance where the conduit is exposed to view
   C. protect the conduit against corrosion
   D. provide good contact for grounding the conduit

8. If a hacksaw blade becomes worn so that the teeth are no longer properly set, the

   A. blade will tend to bind in the cut
   B. cut will have jagged edges
   C. cutting must all be done on the back stroke
   D. blade will lose its temper

9. If you and another helper are assigned to a hard and tedious job and your co-worker is not doing a reasonable share of the work, your best procedure is to

   A. slow down to his rate
   B. do your share and quit
   C. try to persuade him to do his share
   D. stop and register a complaint with the foreman before continuing

10. The most informative way for John Doe, the helper on duty at the 19th Street Lighting Section headquarters in the subway, to answer the telephone would be to say,

    A. "19th Street, who's calling?"
    B. "John Doe speaking."
    C. "Lighting Section, 19th Street."
    D. "Hello, this is Lighting Section."

11. Assume that the field leads of a large, completely disconnected d.c. motor are not tagged or otherwise marked. You could readily tell the shunt field leads from the series field leads by the

    A. length of the leads
    B. size of wire
    C. thickness of insulation
    D. type of insulation

12. Standard electrician's pliers should *NOT* be used to

    A. bend thin sheet metal
    B. crush Insulation on wires to be skinned
    C. cut off nail points sticking through a board
    D. hold a wire in position for soldering

13. The device used to change a.c. to d.c. is a

    A. frequency   B. regulator
    C. transformer   D. rectifier

14. The chief advantage of using stranded rather than solid conductors for electrical wiring is that stranded conductors are

    A. more flexible   B. easier to skin
    C. smaller   D. stronger

15. One identifying feature of a squirrel-cage induction motor is that it has no

    A. windings on the stationary part
    B. commutator or slip rings
    C. air gap
    D. iron core in the rotating part

16. It is advisable to close a knife switch firmly and rapidly because then there is less

    A. danger of shock to the operator
    B. chance of making an error
    C. mechanical wear of the contacts
    D. likelihood of arcing

17. If a cartridge fuse is hot to the touch when you remove it to do some maintenance on the circuit, this most probably indicates that the

    A. voltage of the circuit is too high
    B. fuse clips do not make good contact
    C. equipment on the circuit starts and stops frequently
    D. fuse is oversize for the circuit

18. The instrument most commonly used to determine the state of charge of a lead-acid storage battery is the

    A. thermometer
    B. hydrometer
    C. voltmeter
    D. ammeter

19. Smoking is forbidden in rooms housing storage batteries mainly because of the inflammable gas given off when the batteries are being charged. This gas is

    A. hydrogen
    B. carbon monoxide
    C. ammonia
    D. chlorine

20. Rigid conduit must be so installed as to prevent the collection of water in it between outlets. In order to meet this requirement, the conduit should NOT have a

    A. low point between successive outlets
    B. high point between successive outlets
    C. low point at an outlet
    D. high point at an outlet

21. When a test lamp is connected to the two ends of a cartridge fuse on an operating switchboard, the indication in ALL cases will be that this fuse is

    A. blown if the test lamp remains dark
    B. good if the test lamp lights
    C. blown if the test lamp lights
    D. good if the test lamp remains dark

22. If one copper wire has a diameter of 0.128 inch, and another copper wire has a diameter of 0.064 inch, the resistance of 1,000 feet of the first wire compared to the same length of the second wire is

    A. one half
    B. one quarter
    C. double
    D. four times

4 (#1)

23. The area of a circle having a diameter of one inch is closest to   23.____

   A. 3/4 square inch   B. 1 square inch
   C. 1 1/3 square inches   D. 1 1/2 square inches

24. If the allowable current In a copper bus bar is 1,000 amperes per square inch of cross-   24.____
   section, the width of a standard 1/4" bus bar designed to carry 1500 amperes would be

   A. 2"   B. 4"   C. 6"   D. 8"

25. It is now possible to obtain a 200-watt light-bulb that is as small in all dimensions as the   25.____
   standard 150-watt light-bulb. The principal advantage to users resulting from this reduction in size is that

   A. maintenance electricians can carry many more light-bulbs
   B. two sizes of light-bulbs can be kept in the same storage space
   C. the higher wattage bulb can now fit into certain lighting fixtures
   D. less breakage is apt to occur in handling

26. A carbon brush in a d.c. motor should exert a pressure of about 1 1/2 lbs. per square   26.____
   inch on the commutator.
   A much lighter pressure would be most likely to result in

   A. sparking at the commutator
   B. vibration of the armature
   C. the brush getting out of line
   D. excessive wear of the brush holder

27. The number of watts of heat given off by a resistor is expressed by the formula I^2R. If 10   27.____
   volts is applied to a 5-ohm resistor, the heat given off will be

   A. 500 watts   B. 250 watts
   C. 50 watts   D. 20 watts

Questions 28 - 36.

Questions 28 through 36 in Column I are electrical instruments and devices each of which is represented by one of the symbols in the schematic wiring diagram shown in Column II. For each instrument or device in Column I, select the corresponding symbol from Column II. *PRINT*, in the correspondingly numbered item space at the right, the letter given beside your selected symbol.

5 (#1)

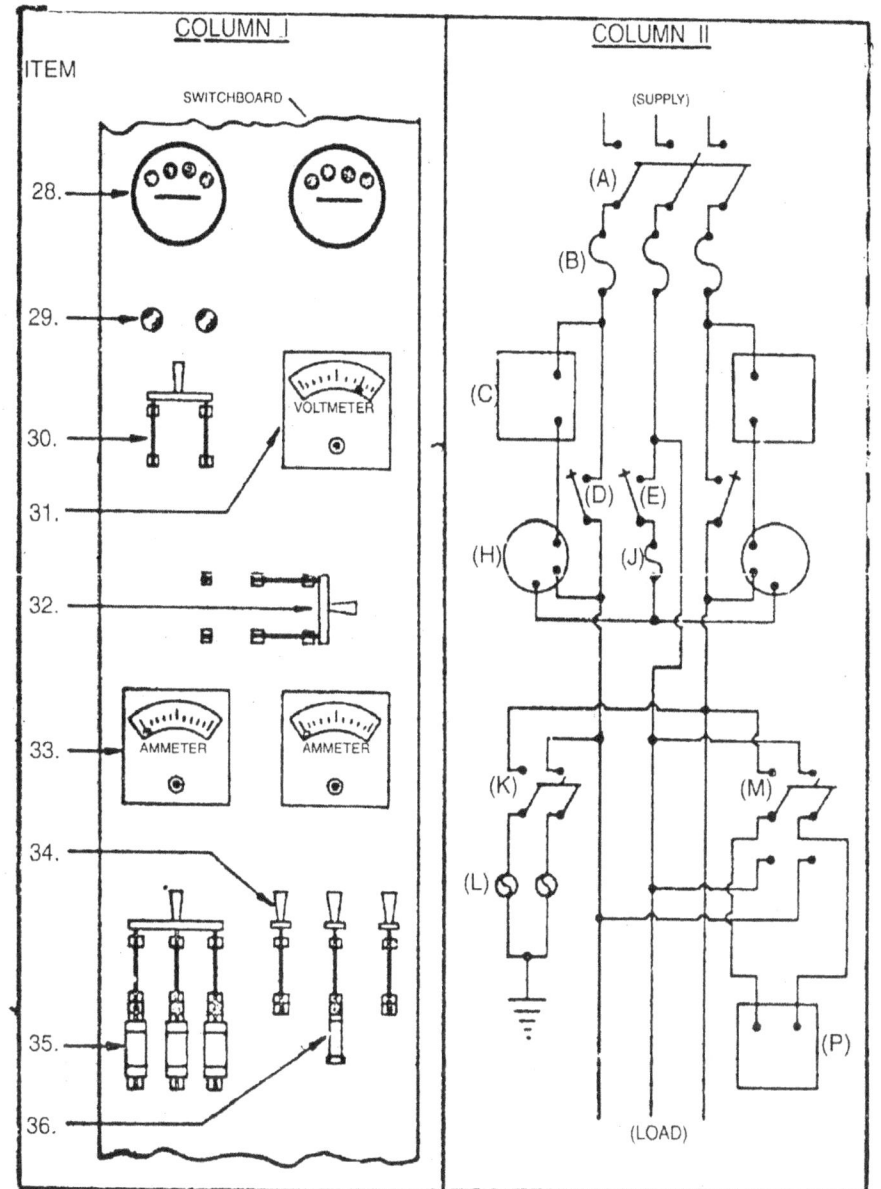

28. _____
29. _____
30. _____
31. _____
32. _____
33. _____
34. _____
35. _____
36. _____

Questions 37-40.

Questions 37 through 40 in Column I are wiring diagrams of the various positions of two rotary snap-switches each of which is shown in simplified form by one of the circuit diagrams in Column II. For each wiring diagram in Column I, select the simplified circuit diagram from Column II. *PRINT,* in the correspondingly number item space at the right, the letter given beside your selected circuit diagram.

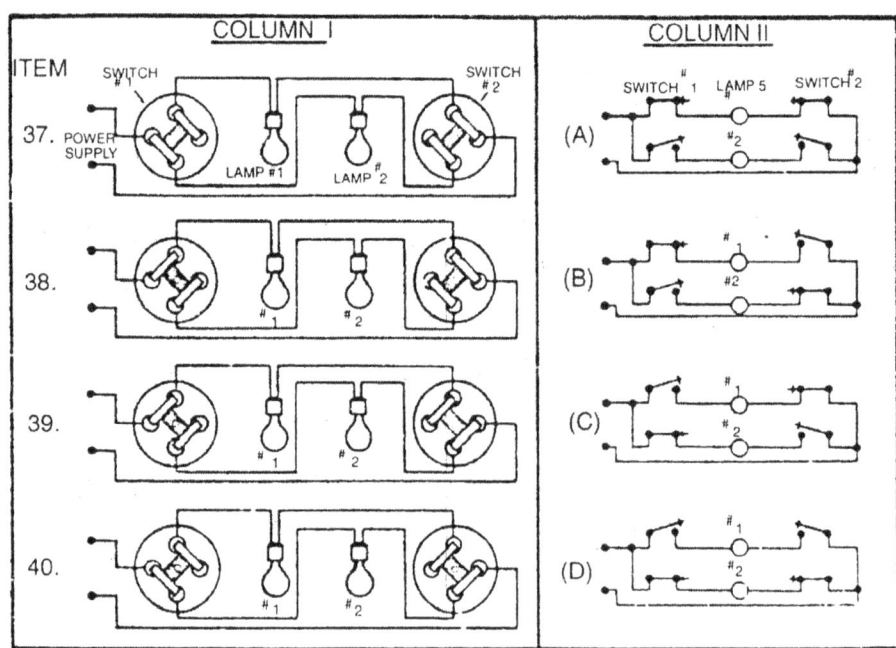

37.____

38.____

39.____

40.____

Questions 41 - 45.

Questions 41 through 45 in Column I are rating-terms each of which is commonly used in association with one of the electrical devices listed in Column II. For each rating-term in Column I, select the most closely associated electrical device from Column II. *PRINT*, in the correspondingly number item space at the right, the letter given beside your selected device.

Column I
(rating-terms)

Column II
(electrical devices)

41. 120 watts; 5 ohms
42. 120 to 13,800 volts
43. 120 volts; 100 watts
44. 120 volts; 100 amp.-hrs.
45. 120 volts; 10 amp.

A. resistor
B. toggle switch
C. transformer
D. light-bulb
E. storage battery

41.____
42.____
43.____
44.____
45.____

46. Assuming that the same kind of insulating material is used on each of the four copper conductors shown, the one intended for the highest voltage service is number
   A. 1
   B. 2
   C. 3
   D. 4

46.____

47. The convenience outlet that is known as a *POLARIZED* outlet is number
   A. 1
   B. 2
   C. 3
   D. 4

47.____

48. The group of 1 1/2-volt dry cells which is properly connected to deliver 6 volts is number
   A. 1
   B. 2
   C. 3
   D. 4

48.____

49. Each of the four sketches shows the proper schematic connections for one kind of d.c. motor. The one showing the connections for a shunt motor is number
    A. 1
    B. 2
    C. 3
    D. 4

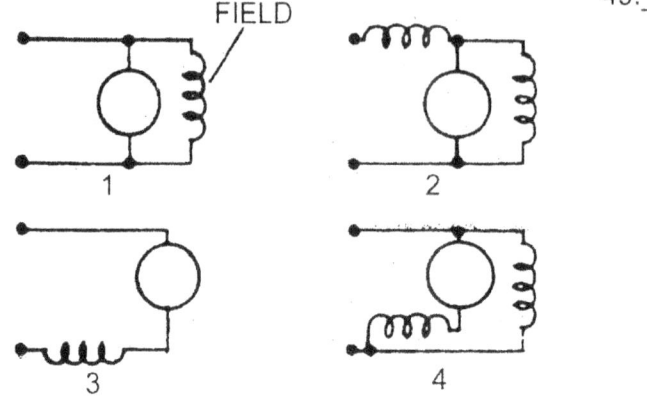

50. The four illustrations show pairs of equal strength permanent magnets on pivots, each magnet being held in the position shown by a mechanical locking device. When they are mechanically unlocked, the magnets which are LEAST likely to change their positions are pair number
    A. 1
    B. 2
    C. 3
    D. 4

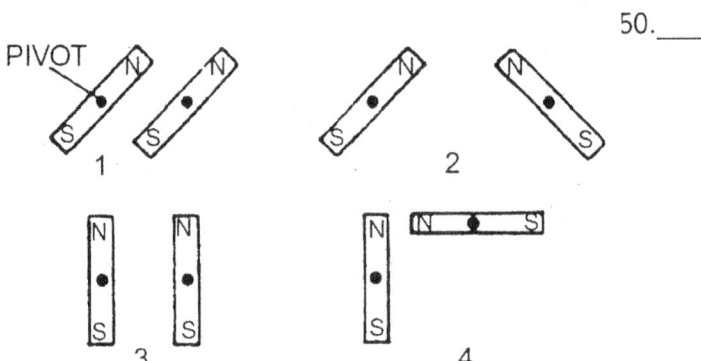

KEY (CORRECT ANSWERS)

1. D	11. B	21. C	31. P	41. A
2. D	12. C	22. B	32. M	42. C
3. B	13. D	23. A	33. C	43. D
4. A	14. A	24. C	34. D	44. E
5. A	15. B	25. C	35. B	45. B
6. C	16. D	26. A	36. J	46. D
7. C	17. B	27. D	37. C	47. A
8. A	18. B	28. H	38. A	48. B
9. C	19. A	29. L	39. B	49. A
10. C	20. A	30. K	40. D	50. C

TEST 2

DIRECTIONS: Each question or incomplete statement is followed by several suggested answers or completions. Select the one that BEST answers the question or completes the statement. *PRINT THE LETTER OF THE CORRECT ANSWER IN THE SPACE AT THE RIGHT.*

1. If the currents in resistors nos. 1, 2, and 3 are 4.8, 7.5, and 6.2 amperes respectively, then the current (in amperes) in resistor no. 4 is
   A. 1.3
   B. 2.7
   C. 3.5
   D. 6.1

   1.____

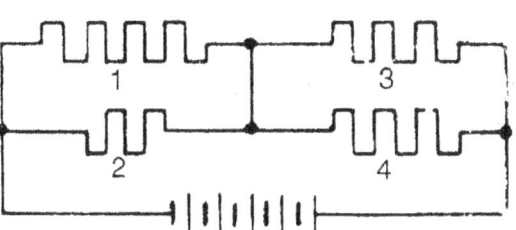

2. If the mercury switch is turned to the horizontal position, the mercury will flow and break the connection between the lead-in wires, thus opening the circuit. By logical reasoning, such a switch would be most useful when

   2.____

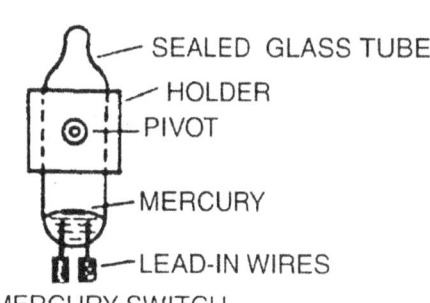

   A. the circuit must be opened quickly
   B. there is likely to be explosive gas near the switch location
   C. there is no restriction on noise
   D. the switch need not be operated often

3. The device shown is clearly intended for use in electrical construction to
   A. support conduit on a wall
   B. join cable to a terminal block
   C. ground a wire to a water pipe
   D. attach a chain-hung lighting fixture to an outlet box

   3.____

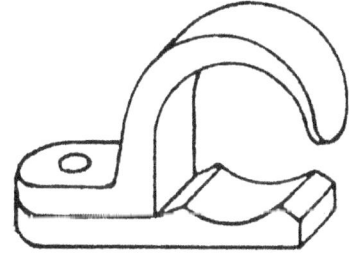

4. The fitting shown is used in electrical construction to
   A. clamp two adjacent junction boxes together
   B. act as a ground clamp for the conduit system
   C. attach flexible metallic conduit to a junction box
   D. protect exposed wires where they pass through a wall

   4.____

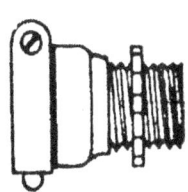

5. The electrical connector shown would most likely be used in a power plant to connect
   A. two branch cables to a main cable
   B. a single cable to the terminals of two devices
   C. a single cable to a flat bus bar
   D. a round bus bar to a flat one

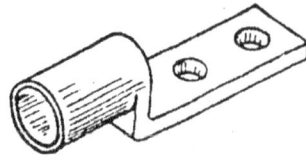

5._____

6. If switch S is closed, the resulting change in the ammeter readings will be that
   A. both will increase
   B. both will decrease
   C. #1 will increase and #2 will decrease
   D. #1 will decrease and #2 will increase

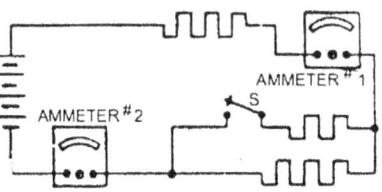

6._____

7. If the 10-ohm resistor marked X burns out, the reading of the voltmeter will become
   A. 0
   B. 20
   C. 80
   D. 100

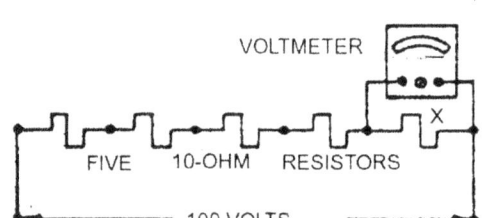

7._____

8. The width of the bar, in inches, is
   A. 1 1/8
   B. 1 5/16
   C. 1 7/16
   D. 2 5/16

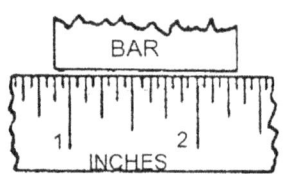

8._____

9. The total resistance, in ohms, between points X and Y is
   A. 2.5
   B. 5
   C. 10
   D. 20

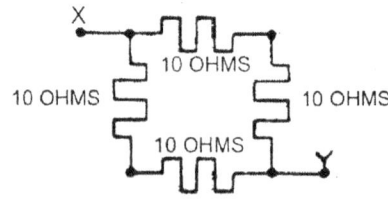

9._____

10. The range of both voltmeters shown is 0-150 volts. In this case, the a.c. meter will indicate the correct voltage and the d.c. meter will indicate
    A. the same
    B. a few volts more
    C. a few volts less
    D. zero

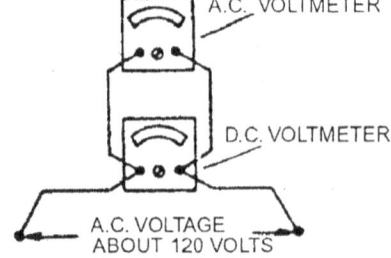

10._____

11. The six wires shown are to be properly connected so that the lighting fixture can be controlled by a single-pole on-off switch. The correct connections in accordance with established good practice are

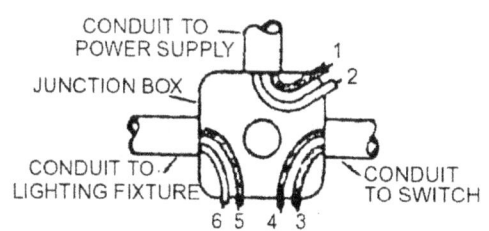

11._____

   A. 1 to 3 and 5; 2 to 4 and 6
   B. 1 to 5; 2 to 3; 4 to 6
   C. 1 to 3 and 6; 2 to 4 and 5
   D. 1 to 3; 4 to 5; 2 to 6

12. In the right-angled triangle shown, the angle marked X is

   A. 45°
   B. 60°
   C. 75°
   D. 90°

12._____

13. The distance from the top of the desk to the bottom of the lighting fixture is
   A. 94"
   B. 81"
   C. 72"
   D. 64"

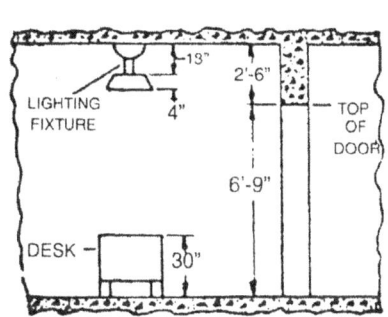

13._____

14. When the movable arm of the uniformly wound resistor is in the position shown, the resistance in ohms between terminals 2 and 3 is
   A. 2000
   B. 1800
   C. 1500
   D. 1200

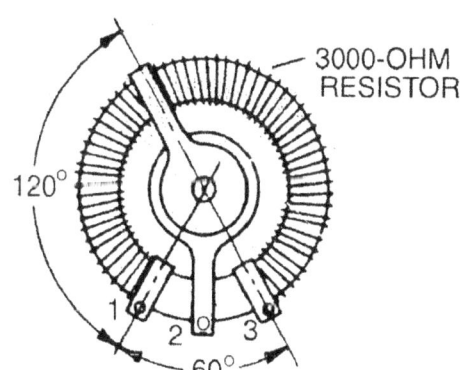

14._____

15. If each of the 19 strands of the conductor shown has a diameter of 0.024", and the thickness of the insulation is 0.047", the diameter over the insulation is
   A. 0.107"
   B. 0.167"
   C. 0.214"
   D. 0.238"

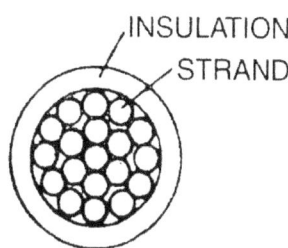

15._____

16. After no. 4, the next larger American Wire Gage size is no.   16._____

    A. 2   B. 3   C. 5   D. 6

17. When steadying a straight wooden ladder for a co-worker who is on it chipping a concrete wall, it would be *LEAST* essential for you to wear   17._____

    A. rubber gloves
    B. hard top shoes
    C. goggles
    D. a helmet

18. It would *NOT* be good practice to use the cutting blade of an electrician's knife to   18._____

    A. cut a template out of cardboard
    B. sharpen a pencil
    C. cut copper wires
    D. remove the braid from an insulated wire

19. You are more likely to receive a shock as the result of a wiring defect in a portable electrical device than as the result of a similar defect in a permanently installed device. This is so primarily because the   19._____

    A. workers on permanent installations are more careful
    B. insulation on portable equipment is usually thinner
    C. metal parts of portable equipment are usually light weight
    D. metal frames of permanent installations are usually grounded

20. If a co-worker is in contact with the 600-volt third rail in the subway, your first action should be to either try to free the man from contact or cut off the power. The action to be taken in a particular case will depend primarily on whether   20._____

    A. cutting off the power will interfere with train operation
    B. the means of cutting off the power Is nearby
    C. there is any arcing at the point of contact
    D. you can free the man in time to do any good

21. When a number of rubber insulated wires are being pulled into a run of conduit having several sharp bends between the two pull boxes, the pulling is likely to be hard and the wires are subjected to considerable strain. For these reasons it is advisable in such a case to   21._____

    A. push the wires into the feed end of the conduit at the same time that pulling is being done
    B. pull in only one wire at a time
    C. use extra heavy grease
    D. pull the wires back a few inches after each forward pull to gain momentum

22. The plug of a portable tool should be removed from the convenience outlet by grasping the plug and not by pulling on the cord because   22._____

    A. the plug is easier to grip than the cord
    B. pulling on the cord may allow the plug to fall on the floor and break
    C. pulling on the cord may break the wires off the
    D. plug terminals
    E. the plug is generally better insulated than the cord

23. The best *IMMEDIATE* first aid if electrolyte splashes into the eyes when filling a storage battery is to

    A. bandage the eyes to keep out light
    B. wipe the eyes dry with a soft towel
    C. induce tears to flow by staring at a bright light
    D. bathe the eyes with plenty of clean water

24. Extreme care must be taken when cleaning electrical machine parts indoors with carbon tetrachloride mainly because the fumes

    A. are poisonous
    B. are highly flammable
    C. attack insulation
    D. conduct electricity

25. When using a pipe wrench, the hand should be placed so as to pull instead of push on the wrench. The basis for this recommendation is that there is less likelihood of

    A. the wrench slipping
    B. injury to the hand if the wrench slips
    C. injury to the pipe if the wrench slips
    D. stripped pipe threads

26. In telephoning for assistance because of an accident to a fellow-employee, it is probably most important for you to report the

    A. name of the injured man
    B. time when the accident occurred
    C. cause of the accident
    D. location of the injured man

27. The electrical power for each section of the subway signal system is arranged to come from either one of two supply feeders. The most likely reason for this arrangement is to

    A. divide the load between two power plants
    B. provide continuing service if one feeder goes dead
    C. keep the supply voltage as low as possible
    D. avoid the use of very large cables

28. Present practice with respect to subway lighting switchboards is to make them "dead front." This means that the front of the switchboard has no

    A. metal parts fastened to it
    B. exposed live parts on it
    C. operating handles extending through it
    D. circuit identification markings on it

29. High-voltage switches in power plants are commonly so constructed that their contacts are submerged in oil. The purpose of the oil is to

    A. help quench arcing
    B. lubricate the contacts
    C. cool the switch mechanism
    D. insulate the contacts from the switch framework

30. One type of fire extinguisher used in the subway consists of a steel tank containing compressed carbon dioxide; it has a valve at the top to which is connected a hose and a directing nozzle. The logical way to tell whether such an extinguisher is fully charged is to

    A. tap it lightly
    B. check the inspection tag
    C. weigh it
    D. try it out on a small fire

31. In a storage battery installation consisting of twenty 2-volt cells connected in series, a leak develops in one of the cells and all the electrolyte runs out of it. The terminal voltage across the twenty cells will now be

    A. 40   B. 38   C. 2   D. 0

32. If your foreman gives you an oral order which you do not understand, you should

    A. ask the foreman to put the order in writing
    B. ask the foreman to explain further
    C. ask a fellow employee what he thinks the foreman meant
    D. use your best judgment as that is all that can be expected

33. It is advisable to use a wooden rather than a steel rule when making measurements in the vicinity of electrical machinery. One good reason for this advice is that a wooden rule

    A. will not conduct electricity
    B. can be held in a position by using only one hand
    C. cannot become magnetized
    D. will not damage the machinery if it becomes caught

Items 34-39.

Items 34 through 39 in Column I are insulating materials each of which is commonly employed for one of the uses listed in Column II. For each insulating material in Column I select its most common use from Column II. *PRINT,* in the correspondingly number item space at the right, the letter given beside your selected use.

Column I (insulating materials)	Column II (uses)
34. Porcelain	A. knive-switch handles
35. Transite	B. commutator-bar separators
36. Wood	C. high voltage line insulators
37. Soft rubber	D. wire and cable insulation
38. Fiber	E. cartridge fuse cases
39. Mica	F. arc chutes

40. If the blade in a hacksaw snaps in two when making a cut, the cause is NOT likely to be that the

    A. teeth were too coarse for work
    B. pressure applied was too great
    C. saw was twisted in the cut
    D. blade was too short for the job

41. When removing the insulation from a wire before making a splice, care should be taken to avoid nicking the wire mainly because then the

    A. current carrying capacity will be reduced
    B. resistance will be increased
    C. insulation will be harder to remove
    D. wire is more likely to break

42. Good practice dictates that an adjustable open end wrench should be used primarily when the

    A. nut to be turned is soft and must not be scored
    B. proper size of fixed wrench is not available
    C. extra leverage is needed
    D. location is cramped permitting only a small turning angle

43. Insulated electrical cables in the subway are sometimes suspended from a tightly strung messenger wire which is supported on brackets attached to the subway structure at intervals of 10 to 20 feet; the electrical cables are strapped to the messenger wire every few inches. By logical reasoning, it is clear that such electrical cables are not suspended overhead without being supported by a messenger wire because the

    A. messenger wire is needed as a continuous ground return
    B. current carrying capacity of unsupported electrical cables would be lower
    C. messenger wire places less strain on the structure
    D. longer spans of electrical cables would sag too much

44. It would generally be poor practice to use ordinary slip-joint pliers to

    A. pull a small nail
    B. bend a wire
    C. remove a cotter pin
    D. tighten a machine bolt

45. The a.c. motor which has exactly the same speed at full-load as at no load is the

    A. synchronous motor
    B. repulsion motor
    C. induction motor
    D. condenser motor

46. A metal bushing is usually screwed on to the end of rigid conduit inside of a junction box. The bushing serves to

    A. center the wires in the conduit
    B. separate the wires where they leave the conduit
    C. protect the wires against abrasion
    D. prevent sagging of the conduit

47. The proper abrasive for cleaning the commutator of a d.c. generator is

    A. steel wool
    B. emery cloth
    C. sand paper
    D. soapstone

48. If a "live" 120-volt d.c. lighting circuit is connected to the 120-volt winding of an otherwise disconnected power transformer, the result will be

   A. blowing of the d.c. circuit fuse
   B. magnetization of the transformer case
   C. sparking at the transformer secondary terminals
   D. burning out of lights on the d.c. circuit

49. Threaded joints in rigid conduit runs are made watertight through the use of

   A. petroleum jelly
   B. solder
   C. red lead
   D. paraffin wax

50. The most important reason for insisting on neatness in maintenance quarters is that it

   A. decreases the chances of accidents to employees
   B. makes for good employee morale
   C. prevents tools from becoming rusty
   D. increases the available storage space

KEY (CORRECT ANSWERS)

1. D	11. D	21. A	31. D	41. D
2. B	12. B	22. C	32. B	42. B
3. A	13. D	23. D	33. A	43. D
4. C	14. B	24. A	34. C	44. D
5. C	15. C	25. B	35. F	45. A
6. A	16. B	26. D	36. A	46. C
7. D	17. A	27. B	37. D	47. C
8. C	18. C	28. B	38. E	48. A
9. C	19. D	29. A	39. B	49. C
10. D	20. B	30. C	40. D	50. A

EXAMINATION SECTION
TEST 1

DIRECTIONS: Each question or incomplete statement is followed by several suggested answers or completions. Select the one that BEST answers the question or completes the statement. PRINT THE LETTER OF THE CORRECT ANSWER IN THE SPACE AT THE RIGHT.

1. Of the following, the best conductor of electricity is

    A. aluminum
    B. carbon
    C. copper
    D. water

2. Good practice requires that the end of a piece of conduit be reamed after it has been cut to length. The purpose of the reaming is to

    A. prevent insulation damage when pulling in the wires
    B. finish the conduit accurately to length
    C. make the threading easier
    D. remove loose rust

3. According to the national electrical code, a run of conduit between two outlet boxes should not contain more than four quarter-bends. The most likely reason for this limitation is that more bends will

    A. result in cracking the conduit
    B. make the pulling of the wire too difficult
    C. increase the wire length unnecessarily
    D. not be possible in one standard length of conduit

4. Asbestos is commonly used as the covering of electric wires in locations where there is likely to be high

    A. voltage
    B. temperature
    C. humidity
    D. current

5. The LEAST likely result of a severe electric shock is

    A. unconsciousness
    B. a burn
    C. stoppage of breathing
    D. bleeding

6. Electrical helpers on the subway system are instructed in the use of fire extinguishers. The probable reason for including helpers in this instruction is that the helper

    A. cannot do the more important work
    B. may be the cause of a fire because of his inexperience
    C. may be alone when a fire starts
    D. will become interested in fire prevention

7. Transit employees are cautioned, as a safety measure, not to use water to extinguish fires involving electrical equipment. One logical reason for this caution is that the water

    A. will cause harmful steam
    B. will not extinguish a fire started by electricity

C. may transmit electrical shock to the user
D. may crack hot insulators

8. When the level of the liquid in a lead-acid storage cell is low, a maintainer should normally add

   A. alkaline solution
   B. diluted alcohol
   C. battery acid
   D. distilled water

9. Portable lamp cord is likely to have

   A. steel armor
   B. stranded wires
   C. paper insulation
   D. number 8 wire

10. The one of the following terms which could NOT correctly be used in describing a knife switch is

    A. quick-break
    B. single throw
    C. four-pole
    D. toggle

11. A transit employee is required to make a written report of any unusual occurrence promptly. The best reason for requiring such promptness is that

    A. the report will tend to be more accurate as to facts
    B. the employee will not be as likely to forget to make the report
    C. there is always a tendency to do a better job under pressure
    D. the report may be too long if made at an employee's convenience

12. With respect to common electric light bulbs, it is correct to state that the

    A. circuit voltage has no effect on the life of the bulb
    B. filament is made of carbon
    C. base has a left hand thread
    D. lower wattage bulb has the higher resistance

13. It is generally known that the voltage of the third rail on the New York City Transit System is about

    A. 3000
    B. 1000
    C. 600
    D. 120

14. The resistance of a 1000-foot coil of a certain size copper wire is 10 ohms. If 300 feet is cut off, the resistance of the remainder of the coil is

    A. 7 ohms
    B. 3 ohms
    C. 0.7 ohms
    D. 0.3 ohm

15. The term "15-ampere" is commonly used in identifying

    A. an insulator
    B. a fuse
    C. a conduit
    D. an outlet box

16. When you are first appointed as a helper and are assigned to work with a maintainer, he will probably expect you to

    A. do very little work
    B. make plenty of mistakes
    C. pay close attention to instructions
    D. do all of the unpleasant work

17. When connecting the two lead wires of a test instrument to a live d.c. circuit, the best procedure is to first make the negative or ground connection and then the positive connection. The reason for this procedure is that

   A. electricity flows from positive to negative
   B. there is less danger of accidental shock
   C. the reverse procedure may blow the fuse
   D. less arcing will occur when the connection is made

17.____

Questions 18 - 24.

Questions 18 through 24 in Column I are materials each of which is commonly used for one of the electrical equipment parts listed in Column II. For each material in Column I, select the most closely associated part from Column II. *PRINT,* in the correspondingly numbered item space at the right, the letter given beside your selected part.

COLUMN I (materials)	COLUMN II (electrical equipment parts)	
18. steel	A. acid storage battery plates	18.____
19. lead	B. transformer cores	19.____
20. mica	C. d.c. motor brushes	20.____
21. porcelain	D. insulating tape	21.____
22. rubber	E. cartridge fuse cases	22.____
23. copper	H. commutator insulation	23.____
24. carbon	J. strain insulators	24.____
	K. knife-switch blades	

25. To make a good soldered connection between two stranded wires, it is *LEAST* important to

   A. twist the wires together before soldering
   B. use enough heat to make the solder flow freely
   C. clean the wires carefully
   D. apply solder to each strand before twisting the two wires together

25.____

26. When a step-up transformer is used, it increases the

   A. voltage   B. current
   C. power   D. frequency

26.____

27. Lock nuts are frequently used in making electrical connections on terminal boards. The purpose of such lock nuts is to

   A. make tighter connections with less effort
   B. make it difficult to tamper with the connections
   C. avoid stripping the threads
   D. keep the connections from loosening through vibration

27.____

28. If a fellow worker has stopped breathing after an electric shock, the best first-aid treatment is

    A. massage his chest
    B. a hot drink
    C. an application of cold compresses
    D. artificial respiration

29. According to a recent safety report, an outstanding cause of accidents to workers is the improper use of tools. The most helpful conclusion that you can draw from this statement is that

    A. most tools are dangerous to use
    B. most tools are difficult to use properly
    C. many accidents from tools occur because of poor working habits
    D. many accidents from tools are unavoidable

Questions 30 - 39.

Questions 30 through 39 refer to the use of tools shown on the next page. Read the item, and for the operation given, select the proper tool to be used from those shown. *PRINT,* in the correspondingly numbered item space at the right, the letter given below your selected tool.

30. Tightening a coupling on a piece of one-inch conduit.

31. Drilling a hole in a concrete wall for a lead anchor.

32. Bending a piece of 3/4-inch conduit.

33. Tightening a wire on the terminal of a standard electric light socket.

34. Cutting off a piece of 4/0 insulated copper cable.

35. Measuring the length of a proposed long conduit run.

36. Tightening a small nut on a terminal board.

37. Removing the burrs from the end of a piece of conduit after cutting.

38. Removing the flat rubber gasket stuck to the cover of a watertight pull box.

39. Knocking the head off a bolt that is rusted in place.

5 (#1)

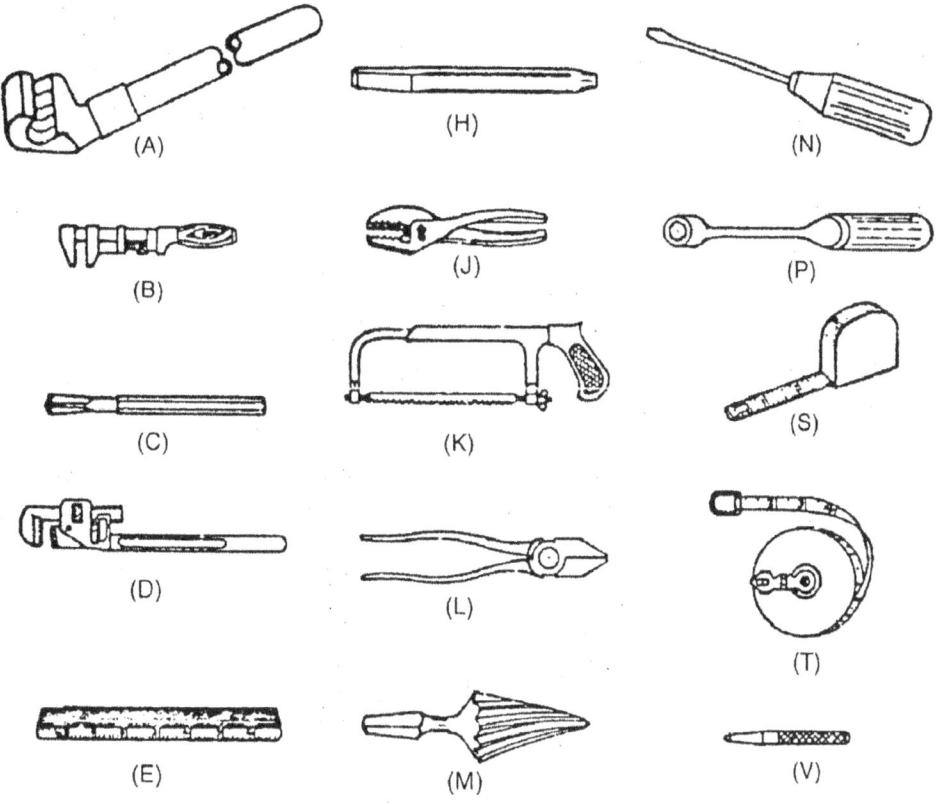

Questions 40 - 45.

Questions 40 through 45 show common electrical jobs. Each item shows four methods (A), (B), (C), and (D) of doing the particular job. Only ONE of the four methods is entirely CORRECT in accordance with good practice. For each item, examine the four sketches and select the sketch showing the correct method. PRINT, in the correspondingly numbered item space at the right, the letter given below your selected sketch.

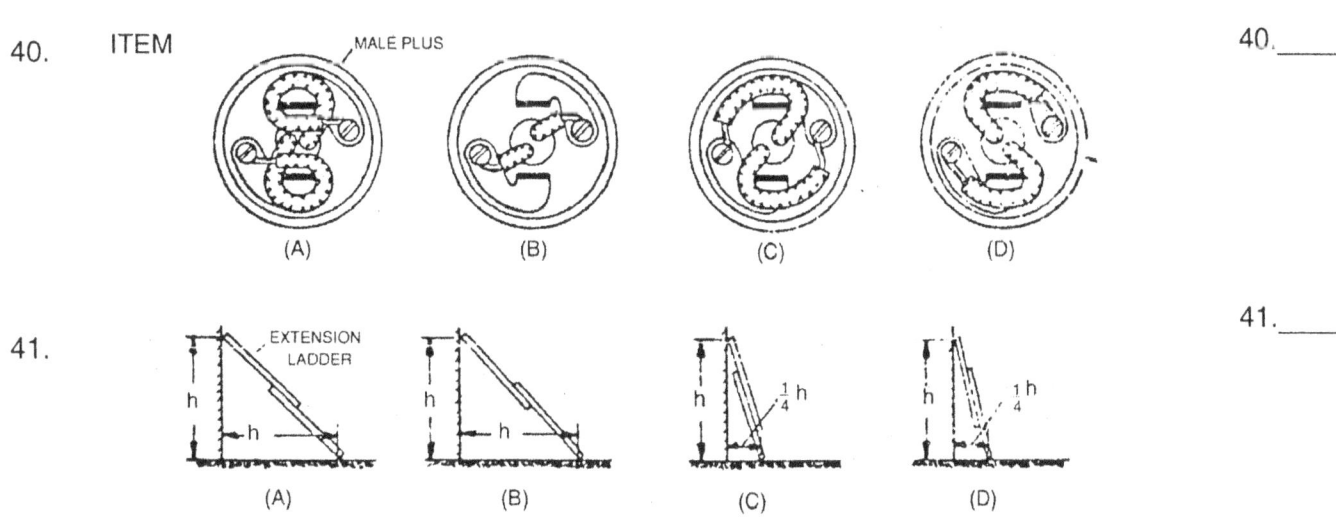

40. _____

41. _____

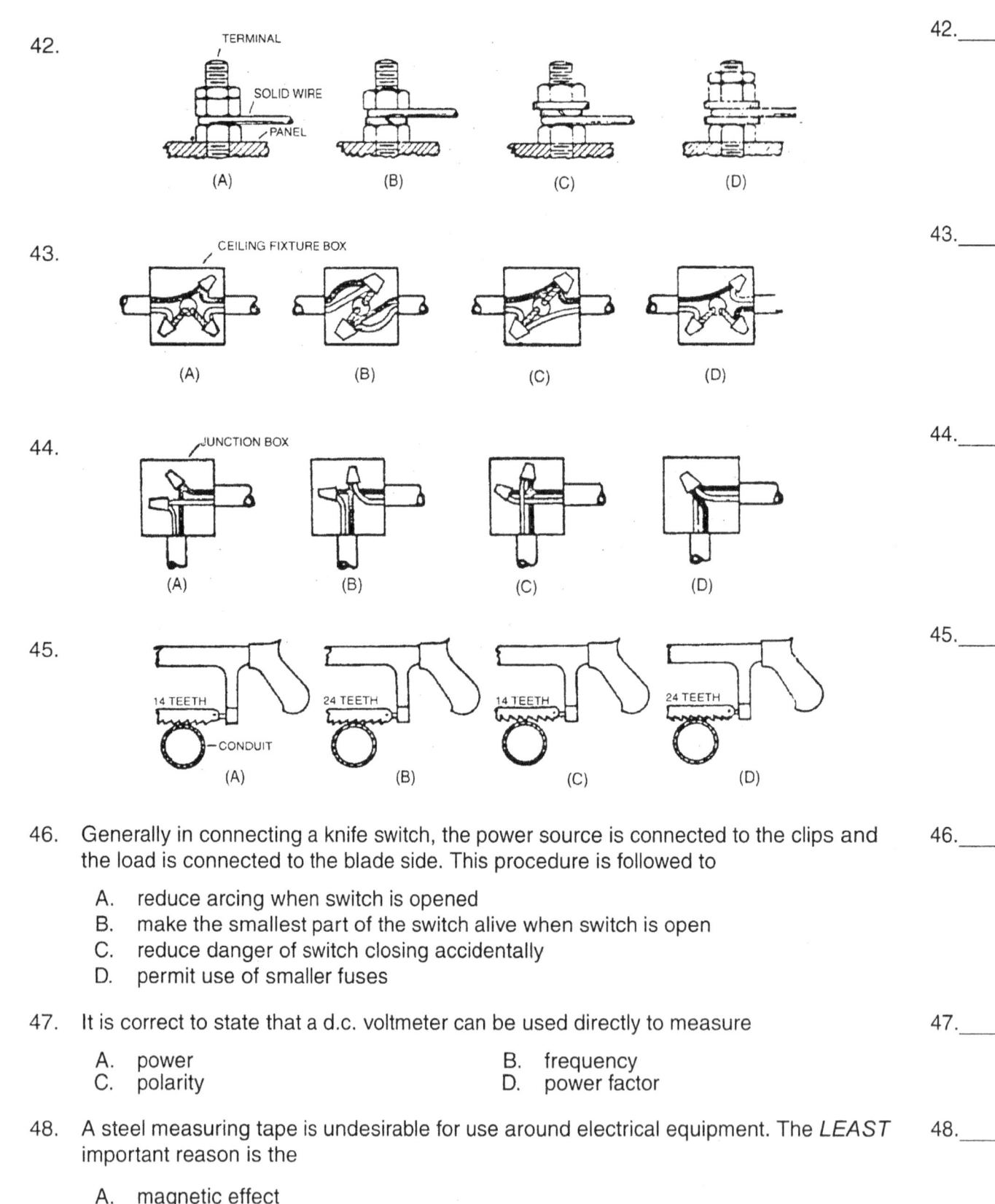

46. Generally in connecting a knife switch, the power source is connected to the clips and the load is connected to the blade side. This procedure is followed to

   A. reduce arcing when switch is opened
   B. make the smallest part of the switch alive when switch is open
   C. reduce danger of switch closing accidentally
   D. permit use of smaller fuses

47. It is correct to state that a d.c. voltmeter can be used directly to measure

   A. power   B. frequency
   C. polarity   D. power factor

48. A steel measuring tape is undesirable for use around electrical equipment. The LEAST important reason is the

   A. magnetic effect
   B. short circuit hazard
   C. shock hazard
   D. danger of entanglement in rotating machines

49. If you had to telephone for an ambulance because of an accident, the most important information for you to give the person who answered the telephone would be the

    A. exact time of the accident
    B. place where the ambulance is needed
    C. cause of the accident
    D. names and addresses of those injured

50. The book of rules and regulations states that employees must give notice in person or by telephone of their intention to be absent from work at least two hours before they are scheduled to report for duty. The most logical reason for having this rule is that

    A. it allows time to check the employee's excuse
    B. it has a nuisance value in limiting absences
    C. the employee's time record can be corrected in advance
    D. a substitute can be provided

KEY (CORRECT ANSWERS)

1. C	11. A	21. J	31. C	41. C
2. A	12. D	22. D	32. A	42. D
3. B	13. C	23. K	33. N	43. C
4. B	14. A	24. C	34. K	44. A
5. D	15. B	25. D	35. T	45. B
6. C	16. C	26. A	36. P	46. B
7. C	17. B	27. D	37. M	47. C
8. D	18. B	28. D	38. N	48. A
9. B	19. A	29. C	39. H	49. B
10. D	20. H	30. D	40. D	50. D

TEST 2

DIRECTIONS: Each question or incomplete statement is followed by several suggested answers or completions. Select the one that *BEST* answers the question or completes the statement. *PRINT THE LETTER OF THE CORRECT ANSWER IN THE SPACE AT THE RIGHT.*

Questions 1-7.

Questions 1 through 7 are based on the fuse information given below. Read this information carefully before answering these items.

FUSE INFORMATION

Badly bent or distorted fuse clips cannot be permitted. Sometimes the distortion or bending is so slight that it escapes notice, yet it may be the cause for fuse failures through the heat that is developed by the poor contact. Occasionally the proper spring tension of the fuse clips has been destroyed by overheating from loose wire connections to the clips. Proper contact surfaces must be maintained to avoid faulty operation of the fuse. Maintenance men should remove oxides that form on the copper and brass contacts, check the clip pressure, and make sure that contact surfaces are not deformed or bent in any way. When removing oxides, use a well-worn file and remove only the oxide film. Do not use sandpaper or emery cloth as hard particles may come off and become embedded in the contact surfaces. All wire connections to the fuse holders should be carefully inspected to see that they are tight.

1. Fuse failure because of poor clip contact or loose connections is due to the resulting   1.____

   A. excessive voltage B. increased current
   C. lowered resistance D. heating effect

2. Oxides should be removed from fuse contacts by using   2.____

   A. a dull file B. emery cloth
   C. fine sandpaper D. a sharp file

3. One result of loose wire connections at the terminal of a fuse clip is stated in the above paragraph to be   3.____

   A. loss of tension in the wire
   B. welding of the fuse to the clip
   C. distortion of the clip
   D. loss of tension of the clip

4. Simple reasoning will show that the oxide film referred to is undesirable chiefly because it   4.____

   A. looks dull
   B. makes removal of the fuse difficult
   C. weakens the clips
   D. introduces undesirable resistance

5. Fuse clips that are bent very slightly   5.____

   A. should be replaced with new clips
   B. should be carefully filed

116

C. may result in blowing of the fuse
D. may prevent the fuse from blowing

6. Prom the fuse information paragraph it would be reasonable to conclude that fuse clips   6.____

   A. are difficult to maintain
   B. must be given proper maintenance
   C. require more attention than other electrical equipment
   D. are unreliable

7. A safe practical way of checking the tightness of the wire connection to the fuse clips of a   7.____
   live 120-volt lighting circuit is to

   A. feel the connection with your hand to see if it is warm
   B. try tightening with an insulated screwdriver or socket wrench
   C. see if the circuit works
   D. measure the resistance with an ohmmeter

Questions 8 - 11.

Questions 8 through 11 in Column I below are wiring diagrams of the various positions of a 4-position switch each of which is shown in simplified form by one of the circuit diagrams in Column II below. For each wiring diagram in Column I, select the simplified circuit diagram from Column II. *PRINT,* in the correspondingly numbered item space at the right, the letter given beside your selected circuit diagram.

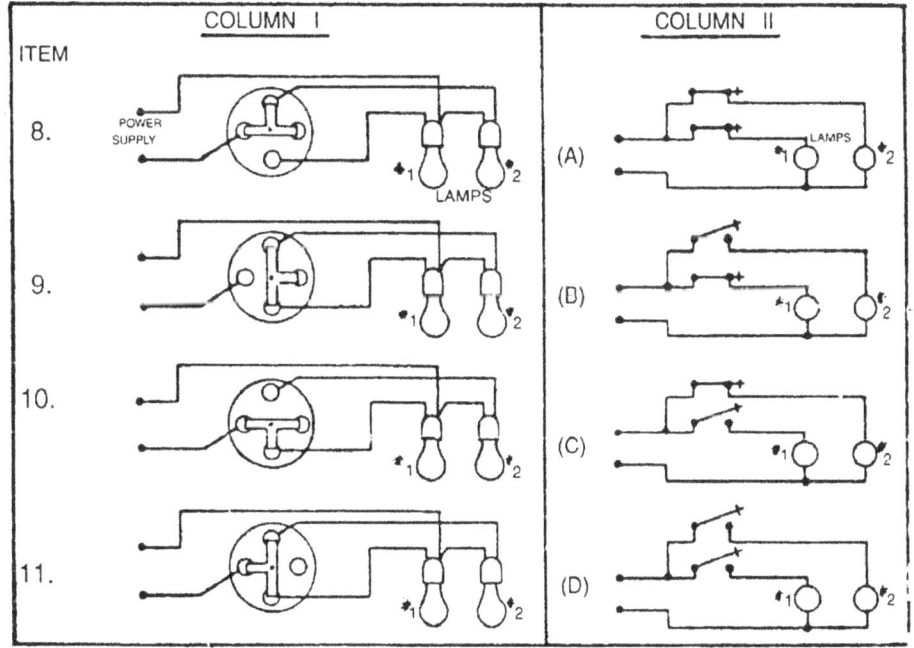

Questions 12 - 16.
Questions 12 through 16 in Column I are supply voltages each of which can be obtained by one of the dry cell battery connections in Column II. For each voltage in Column I, select the proper battery connections from Column II. *PRINT,* in the correspondingly numbered item space at the right, the letter given below your selected battery connections.

COLUMN I
(supply voltages)

COLUMN II
(battery connections)
Note: Each dry cell - 1 1/2 volts.

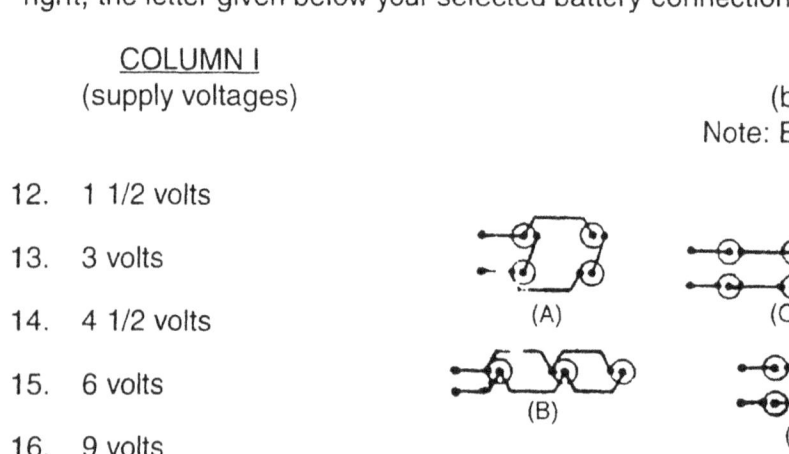

12. 1 1/2 volts   12.____

13. 3 volts   13.____

14. 4 1/2 volts   14.____

15. 6 volts   15.____

16. 9 volts   16.____

17. The sketch shows the ends of 4 bare copper wires full size with diameters as given. From left to right, the #14 wire is   17.____

    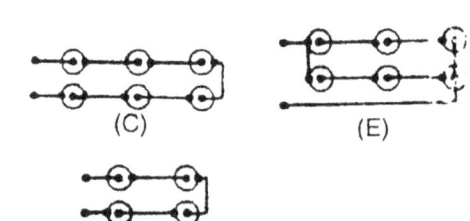

    A. first   B. second
    C. third   D. fourth

18. Regardless of the battery voltage, it is clear by inspection that the highest current is in the   18.____
    A. 1-ohm resistor
    B. 2-ohm resistor
    C. 3-ohm resistor
    D. 4-ohm resistor

    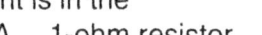

19. On the transformer, the dimension marked X is   19.____
    A. 29 1/2"
    B. 27"
    C. 25 1/2"
    D. 21 1/2"

    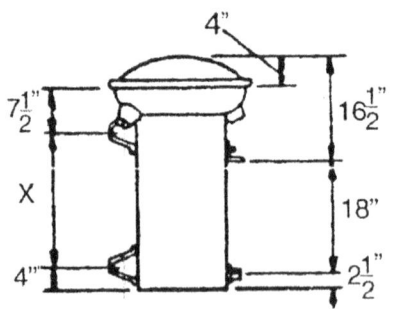

20. The reading of the voltmeter in the accompanying sketch will be   20.____
    A. 0 volts
    B. 80 volts
    C. 120 volts
    D. 240 volts

    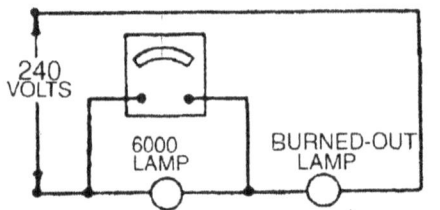

21. The total resistance in ohms between points X and Y is
    A. 0.30
    B. 3.33
    C. 15
    D. 30

    21.____

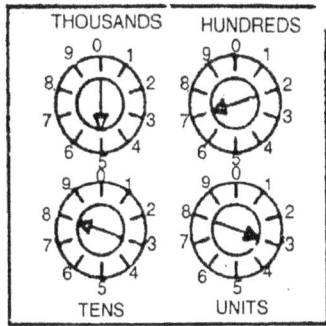

22. The resistance box shown can be set to any value of resistance up to 10,000 ohms. The reading shown is
    A. 3875
    B. 5738
    C. 5783
    D. 8375

    22.____

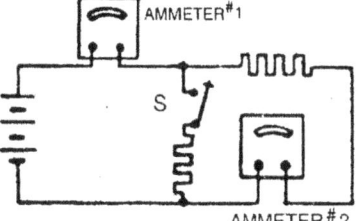

23. If switch "S" is closed, the ammeter readings will change as follows
    A. both will increase
    B. #1 only will increase
    C. both will decrease
    D. #2 only will increase

    23.____

24. The reading on the meter scale shown is
    A. 56
    B. 52
    C. 51
    D. 46

    24.____

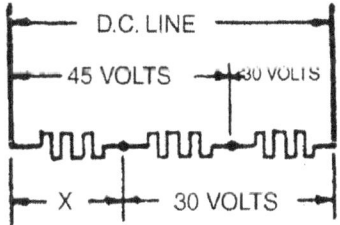

25. The voltage "X" is
    A. 25
    B. 20
    C. 15
    D. 5

    25.____

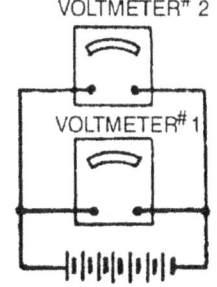

26. The two voltmeters shown are identical. If the battery voltage is 120 volts, the readings of the voltmeters should be
    A. 120 volts on each meter
    B. 60 volts on each meter
    C. 120 volts on meter #1 and 240 volts on #2
    D. 120 volts on meter #1 and zero on #2

    26.____

27. Standard tables are available showing the safe carrying capacity of copper wire of various sizes to avoid damage to insulation from overheating. The allowable current given is dependent on the

    A. voltage
    B. length of wire
    C. type of current (a.c. or d.c.)
    D. room temperature

28. A test lamp using an ordinary lamp bulb can *NOT* be used to test for

    A. live circuits
    B. overloads
    C. grounds
    D. blown fuses

29. Consumers are warned never to use a coin instead of a spare fuse. The reason for this warning is that

    A. the protection of the fuse will be lost
    B. additional resistance will be placed in the circuit
    C. mutilating coins is illegal
    D. shock hazard is increased

30. Maintainers are cautioned not to smoke or permit open flames in a storage battery room. The probable reason for this caution is that

    A. the liquid in the battery is inflammable
    B. the terminals are greased
    C. batteries give off an explosive gas when charging
    D. fire extinguishers are not permitted in battery rooms

31. Safety on the job is best assured by

    A. working very slowly
    B. following every rule
    C. never working alone
    D. keeping alert

32. If you think you have found an improvement for a piece of standard equipment used in your department, the most sensible course for you to follow would be to

    A. examine it critically before making the suggestion
    B. try to sell it to an outside company
    C. forget it because you will probably get no credit
    D. get a definite promise of reward from the management before disclosing it

33. As a helper you will be assigned to a maintainer under the general supervision of a foreman. If you do not understand the operation of some special equipment on which you work, your best procedure would be to

    A. ask the foreman since he is more competent
    B. study up at home
    C. forget the matter until you are more experienced
    D. ask the maintainer first

34. A proper use for an electrician's knife is to

    A. cut small wires
    B. mark the point where a conduit is to be cut
    C. pry out a small cartridge fuse
    D. skin wires

35. Specifying a machine screw as an 8-32 screw fixes the

   A. material
   B. type of head
   C. diameter
   D. length

36. It is good practice to connect the ground wire for a building electrical system to a

   A. gas pipe
   B. cold water pipe
   C. vent pipe
   D. steam pipe

37. When removing the insulation from a wire before making a splice, care should be taken to avoid nicking the wire mainly because the

   A. current carrying capacity will be reduced
   B. resistance will be increased
   C. wire is more likely to break
   D. tinning on the wire will be injured

38. The term "ampere-hours" is associated with

   A. motors
   B. transformers
   C. electromagnets
   D. storage batteries

39. It is generally true that most accidents to employees result because of

   A. too heavy work schedules
   B. poor light
   C. carelessness
   D. complicated equipment

40. It is NOT correct to state that

   A. current flowing through a resistor causes heat
   B. rectifiers change d.c. to a.c.
   C. the conduit of an electrical system should be grounded
   D. ammeters are used in series in the circuit

41. When a d.c. voltage of 1.50 volts is applied to a certain coil, the current in the coil is 6 amperes. The resistance of this coil is

   A. 1/4 ohm   B. 4 ohms   C. 7 1/2 ohms   D. 9 ohms

Questions 42 - 50.

Questions 42 through 50 in Column I (on the next page) are electrical symbols, each of which represents one of the electrical devices shown in Column II (on the next page). For each symbol shown in Column I, select the corresponding device from Column II. PRINT, in the correspondingly numbered item space at the right, the letter given below your selected device.

42.		42.
43.	ITEM	43.
44.		44.
45.		45.
46.		46.
47.		47.
48.		48.
49.		49.
50.		50.

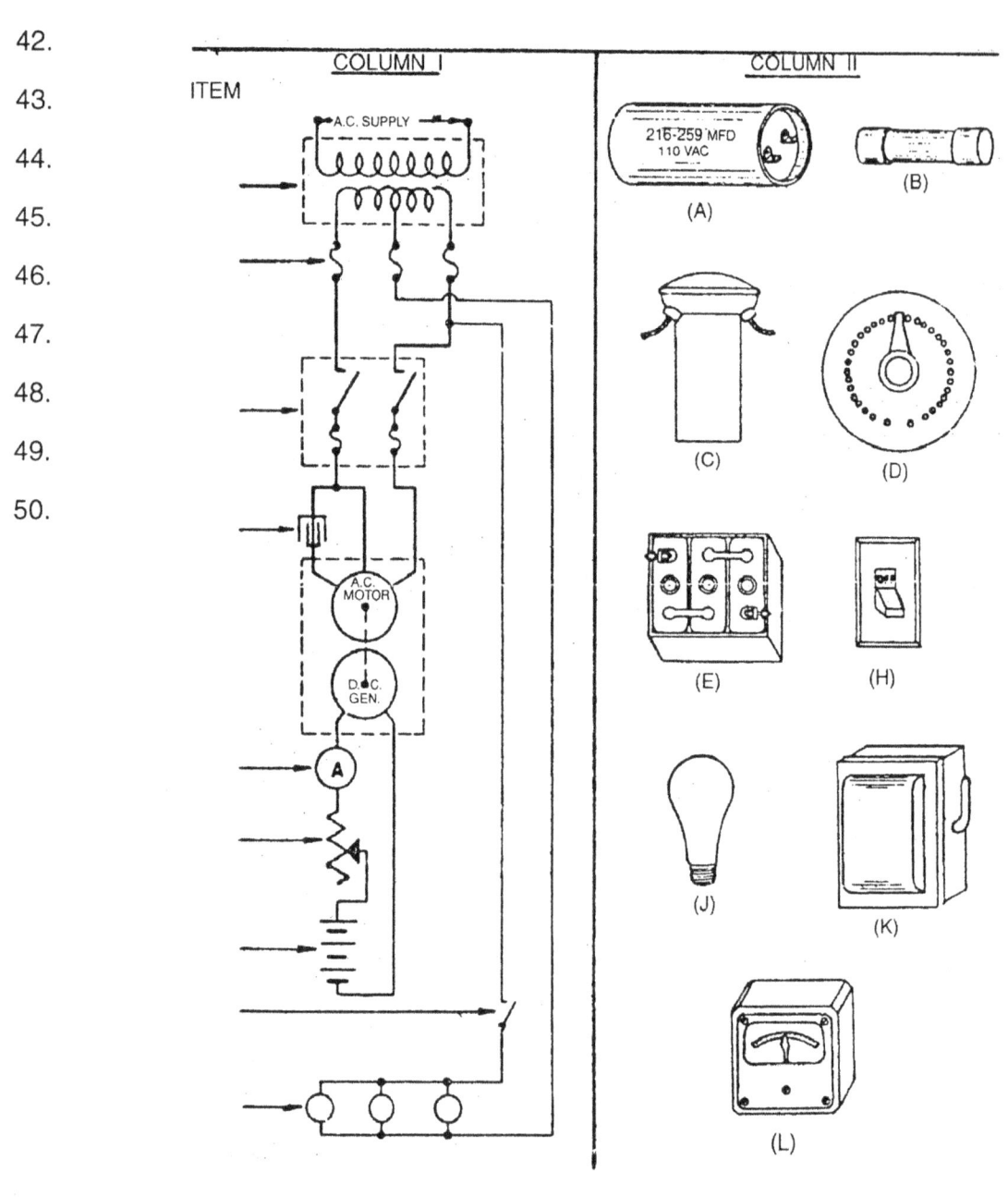

KEY (CORRECT ANSWERS)

1. D	11. A	21. B	31. D	41. A
2. A	12. B	22. C	32. A	42. C
3. D	13. A	23. B	33. D	43. B
4. D	14. E	24. B	34. D	44. K
5. C	15. D	25. A	35. C	45. A
6. B	16. C	26. A	36. B	46. L
7. B	17. C	27. D	37. C	47. D
8. C	18. D	28. B	38. D	48. E
9. D	19. D	29. A	39. C	49. H
10. B	20. A	30. C	40. B	50. J

SPATIAL RELATIONS
EXAMINATION SECTION
TEST 1

DIRECTIONS: In each of Questions 1 to 11 the front and top views of an object are given. Of the views labeled 1, 2, 3, and 4, select the one that CORRECTLY represents the right side view of each object for third angle projection.

1.

   A. 1   B. 2   C. 3   D. 4   1.____

2.

   A. 1   B. 2   C. 3   D. 4   2.____

3.

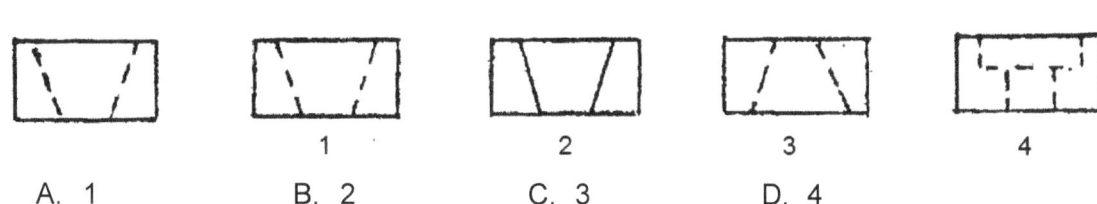

   A. 1   B. 2   C. 3   D. 4   3.____

125

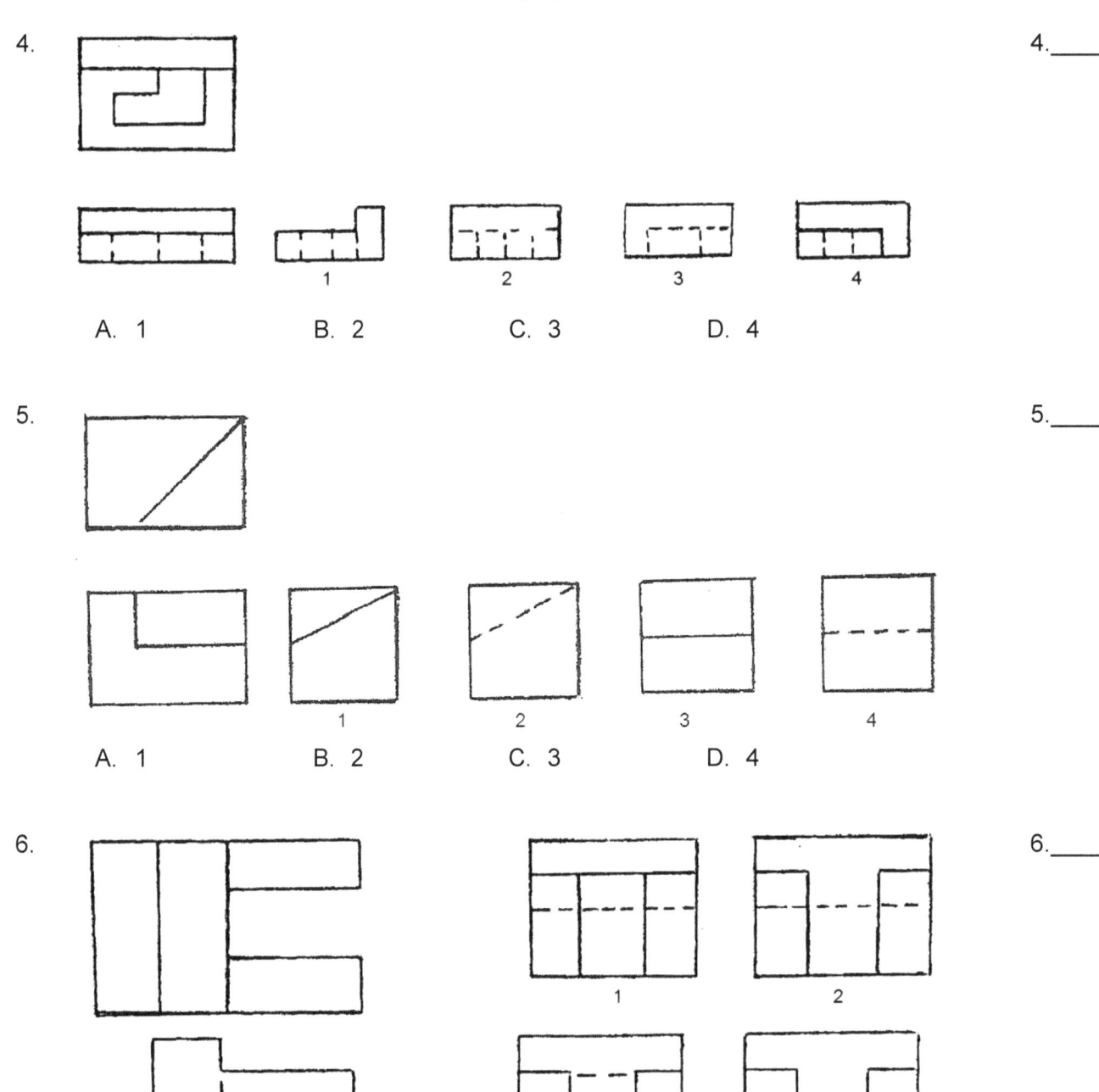

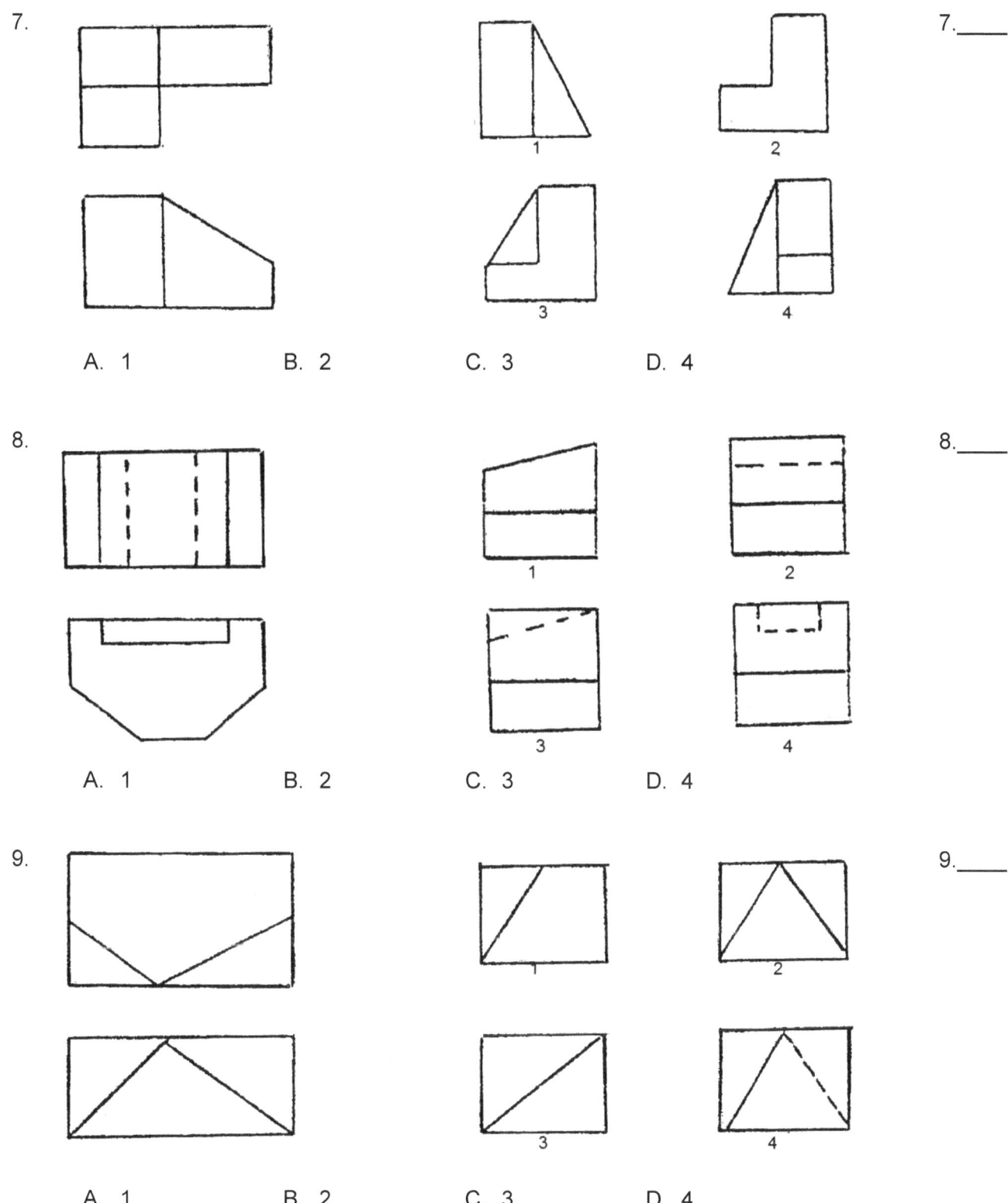

10.   A. 1   B. 2   C. 3   D. 4   10.____

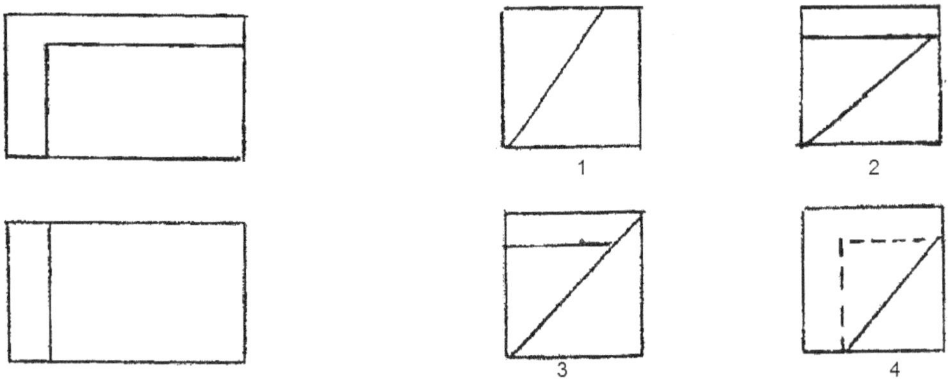

11.   A. 1   B. 2   C. 3   D. 4   11.____

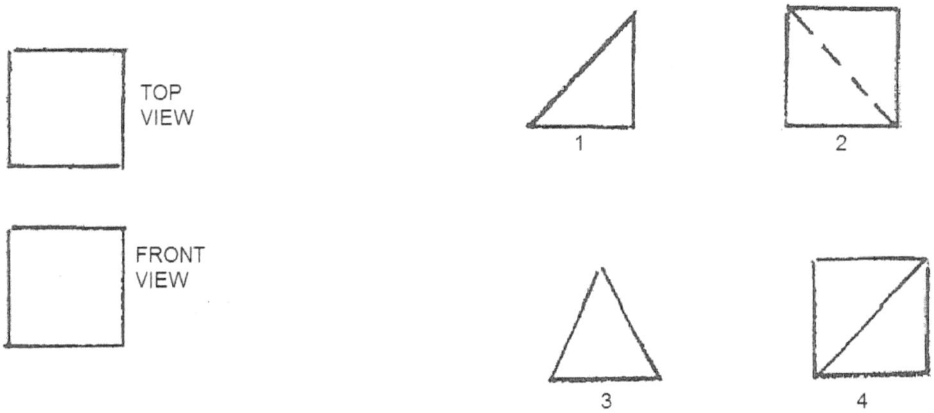

Questions 12-16.

DIRECTIONS: In each of Questions 12 to 25 inclusive, two views of an object are given. Of the views labeled 1, 2, 3, and 4, select the one that CORRECTLY represents the right side view of each object.

12.   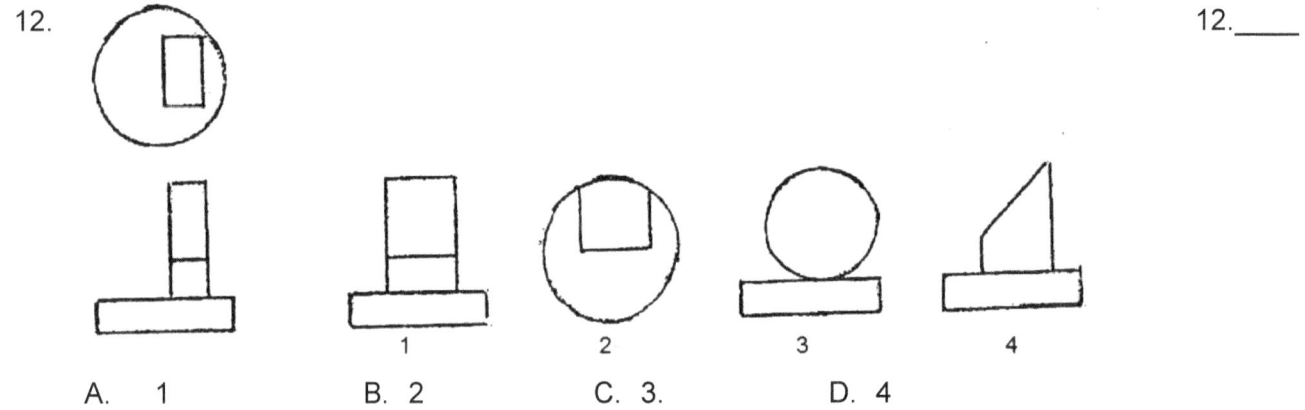   12.____

A. 1   B. 2   C. 3.   D. 4

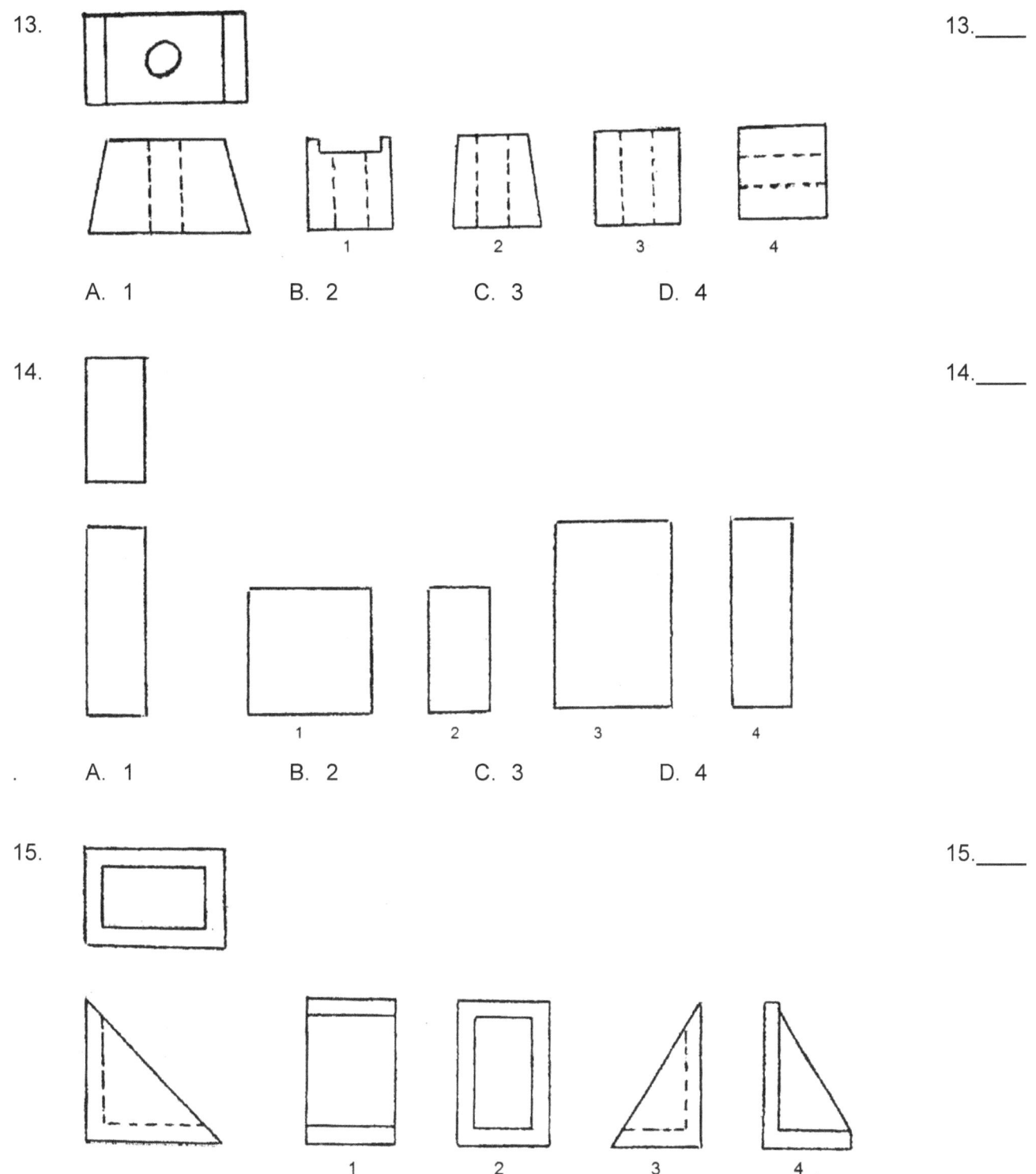

13.

A. 1 B. 2 C. 3 D. 4

14.

A. 1 B. 2 C. 3 D. 4

15.

A. 1 B. 2 C. 3 D. 4

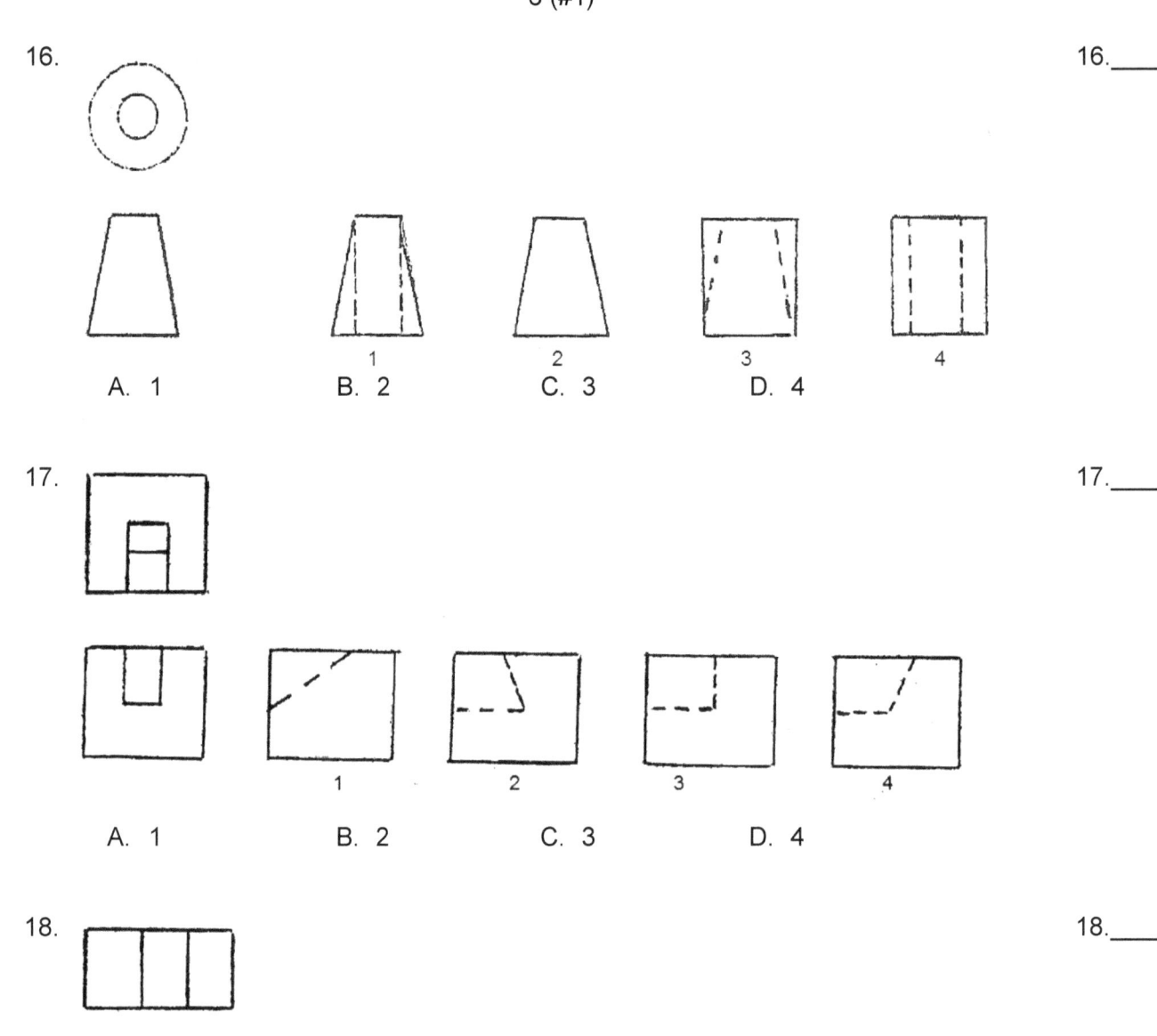

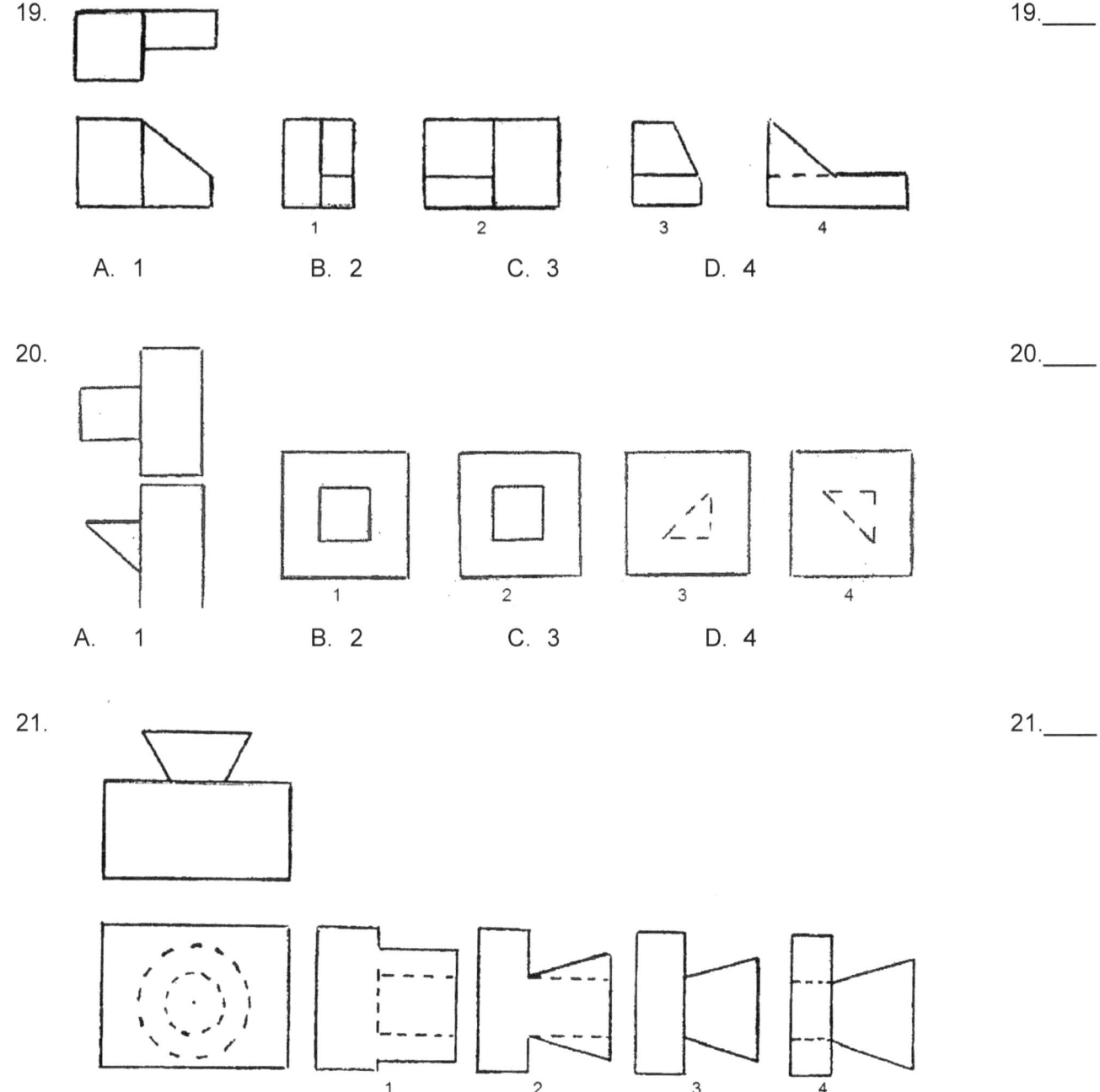

19. _____

20. _____

21. _____

22.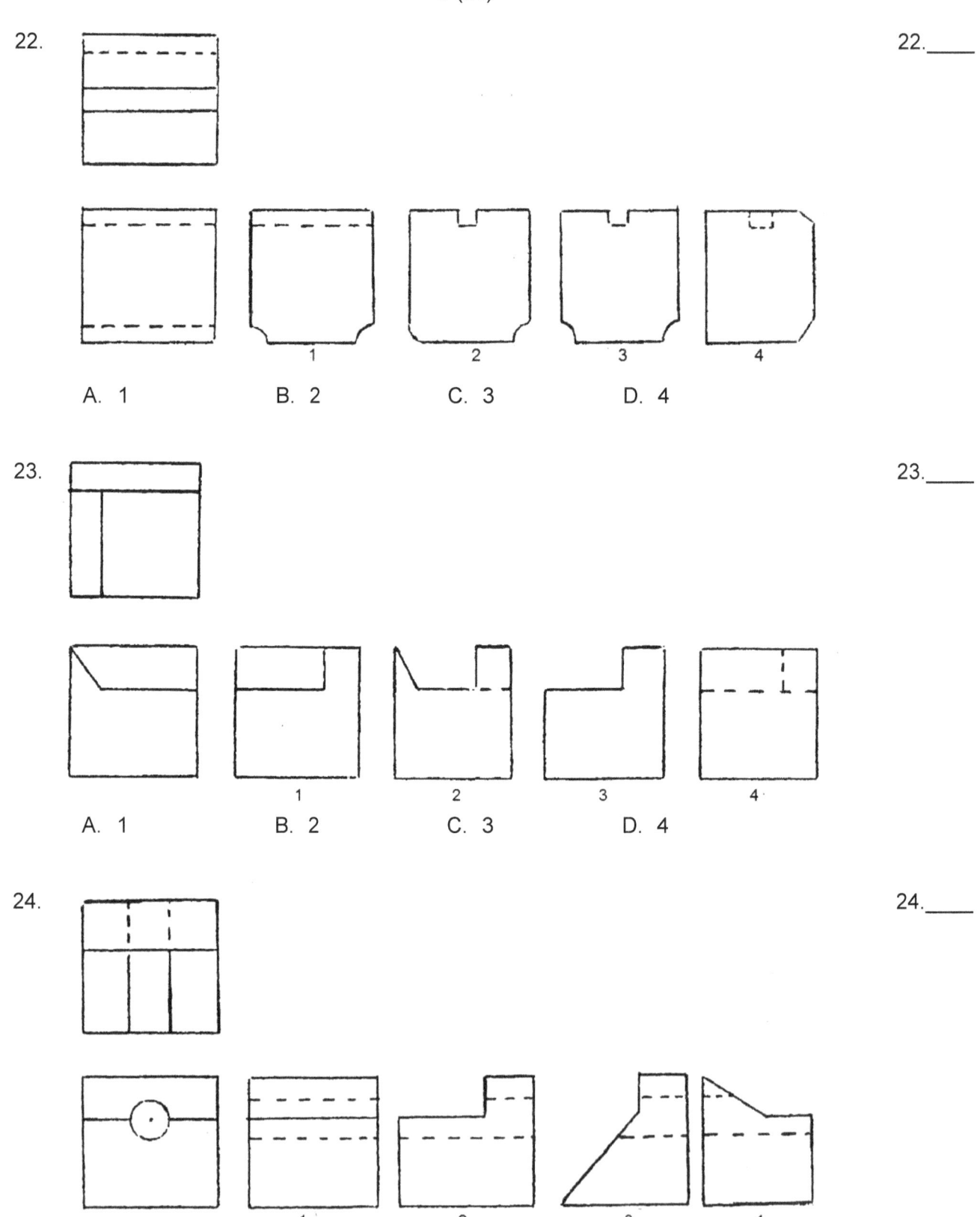

A. 1   B. 2   C. 3   D. 4

23.

A. 1   B. 2   C. 3   D. 4

24.

25.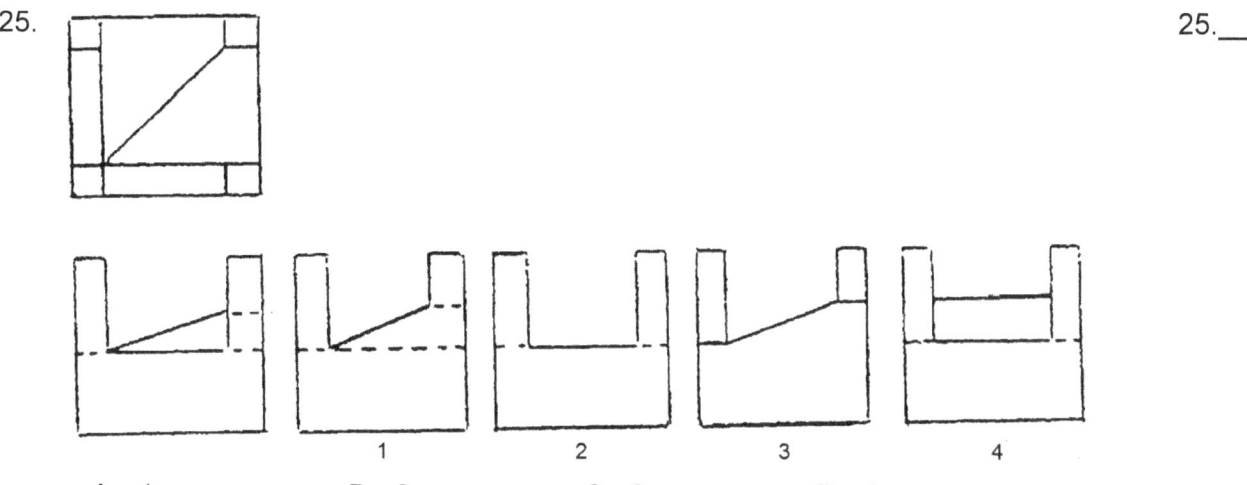

A. 1   B. 2   C. 3   D. 4

Questions 26-30.

DIRECTIONS: In Questions 26 through 30 which follow, the plan and front elevation of an object are shown on the left, and on the right are shown four figures, one of which and only one represents the right side elevation. Mark in the space at the right the letter which represents the right side elevation. In the sample below, which figure correctly represents the right side elevation?

SAMPLE QUESTION

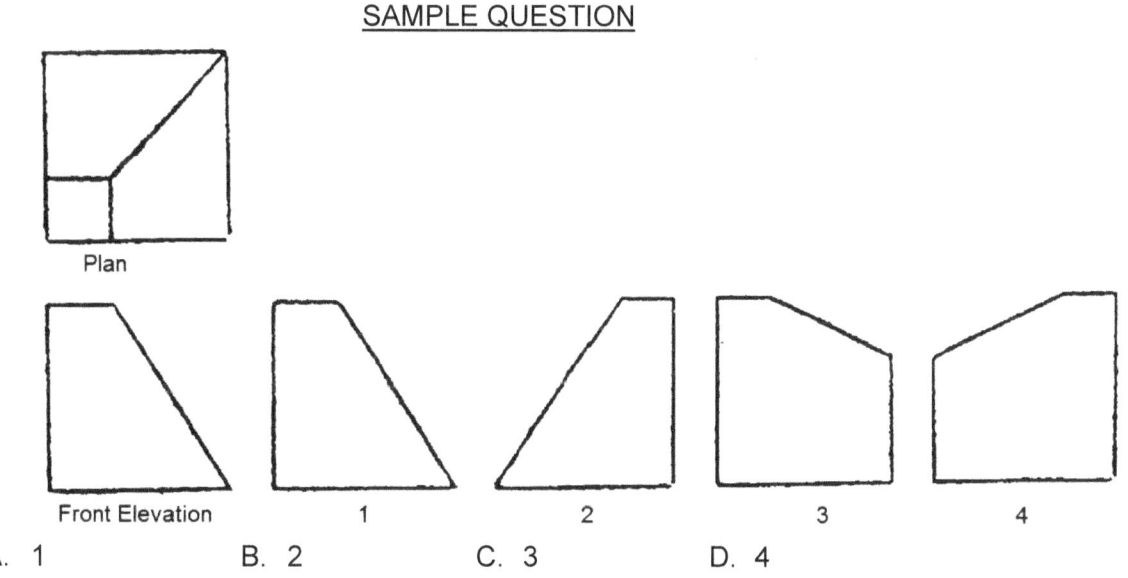

A. 1   B. 2   C. 3   D. 4

The correct answer is A.

26. ____

27. ____

28. ____

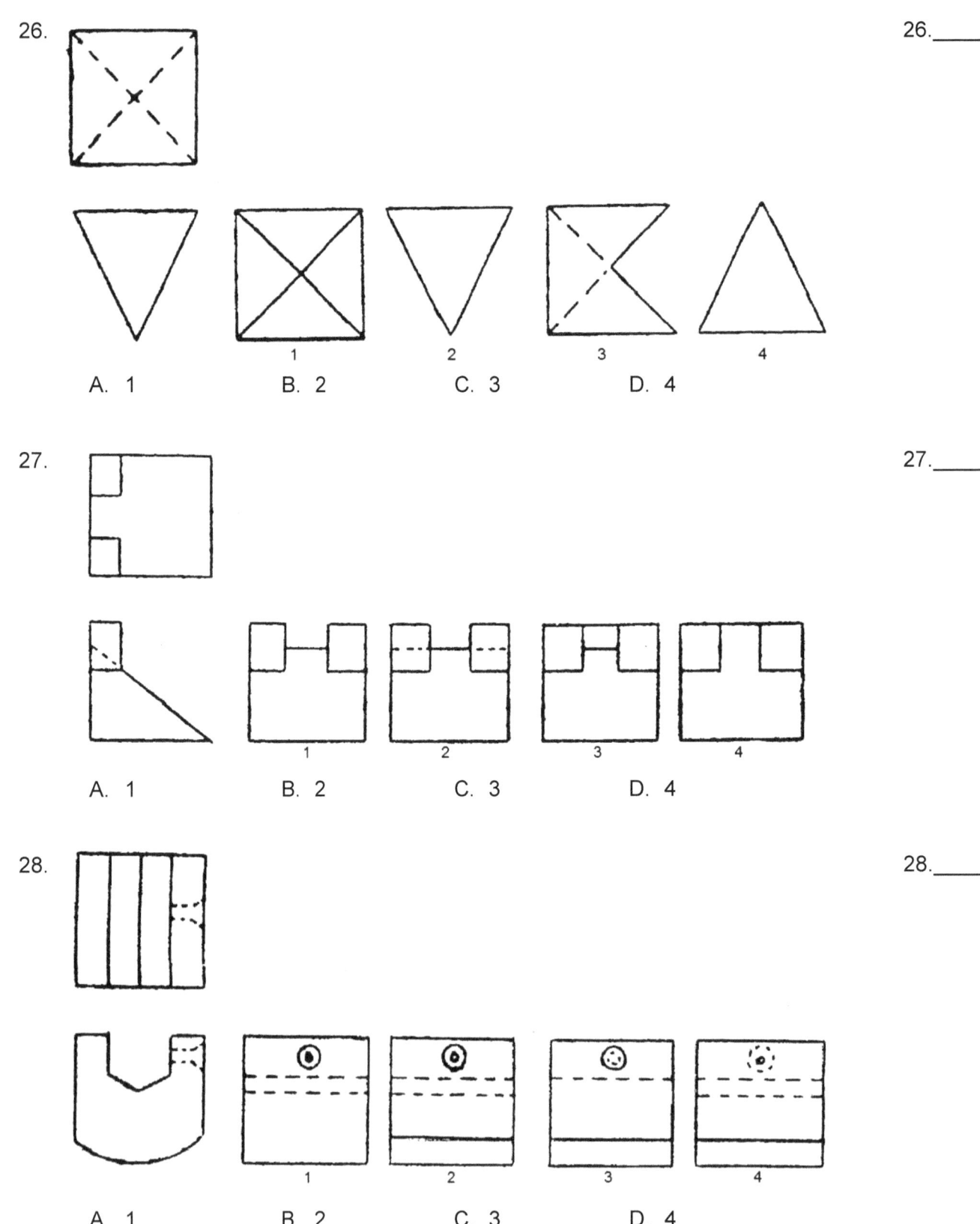

134

29.

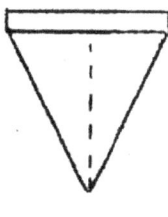 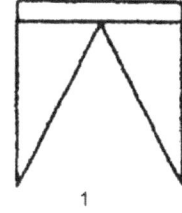 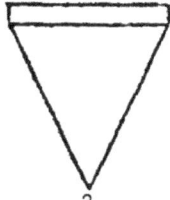 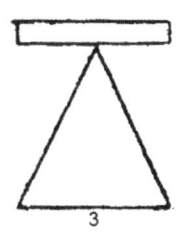 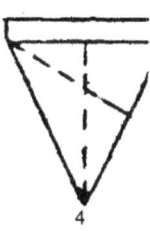

A. 1   B. 2   C. 3   D. 4

30.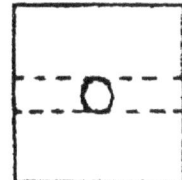

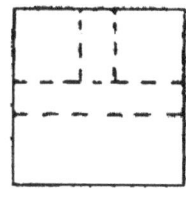 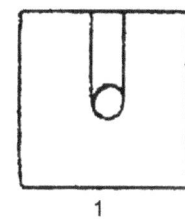 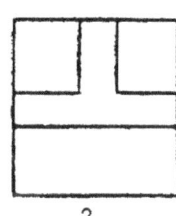  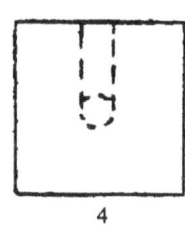

A. 1   B. 2   C. 3   D. 4

KEY (CORRECT ANSWERS)

1.	B	11.	A	21.	C
2.	D	12.	D	22.	B
3.	A	13.	C	23.	A
4.	A	14.	C	24.	B
5.	C	15.	B	25.	A
6.	B	16.	B	26.	B
7.	D	17.	D	27.	A
8.	C	18.	C	28.	B
9.	A	19.	A	29.	A
10.	A	20.	B	30.	C

TEST 2

Questions 1-10.

DIRECTIONS: Questions 1 through 10 deal with relationships between sets of figures. For each question, select that choice (A, or B, or C, or D) which has the SAME relationship to Figure 3 that Figure 2 has to Figure 1.

SAMPLE: Study Figures 1 and 2 in the Sample. Notice that Figure 1 has been turned clockwise 1/4 of a turn to get Figure 2. Taking Figure 3 and turning it clockwise 1/4 of a turn, we get choice A, the correct answer.

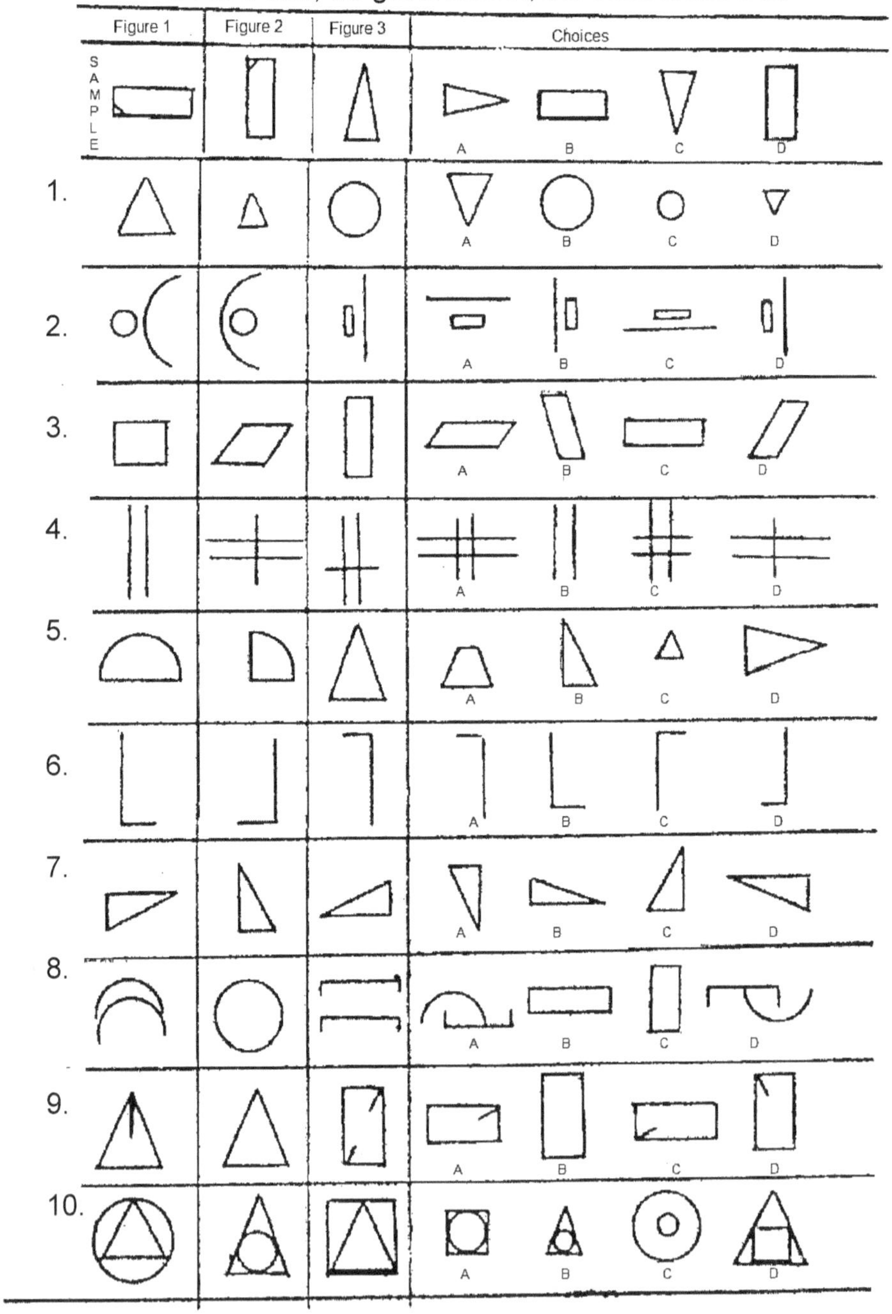

Questions 11-16.

DIRECTIONS: Questions 11 through 16 show the top view of an object in the first column, the front view of the same object in the second column and four drawings in the third column, one of which correctly represents the RIGHT side of the object. Select the CORRECT right side view.

As a guide, the first one is an illustrative example, the correct answer of which is C.

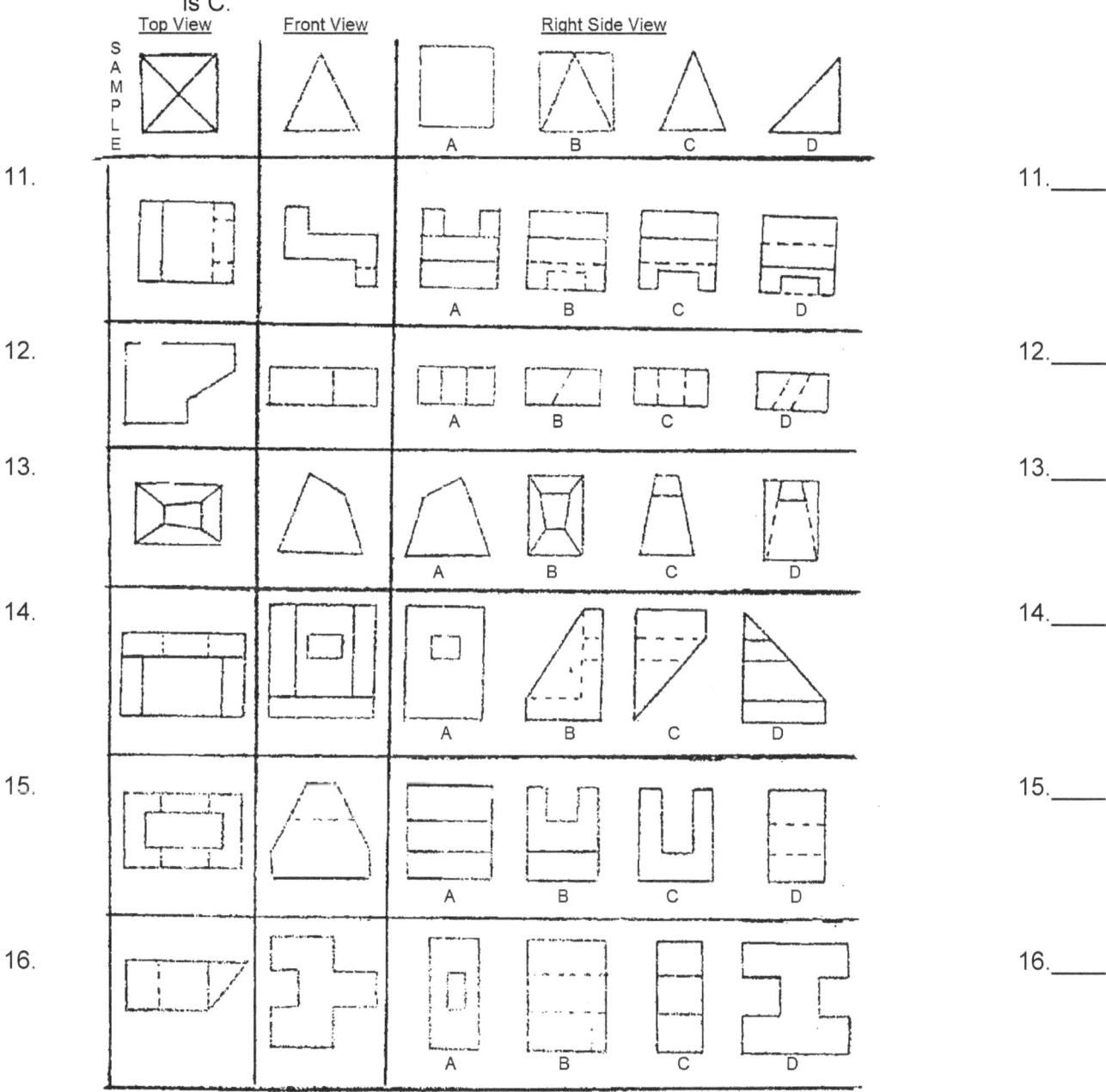

Questions 17-20.

DIRECTIONS: In each of the following groups of drawings, the top view and front elevation of an object are shown on the left. At the right are four drawings, one of which represents the end elevation of the object as seen from the right. Select the drawing which represents the correct end elevation and print the letter in the space at the right.

The first group is shown as an example only.
The correct answer in this group is C.

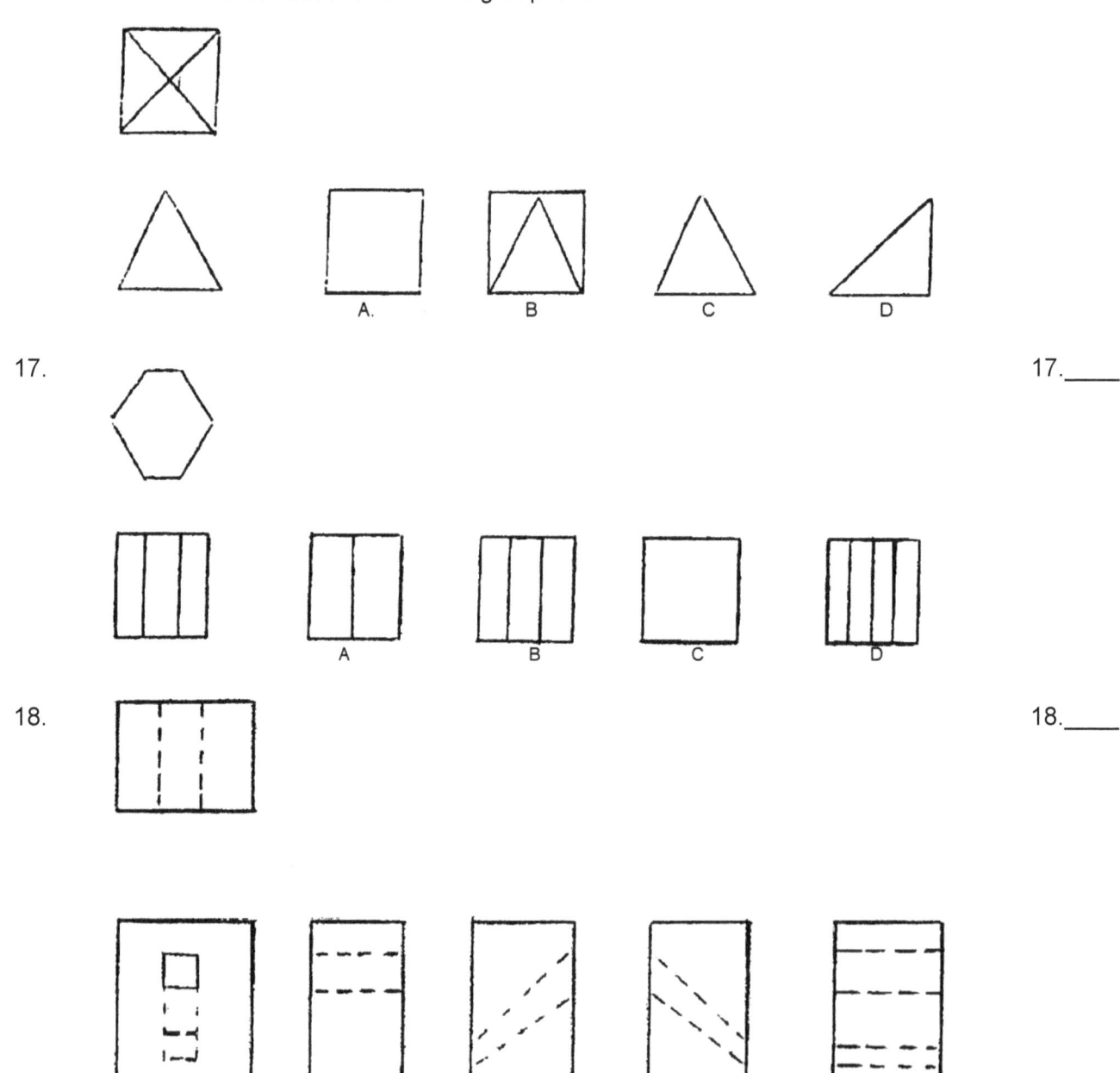

17. _____

18. _____

4 (#2)

19. 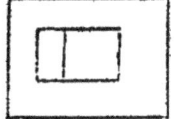 19.____

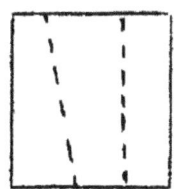   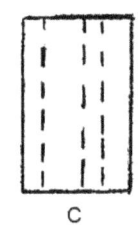 
                    A   B   C   D

20.  20.____

 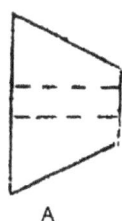 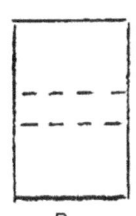  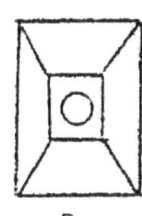
                    A   B   C   D

KEY (CORRECT ANSWERS)

1.	C	6.	C	11.	C	16.	C
2.	B	7.	A	12.	A	17.	A
3.	D	8.	B	13.	C	18.	C
4.	A	9.	B	14.	B	18.	D
5.	B	10.	D	15.	B	19.	A

ARITHMETICAL REASONING

EXAMINATION SECTION
TEST 1

DIRECTIONS: Each question or incomplete statement is followed by several suggested answers or completions. Select the one that BEST answers the question or completes the statement. *PRINT THE LETTER OF THE CORRECT ANSWER IN THE SPACE AT THE RIGHT.*

1. A canvas tarpaulin measures 6 feet by 9 feet.
   The LARGEST circular area that can be covered completely by this tarpaulin is a circle with a diameter of _____ feet.

   A. 9   B. 8   C. 7   D. 6

2. The population of Maple Grove was 1,000 in 2006. In 2007, the population increased 40 percent, but in 2008, 2009, and 2010, the population decreased 20 percent, 10 percent, and 25 percent, respectively. (For each year, the percentage change in population is based upon a comparison with the preceding year.)
   At the end of this period, the population was MOST NEARLY

   A. 900   B. 850   C. 800   D. 750

3. The ratio of boys to girls in one school is 6 to 4. A second school contains half as many boys and twice as many girls as the first.
   The one of the following statements that is MOST accurate is that

   A. both schools have the same number of pupils
   B. the first school has 10 percent more pupils than the second
   C. the second school has 10 percent more pupils than the first
   D. there is not sufficient information to reach any conclusion about which school has more pupils

4. In a certain city, X number of cases of malaria have occurred over a 10-year period, resulting in Y number of deaths.
   The AVERAGE annual death rate from malaria in this city is

   A. $Y/10$ B. $10/X$ C. $10-X/Y$ D. $\dfrac{Y(10X)}{X+Y}$

5. A fireman's softball team wins 6 games out of the first 9 played. They go on to win all their remaining games and finish the season with a final average of games won of .750.
   The TOTAL number of games they played that season was

   A. 10   B. 12   C. 15   D. 18

6. While inspecting a cylindrical gravity tank for an automatic sprinkler system, a chief observes that the water in the tank is 10 feet deep and that the tank has a diameter of 9 feet. He asks the building manager how many gallons are in the tank and receives the reply, *About 10,000.* (Cubic foot of water contains 7 1/2 gallons.) Based on his own observation and calculations, the chief should

A. agree that the manager's answer is probably correct
B. disagree with the manager's answer; the answer is more nearly 20,000 gallons
C. disagree with the manager's answer; the answer is more nearly 15,000 gallons
D. disagree with the manager's answer; the answer is more nearly 5,000 gallons

7. The diagram at the right represents the storage space of a fire engine. The amount of space available for the storage of hose in the fire engine is MOST NEARLY _____ cubic feet.
   A. 40
   B. 75
   C. 540
   D. 600

8. If a piece of rope 100 feet long is cut so that one piece is 2/3 as long as the other piece, the length of the longer piece must be _____ feet.
   A. 60
   B. 66 2/3
   C. 70
   D. 75

9. A water tank has a discharge valve which is capable of emptying the tank when full in two hours. It also has an inlet valve which can fill the tank, when empty, in four hours and a second inlet valve which can fill the tank, when empty, in six hours.
   If the tank is full and all three valves are opened fully, with water flowing through each valve to capacity, the tank will be emptied in _____ hours.

   A. 2
   B. 6
   C. 12
   D. a period of time which cannot be determined from the information given

10. Final grades in a history course are determined as follows:
    Class recitations - weight 50
    Weekly quizzes - weight 25
    Final examination - weight 25
    A student has an average of 60 on a class recitation and 80 on weekly quizzes.
    In order to receive a final grade of 75, he must obtain on his final examination a grade of
    A. 75
    B. 80
    C. 90
    D. 100

11. Suppose that 8 inches of snow contribute as much water to the reservoir system as one inch of rain.
    If, during a snowstorm, an average of 12 inches of snow fell during a six-hour period, with drifts as high as three feet, the addition to the water supply as a result of this snowfall ultimately will be the equivalent of _____ inches of rain.

    A. 1 1/2
    B. 3
    C. 4 1/2
    D. an amount of rain which cannot be determined from the information given

12. A fire engine carries 900 feet of 2 1/2" hose, 500 feet of 2" hose, and 350 feet of 1 1/2" hose.
    Of the total hose carried, the percentage of 1 1/2" hose is MOST NEARLY

    A. 35   B. 30   C. 25   D. 20

    12.____

13. An engine company made 96 runs in the month of April, which was a decrease of 20% from the number of runs made in March.
    The number of runs made in March was MOST NEARLY

    A. 136   B. 128   C. 120   D. 110

    13.____

14. A water tank has a capacity of 6,000 gallons. Connected to the tank is a pump capable of supplying water at the rate of 25 gallons per minute, which goes into operation automatically when the water in the tank falls to the one-half mark.
    If we start with a full tank and drain the water from the tank at the rate of 50 gallons a minute, the tank can continue supplying water at the required rate for_____ hours.

    A. 2 1/2   B. 3   C. 3 1/2   D. 4

    14.____

15. Three firemen are assigned the task of cleaning fire apparatus which usually takes three men five hours to complete. After they have been working three hours, three additional firemen are assigned to help them. Assuming that they all work at the normal rate, the assignment of the additional men will reduce the time required to complete the task by _____ minutes.

    A. 20   B. 30   C. 50   D. 60

    15.____

16. Assume that at the beginning of the calendar year, an employee was earning $48,000 per year. On July 1st, he received an increase of $2,400 per year. On November 1st, he was promoted to a position paying $60,000 per year. The total earnings for the year were MOST NEARLY

    A. $51,000   B. $49,000   C. $50,000   D. $53,000

    16.____

17. Engine A leaves its firehouse at 1:48 P.M. and travels 3 miles to a fire at an average speed of 30 miles per hour. Engine B leaves its firehouse at 1:51 P.M. and travels 6 miles to the same fire at an average speed of 40 miles per hour.
    From the above facts, we may conclude that Engine A arrives _____ minutes _____ Engine B.

    A. 3; before   B. 6; before
    C. 3; after   D. 6; after

    17.____

18. A widely used formula for calculating the quantity of water discharged from a hose is $GPM = 29.7d^2/P$, where GPM = gallons per minute, d = diameter of the nozzle in inches, and P = pressure at the nozzle in pounds per square inch.
    If it takes 1 minute to extinguish a fire using a 1 1/2" nozzle at 100 pounds pressure per square inch, the number of gallons discharged is, according to the above formula, MOST NEARLY

    A. 730   B. 650   C. 690   D. 670

    18.____

19. The spring of a spring balance will stretch in proportion to the amount of weight placed on the balance.
    If a 2-pound weight placed on a certain balance stretches the spring 1/4", then a stretch in the spring of 1 3/4" will be caused by a weight of _____ lbs.

    A. 10	B. 12	C. 14	D. 16

20. In a yard 100 feet by 60 feet, a dog is tied by a leash to a stake driven into the ground in the center of the yard.
    If the dog is to be kept from going off the property, the MAXIMUM acceptable length of the leash is _____ feet.

    A. 60	B. 50	C. 30	D. 28

21. From a length of pipe 10 feet long, a 3 1/3 foot piece is to be cut.
    If the diameter of the 10-foot length is 5 inches, the diameter of the piece to be cut will be

    A. 5"	B. 2 1/3"	C. 2"	D. 1 2/3"

22. A certain crew consists of one foreman who is paid $15.00 per hour, 2 carpenters who are paid $12.60 per hour, 4 helpers who are paid $10.50 per hour, and 10 laborers who are paid $7.50 per hour.
    The average hourly earnings of the members of the crew is MOST NEARLY

    A. $11.40	B. $10.50	C. $10.05	D. $9.30

23. The fraction which is equivalent to the sum of .125, .25, .375, and .0625 is

    A. 5/8	B. 13/16	C. 7/8	D. 15/16

24. If the pay period of an employee is changed from every two weeks to twice a month, his gross pay (before deductions) from each pay period will

    A. increase by one-tenth
    B. increase by one-twelfth
    C. decrease by one-thirteenth
    D. decrease by one-fifteenth

25. In a certain state, the automobile license tags consist of two letters followed by three digits, e.g., AA-122. The MAXIMUM number of different combinations of numbers and letters which can be obtained under this system is MOST NEARLY

    A. 13,500	B. 75,000	C. 325,000	D. 675,000

KEY (CORRECT ANSWERS)

1. D
2. D
3. C
4. A
5. B

6. D
7. C
8. A
9. C
10. D

11. A
12. D
13. C
14. B
15. D

16. A
17. B
18. D
19. C
20. C

21. A
22. D
23. B
24. B
25. D

SOLUTIONS TO PROBLEMS

1. The largest circular area completely covered by the tarpaulin would have a diameter of the lesser of 6 ft. and 9 ft.

2. At the end of 2010, the population was $(1000)(1.40)(.80)(.90)(.75) = 756 \approx 750$.

3. Let 6x and 4x represent the number of boys and girls, respectively, at the first school. Then, 3x and 8x will represent the number of boys and girls, respectively, at the second school. The enrollment of the second school, 11x, is 10% higher than the enrollment at the first school, 10x.

4. Since Y deaths have occurred over a 10-year period due to malaria, the annual death rate caused by malaria is Y/10. X, the number of cases of malaria, has no effect on the annual death rate.

5. Let x = number of games played, after the first 9 games. Then, $(6+x)/(9+x) = .750$. Solving, x = 3. The total number of games played = 9 + 3 = 12.

6. Volume = $(\pi)(4.5)^2(10) \approx 636$ cu.ft. Then, $(636)(7\ 1/2) = 4770 \approx 5000$

7. 15x8x3 = 360; 15x6x2 = 180; 360 + 180 = 540 cu.ft.

8. Let 2x and 3x represent the two pieces. Then, 2x + 3x = 100. Solving, x = 20. The longer piece = (3)(20) = 60 ft.

9. Let x = number of hours required. Then, $\frac{x}{2} \cdot \frac{x}{4} \cdot \frac{x}{6} = 1$ Simplifying, x/12 = 1. Thus, x = 12

10. Let x = final exam grade. Then, (60)(.50) + (80)(.25) + (x)(.25) = 75. Simplifying, 50 + ,25x = 75. Solving, x = 100

11. If 8 in. of snow contribute 1 in. of rain, then 12 in. of snow contribute (1)(12/8) = 1 1/2 in. of rain.

12. 350 ÷ (900+500+350) = .20 = 20%

13. The number of runs in March was 96 ÷ .80 = 120

14. The time required to extract 3000 gallons at 50 gallons per minute = 3000 ÷ 50 = 60 min. = 1 hour. At this point, the tank is half full. Also, a pump begins replenishing the tank at 25 gallons per minute. Thus, the effect on draining has been slowed to 50 - 25 = 25 gallons per minute. To drain the remaining 3000 gallons will require 3000 ÷ 25 = 120 minutes = 2 hours. Total draining time = 3 hours.

15. (3)(5) = 15 man-hours. After 3 hours, 9 man-hours have been used. At this point, 6 men are working, and since only 6 man-hours remaining, the time needed is 1 hour = 60 minutes.

16. ($48,000)(1/2) + ($50,400)(1/3) + ($60,000)(1/6) = $50,800 ≈ $51,000

17. Engine A requires (3)(60/30) = 6 minutes to get to the fire.
So, Engine A arrives at 1:54 PM. Engine B requires (6)(60/40) = 9 minutes to get to the fire. So, Engine B arrives at 2:00 PM. Thus, Engine A arrives 6 minutes before Engine B.

18. GPM = $(29.7)(1.5)^2(\sqrt{100})$ = 668.25 ≈ 670

19. Let x = required number of pounds. Then, 2/x = 1/4/1 3/4.
So, 1/4x = 3 1/2. Solving, x = 14

20. The shorter of the two dimensions is 60 ft. If the dog is in the center of the yard, the maximum length allowed for the leash is 60/2 = 30 ft.

21. The diameter of the cut piece = diameter of entire pipe = 5"

22. [($15.00)(1)+($12.60)(2)+($10.50)(4)+($7.50)(10)]/17 = $157.20/17 9.25 (closest answer in answer key is $9.30).

23. .125 + .25 + .375 + .0625 = .8125 = 13/16

24. Let x = annual pay. Then, x/26 = pay every two weeks, whereas pay every half month. His increase is $\frac{x}{24} - \frac{x}{26} = \frac{x}{312}$, which represents a fractional increase of $\frac{x}{312} / \frac{x}{26} = \frac{1}{12}$

25. The number of different license tags = (26)(26)(10)(10)(10) = 676,000 (closest answer in answer key is 675,000).

TEST 2

DIRECTIONS: Each question or incomplete statement is followed by several suggested answers or completions. Select the one that BEST answers the question or completes the statement. *PRINT THE LETTER OF THE CORRECT ANSWER IN THE SPACE AT THE RIGHT.*

1. If cast iron weighs 450 pounds per cubic foot, the weight of a solid cast iron manhole cover 2 feet in diameter and 1 inch thick is MOST NEARLY _____ pounds.

    A. 94 B. 118 C. 136 D. 164

    1._____

2. The sum of 2 5/8, 3 3/16, 1 1/2, and 4 1/4 is

    A. 9 13/16 B. 10 7/16 C. 11 9/16 D. 13 3/16

    2._____

3. A pump is able to fill a tank holding 15,000 gallons in 2 hours and 30 minutes. Pumping at the same rate, an empty 60,000 gallon tank can be filled in

    A. 10 hours
    C. 11 hours
    B. 10 hours, 30 minutes
    D. 11 hours, 30 minutes

    3._____

4. Assume you want to add 10,000 gallons of water to a tank. If you pump water into the tank at the rate of 100 gallons per minute for one hour and 50 gallons per minute after the first hour, the total time required to add the 10,000 gallons is MOST NEARLY

    A. 1 hour, 20 minutes
    C. 2 hours, 20 minutes
    B. 2 hours
    D. 3 hours

    4._____

5. A tank 25 feet long, 15 feet wide, and 10 feet deep is enlarged by extending the length another 25 feet.
    The enlarged tank will be able to hold _____ more than the original tank.

    A. 50% B. 100% C. 150% D. 200%

    5._____

6. If cast iron weighs 450 pounds per cubic foot, the weight of a solid cast iron manhole cover 4 feet in diameter and 1 inch thick is MOST NEARLY _____ pounds.

    A. 188 B. 236 C. 328 D. 471

    6._____

7. If four men work seven hours during the day, the number of man-hours of work done is

    A. 4 B. 7 C. 11 D. 28

    7._____

8. If it takes four men fourteen days to do a certain job, seven men working at the same rate should be able to do the same job in _____ days.

    A. 8 B. 7 C. 6 D. 5

    8._____

9. A truck leaves the garage at 9:26 A.M. and returns the same day at 3:43 P.M. The period of time that the truck was away from the garage is MOST NEARLY _____ hours, _____ minutes.

    A. 5; 17 B. 5; 43 C. 6; 17 D. 6; 26

    9._____

10. Assume that it takes 6 men 8 days to do a certain job. Working at the same speed, the number of days that it will take 4 men to do this job is

    A. 9   B. 10   C. 12   D. 14

11. The sum of 3 5/8 + 4 1/4 + 6 1/2 + 7 1/8 is

    A. 20 7/8   B. 21 1/4   C. 21 1/2   D. 22 1/8

12. The fraction which is equal to .0625 is

    A. 1/64   B. 3/64   C. 1/16   D. 5/8

13. The volume, in cubic feet, of a rectangular coal bin 8 feet long by 5 feet wide by 7 feet high is MOST NEARLY

    A. 40   B. 56   C. 186   D. 280

14. Assume that a car travels at a constant speed of 36 miles per hour.
    The speed of this car, in feet per second, is MOST NEARLY (one mile equals 5,280 ft.)

    A. 3   B. 24.6   C. 52.8   D. 879.8

15. If one-third of a 19-foot length of lumber is cut off, the length of the remaining piece will measure APPROXIMATELY

    A. 8'8"   B. 9'8"   C. 12'8"   D. 13'8"

16. The circumference of a circle having a diameter of 10" is MOST NEARLY _____ inches.

    A. 3.14   B. 18.72   C. 24.96   D. 31.4

17. Assume that in the purchase of paint, the seller quotes a discount of 10%.
    If the price per gallon is $19.05, the actual payment, in dollars per gallon, is MOST NEARLY

    A. $17.15   B. $17.85   C. $18.75   D. $19.50

18. Assume that a cubic foot of water contains 7 1/2 gallons. The number of gallons of water which could be contained in a rectangular tank 3 feet long, 2 feet wide, and 2 feet deep is MOST NEARLY

    A. 12   B. 45   C. 90   D. 120

19. The volume, in cubic feet, of a slab of concrete that is 5'0" wide, 6'0" long, and 0'6" in depth is MOST NEARLY

    A. 15.0   B. 13.5   C. 12.0   D. 10.5

20. The sum of the following pipe lengths, 22 1/8", 7 3/4", 19 7/16", and 43 5/8", is

    A. 91 7/8"   B. 92 1/16"   C. 92 1/2"   D. 92 15/16"

21. The area, in square feet, of a plant floor that is 42 feet wide and 75 feet long is

    A. 3,150   B. 3,100   C. 3.075   D. 2,760

22. The sum of the following dimensions, 1 5/8, 2 1/4, 4 1/16, and 3 3/16, is

    A. 10 15/16   B. 11   C. 11 1/8   D. 11 1/4

23. Assume that six men, working together at the same rate of speed, can complete a certain job in 3 hours.
    If, however, there were only four men available to do this job, and they all worked at the same rate of speed, to complete this job would take MOST NEARLY _____ hours.

    A. 4 1/4   B. 4 1/2   C. 4 3/4   D. 5

24. Due to unforeseen difficulties, a job which would normally take 17 hours to complete was actually completed in 21 hours.
    This represents a percent increase over the normal time of MOST NEARLY

    A. 19%   B. 2.4%   C. 24%   D. 124%

25. Truck A costs $30,000 and gets 12 mpg and truck B costs $35,000 and gets 15 mpg. After 1 year driving 12,000 miles, how much would be saved by purchasing truck A if gasoline costs $1.50 per gallon?

    A. $1,000   B. $3,000   C. $4,700   D. $6,000

KEY (CORRECT ANSWERS)

1. B
2. C
3. A
4. C
5. B
6. D
7. D
8. A
9. C
10. C
11. C
12. C
13. D
14. C
15. C
16. D
17. A
18. C
19. A
20. D
21. A
22. C
23. B
24. C
25. C

SOLUTIONS TO PROBLEMS

1. $(450)(\pi)(1)^2(1/12) \approx 118$ pounds. (Note: $V = \pi R^2 H$)

2. 2 5/8 + 3 3/16 + 1 1/2 + 4 1/4 = 10 25/16 = 11 9/16

3. To fill a 60,000 gallon tank would require (4)(2 1/2 hrs.) = 10 hrs.

4. After 1 hour, (100)(60) = 6000 gallons have been added. To add the remaining 4000 gallons will require 4000 ÷ 50 = 80 minutes = 1 hour 20 minutes. Thus, total time needed is 2 hrs. 20 min.

5. The original volume = (25)(15)(10) = 3750 cu.ft., and the new volume = (50)(15)(10) = 7500 cu.ft. The increased volume of 3750 represents an increase of (3750/3750)(100) = 100%.

6. $(450)(\pi)(2)^2(1/12) \approx 471$ pounds

7. (4)(7) = 28 man-hours

8. (4)(14) = 56 man-days. Then, 56 ÷ 7 = 8 days

9. From 9:26 A.M. to 3:43 P.M. = 6 hrs. 17 min.

10. (6)(8) = 48 man-days. Then, 48 ÷ 4 = 12 days

11. 3 5/8 + 4 1/4 + 6 1/2 + 7 1/8 = 20 12/8 = 21 1/2

12. .0625 = 625/10,000 = 1/16

13. (8)(5)(7) = 280 cu.ft.

14. (36)(5280) = 190,080 ft. per hour. Since there are 3600 seconds in 1 hour, the speed = 190,080 ÷ 3600 = 52.8 ft. per second.

15. 19' - 1/3(19') = 12 2/3, = 12'8"

16. Circumference = $(\pi)(10")$ 31.4"

17. ($19.05)(.90) ≈ $17.15

18. (7 1/2)(3)(2)(2) = 90 gallons

19. (5)(6)(1/2) = 15 cu.ft.

20. 22 1/8" + 7 3/4" + 19 7/16" + 43 5/8" = 91 31/16" = 92 15/16"

21. Area = (42)(75) = 3150 sq.ft.

22. 1 5/8 + 2 1/4 + 4 1/16 + 3 3/16 = 10 18/16 = 11 1/8

23. (6) (3) = 18 man-hours. Then, 18 / 4 = 4 1/2 hours

24. 21 - 17 = 4. Then, 4/17 ≈ 24%

25. For Truck A, the expenses are $30,000 + (1000)($1.50) = $31,500 For Truck B, the expenses are $35,000 + (800)($1.50) = $36,200. $36,200 - $31,500 = $4,700

TEST 3

DIRECTIONS: Each question or incomplete statement is followed by several suggested answers or completions. Select the one that BEST answers the question or completes the statement. *PRINT THE LETTER OF THE CORRECT ANSWER IN THE SPACE AT THE RIGHT.*

1. Assume that a light maintainer and his helper replaced 25 lamps on one round of their assigned territory.
   If it took two hours to complete this round, and the maintainer's pay rate was $9.60 per hour and the helper's rate was $8.40 per hour, the labor cost of replacing each burned out lamp averaged _____ cents.

   A. 18   B. 36   C. 72   D. 144

   1.____

2. A certain power distribution job will require two main-tainers at $16.00 per hour and two helpers at $13.20 per hour. The job will take three 8-hour days to complete and will require 6 hours of planning and supervision by a foreman at $19.60 per hour.
   The TOTAL labor cost for this job is

   A. $264.80   B. $501.60   C. $818.40   D. $1,519.20

   2.____

3. Two identical containers are partly filled with bolts and weigh 40 lbs. and 75 lbs., respectively. To save storage space, all the bolts are put in one of the containers. The two containers now weigh 5 lbs. and 110 lbs., respectively.
   If three bolts weigh 1/2 lb., the TOTAL number of bolts is

   A. 210   B. 450   C. 630   D. 660

   3.____

4. The sum of the following dimensions, 2'7 1/2", 1'8 1/2", 2'1/16", and 3/4", is

   A. 5'15 9/16"   B. 5'15 11/16"
   C. 5'7/16"   D. 6'4 9/16"

   4.____

5. If a 3-foot length of contact rail weighs 150 pounds, then 39 feet of contact rail weighs _____ pounds.

   A. 1,850   B. 1,900   C. 1,950   D. 2,000

   5.____

6. The sum of the following dimensions, 3'2 1/2", 8 7/8", 2'6 3/8", 2'9 3/4", and 1'0", is

   A. 9'3 1/4"   B. 10'3 1/4"   C. 10'7 1/4"   D. 16'7 1/4"

   6.____

7. If a drawing for a contact rail installation is made to a scale of 1 1/2" to the foot, the drawing is said to be one _____ size.

   A. sixteenth   B. eight   C. quarter   D. half

   7.____

8. If a drawing has a scale of 1/4" = 1', a dimension of 1 3/4" on the drawing would be equal to

   A. 4'   B. 5'   C. 6'   D. 7'

   8.____

9. A reel weighs 600 lbs. when fully loaded with cable and 200 lbs. when empty.
   If the cable weighs 2.5 lbs. per foot, the number of reels a foreman should order for a job requiring 700 feet of this cable is _____ reels.

   A. 2   B. 3   C. 4   D. 5

   9.____

10. If the scale on a working drawing is shown as 1/4" = 1', a scaled measurement of 4 1/2 inches represents an actual length of _____ feet.

   A. 8 B. 9 C. 16 D. 18

11. A gap on the third rail starts at a subway column marked 217+79. The gap extends 68 feet to another column marked 217+11.
   A column midway between these columns would be marked 217+_____

   A. 34 B. 39 C. 45 D. 68

12. Assume a foreman decided that 100 contact rail ties need replacing. Each tie measures 9' x 6" x 8".
   In providing room for storing these ties at the job site, the MINIMUM storage volume required is APPROXIMATELY _____ cubic feet.

   A. 300 B. 360 C. 432 D. 576

13. Assume a certain job was done a year ago and took 8 men a total of 5 days to complete. The records show that each day involved 5 hours of overtime for half the men. Your assistant supervisor now assigns you the identical job to be done using 6 men and no overtime.
   The MINIMUM number of regular work days that should be scheduled for this job is _____ days.

   A. 13 B. 11 C. 9 D. 6

14. The sum of the following dimensions, 12'11 3/16", 9'8 5/8", 7'3 3/4", 5'2 1/2", and 3'1 1/4", is

   A. 39'5 9/16"   B. 38'3 5/16"
   C. 36'2 3/8"   D. 35'1 7/8"

15. If the scale on a drawing is 1/4" to the foot, then a 5/8" measurement would represent an actual length of

   A. 5'4" B. 4'8" C. 2'6" D. 1'3"

16. The sum of 1 9/16", 3 1/2", 7 3/8", 10 3/4", and 12 5/8" is

   A. 33 11/16" B. 34 13/16" C. 35 11/16" D. 35 13/16"

17. A reel containing an unknown length of cable weighs 340 pounds.
   If the empty reel weighs 119 lbs. and the cable weighs 0.85 lb. per foot, the number of feet of cable on the reel is

   A. 140 B. 260 C. 400 D. 540

18. If the scale on a shop drawing is 1/4" to the foot, then a part which measures 3 3/8 inches long on the drawing has an actual length of_____ feet _____ inches.

   A. 12; 6 B. 13; 6 C. 13; 9 D. 14; 9

19. Taking into account time and one-half payment for time over 40 hours of work, the gross pay of an employee who works 43 hours in a week at a rate of pay of $5.34 per hour is

   A. $213.60 B. $229.62 C. $237.63 D. $245.64

20. The sum of 0.365 + 3.941 + 10.676 + 0.784 is 20.____

    A. 13.766   B. 15.666   C. 15.756   D. 15.766

21. An air conditioning unit is rated at 1000 watts. The unit is run for 10 hours per day, five 21.____
    days per week. If the cost for electrical energy is 50 cents per kilowatt-hour, the weekly
    cost for electricity should be

    A. $2.50   B. $5.00   C. $25.00   D. $250.00

22. Assume that the cost of a certain wiring installation is broken down as follows: Materials 22.____
    $1,200, Labor $800, and Rental of equipment $400.
    The percentage of the total cost of the job that can be charged to Labor is MOST
    NEARLY

    A. 12.3   B. 33.3   C. 40.0   D. 66.6

23. Assume that it takes 4 electrician's helpers 6 days to do a certain job. 23.____
    Working at the same rate of speed, the number of days it will take 3 electrician's help-
    ers to do the same job is

    A. 6   B. 7   C. 8   D. 9

24. Assume that a 120-volt, 25-cycle magnetic coil is to be rewound to operate properly on 24.____
    60-cycles at the same voltage.
    If the coil at 25-cycles has 1,000 turns, at 60-cycles the number of turns should be
    MOST NEARLY

    A. 2,400   B. 1,200   C. 416   D. 208

25. A light maintainer whose rate is $14.40 per hour is assigned to replace burned-out sta- 25.____
    tion and tunnel lamps. During 4 hours, he replaces 28 lamps.
    The average labor cost for replacing each of these burned-out lamps was NEAREST
    to

    A. 56¢   B. $1.04   C. $2.00   D. $3.60

KEY (CORRECT ANSWERS)

1. D
2. D
3. C
4. D
5. C

6. B
7. B
8. D
9. D
10. D

11. C
12. A
13. C
14. B
15. C

16. D
17. B
18. B
19. C
20. D

21. C
22. B
23. C
24. C
25. C

SOLUTIONS TO PROBLEMS

1. (2)($9.60+$8.40) = $36.00. Then, $36.00 ÷ 25 = $1.44 or 144 cents.

2. (2)($16.00)(24) + (2)($13.20)(24) + (6)($19.60) = $1519.20

3. An empty container weighs 5 lbs., so the container which contains bolts and weighs 110 lbs. actually has 105 lbs. of bolts. Since 3 bolts weigh 1/2 lb., 105 lbs. would contain (105/1/2)(3) = 630 bolts.

4. 2'7 1/4" + 1'8 1/2" + 2'1/16" + 3/4" = 5'15 25/16" = 6 '4 9/16"

5. 39 feet of rail weighs (13)(150) = 1950 pounds

6. 3'2 1/4" + 8 7/8" + 2'6 3/8" + 2'9 3/4" + 1'0" = 8'25 18/8" = 10'3 1/4"

7. 1 1/2"/1" = 3/2.1/12=1/8

8. 1 3/4" ÷ 1/4" = 7 Then, (7)(1') = 7'

9. 600 - 200 = 400. Then, 400 ÷ 2.5 = 160 ft. of cable per reel. Since 700 ft. of cable is needed, 700/160 = 4.375, which means 5 reels will be required (must round up).

10. 4 1/2" ÷ 1/4" = 9/2 4/1 = 18 Then, (18)(1') = 18'

11. Half of 68 = 34; 11 + 34 = 45; 79 - 34 = 45

12. (100)(9')(1/2')(2/3') = 300 cu.ft.

13. Number of man-days = (4)(5) + (4)(5)(1 5/8) =52.5
    For 6 men working only 8-hour days, 52.5 ÷ 6 = 8.75 = 9 days needed.

14. 12'11 3/16" + 9'8 5/8" + 7'3 3/4" + 5'2 1/2" + 3'1 1/4" = 36'25 37/16" = 38'3 5/16"

15. 5/8" ÷ 1/4" = 5/8 . 4/1 = 2 1/2. Then, (2 1/2)(1') = 2'6"

16. 1 9/16" + 3 1/2" + 7 3/8" + 10 3/4" + 12 5/8" = 33 45/16" = 35 13/36"

17. 340 - 119 = 221 lbs. Then, 221 ÷ .85 = 260 ft.

18. 3 3/8" ÷ 1/4" = 27/8 . 4/1 = 13/ 1/2. Then, (13 1/2) (1') = 13 ft. 6 in.

19. (40)($5.34) + (3)($5.34)(1.5) = $237.63

20. 0.365 +3.941 + 10.676 + 0.784 = 15.766

21. (1000)(10)(5) = 50,000 watt-hours = 50 kilowatt-hours. Then, (50)($.50) = $25.00

22. $800 / ($1200+$800+$400) =1/3 ≈ 33.3%

23. (4)(6) = 24. Then, 24/ 3 = 8 days

24. Let x = number of required turns. Since the number of cycles varies inversely as the number of turns, 25/60 = x/1000.
    Solving, x 416 (actually 416 2/3)

25. ($14.40)(4) = $57.60. Then, $57.60 ÷ 28 ≈ $2.06

BASIC ELECTRICITY

FUNDAMENTAL CONCEPTS OF ELECTRICITY
What is Electricity?

The word "electric" is actually a Greek-derived word meaning AMBER. Amber is a translucent (semitransparent) yellowish mineral, which, in the natural form, is composed of fossilized resin. The ancient Greeks used the words "electric force" in referring to the mysterious forces of attraction and repulsion exhibited by amber when it was rubbed with a cloth. They did not understand the fundamental nature of this force. They could not answer the seemingly simple question, "What is electricity?". This question is still unanswered. Though you might define electricity as "that force which moves electrons," this would be the same as defining an engine as "that force which moves an automobile." You would have described the effect, not the force.

We presently know little more than the ancient Greeks knew about the fundamental nature of electricity, but tremendous strides have been made in harnessing and using it. Elaborate theories concerning the nature and behavior of electricity have been advanced, and have gained wide acceptance because of their apparent truth and demonstrated workability.

From time to time various scientists have found that electricity seems to behave in a constant and predictable manner in given situations, or when subjected to given conditions. These scientists, such as Faraday, Ohm, Lenz, and Kirchhoff, to name only a few, observed and described the predictable characteristics of electricity and electric current in the form of certain rules. These rules are often referred to as "laws." Thus, though electricity itself has never been clearly defined, its predictable nature and easily used form of energy has made it one of the most widely used power sources in modern time. By learning the rules, or laws, applying to the behavior of electricity, and by learning the methods of producing, controlling, and using it, you will have "learned" electricity without ever having determined its fundamental identity.

THE MOLECULE

One of the oldest, and probably the most generally accepted, theories concerning electric current flow is that it is comprised of moving electrons. This is the ELECTRON THEORY. Electrons are extremely tiny parts, or particles, of matter. To study the electron, you must therefore study the structural nature of matter itself. (Anything having mass and inertia, and which occupies any amount of space, is composed of matter.) To study the fundamental structure or composition of any type of matter, it must be reduced to its fundamental fractions. Assume the drop of water in figure 1-1 (A) was halved again and again. By continuing the process long enough, you would eventually obtain the smallest particle of water possible-the molecule. All molecules are composed of atoms.

A molecule of water (H_2O) is composed of one atom of oxygen and two atoms of hydrogen, as represented in figure 1-1 (B). If the molecule of water were further subdivided, there would remain only unrelated atoms of oxygen and hydrogen, and the water would no longer exist as such. This example illustrates the following fact-the molecule is the smallest particle to which a substance can be reduced and still be called by the same name. This applies to all substances-liquids, solids, and gases.

When whole molecules are combined or separated from one another, the change is generally referred to as a PHYSICAL change. In a CHEMICAL change the molecules of the substance are altered such that

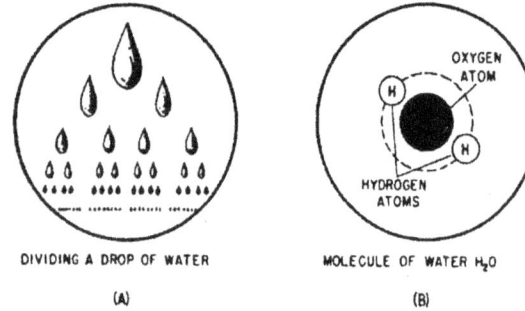

Figure 1-1.—Matter is made up of molecules.

new molecules result. Most chemical changes Involve positive and negative ions and thus are electrical in nature. All matter is said to be essentially electrical in nature.

THE ATOM

In the study of chemistry it soon becomes apparent that the molecule is far from being the ultimate particle into which matter may be subdivided. The salt molecule may be decomposed into radically different substances—sodium and chlorine. These particles that make up molecules can be isolated and studied separately. They are called ATOMS.

The atom is the smallest particle that makes up that type of material called an ELEMENT. The element retains its characteristics when subdivided into atoms. More than 100 elements have been identified. They can be arranged into a table of increasing weight, and can be grouped into families of material having similar properties. This arrangement is called the PERIODIC TABLE OF THE ELEMENTS.

The idea that all matter is composed of atoms dates back more than 2,000 years to the Greeks. Many centuries passed before the study of matter proved that the basic idea of atomic structure was correct. Physicists have explored the interior of the atom and discovered many subdivisions in it. The core of the atom is called the NUCLEUS. Most of the mass of the atom is concentrated in the nucleus. It is comparable to the sun in the solar system, around which the planets revolve. The nucleus contains PROTONS (positively charged particles) and NEUTRONS which are electrically neutral.

Most of the weight of the atom is in the protons and neutrons of the nucleus. Whirling around the nucleus are one or more smaller particles of negative electric charge. THESE ARE THE ELECTRONS. Normally there is one proton for each electron in the entire atom so that the net positive charge of the nucleus is balanced by the net negative charge of the electrons whirling around the nucleus. THUS THE ATOM IS ELECTRICALLY NEUTRAL.

The electrons do not fall into the nucleus even though they are attracted strongly to it. Their motion prevents it, as the planets are prevented from falling into the sun because of their centrifugal force of revolution.

The number of protons, which is usually the same as the number of electrons, determines the kind of element in question. Figure 1-2 shows a simplified picture of several atoms of different materials based on the conception of planetary electrons describing orbits about the nucleus. For example, hydrogen has a nucleus consisting of 1 proton, around which rotates 1 electron. The helium atom has a nucleus containing 2 protons and 2 neutrons with 2 electrons encircling the nucleus. Near the other extreme of the list of elements is curium (not shown in the figure), an element discovered in the 1940's, which has 96 protons and 96 electrons in each atom.

The *Periodic Table of the Elements* is an orderly arrangement of the elements in ascending atomic number (number of planetary electrons) and also in atomic weight (number of protons and neutrons in the nucleus). The various kinds of atoms have distinct masses or

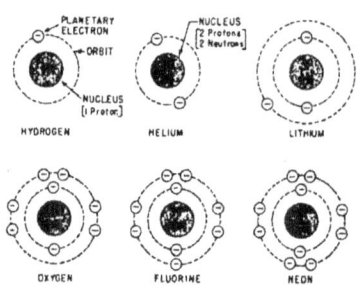

Figure 1-2.—Atomic structure of elements.

weights with respect to each other. The element most closely approaching unity (meaning 1) is hydrogen whose atomic weight is 1.008 as compared with oxygen whose atomic weight is 16. Helium has an atomic weight of approximately 4, lithium 7, fluorine 19, and neon 20, as shown in figure 1-2.

Figure 1-3 is a pictorial summation of the discussion that has just been presented. Visible matter, at the left of the figure, is broken down first to one of its basic molecules, then to one of the molecule's atoms. The atom is then further reduced to its subatomic particles—the protons, neutrons, and electrons. Subatomic particles are electric in nature. That is, they are the particles of matter most affected by an electric force. Whereas the whole molecule or a whole atom is electrically neutral, most subatomic particles are not neutral (with the exception of the neutron). Protons are inherently positive, and electrons are inherently negative. It is these inherent characteristics which make subatomic particles sensitive to electric force.

When an electric force is applied to a conducting medium, such as copper wire, electrons in the outer orbits of the copper atoms are forced out of orbit and impelled along the wire. The direction of electron movement is determined by the direction of the impelling force. The protons do not move, mainly because they are extremely heavy. The proton of the lightest element, hydrogen, is approximately 1,850 times as heavy as an electron. Thus, it is the relatively light electron that is most readily moved by electricity.

When an orbital electron is removed from an atom it is called a FREE ELECTRON. Some of the electrons of certain metallic atoms are so loosely bound to the nucleus that they are comparatively free to move from atom to atom. Thus, a very small force or amount of energy will cause such electrons to be removed from the atom and become free electrons. It is these free electrons that constitute the flow of an electric current in electrical conductors.

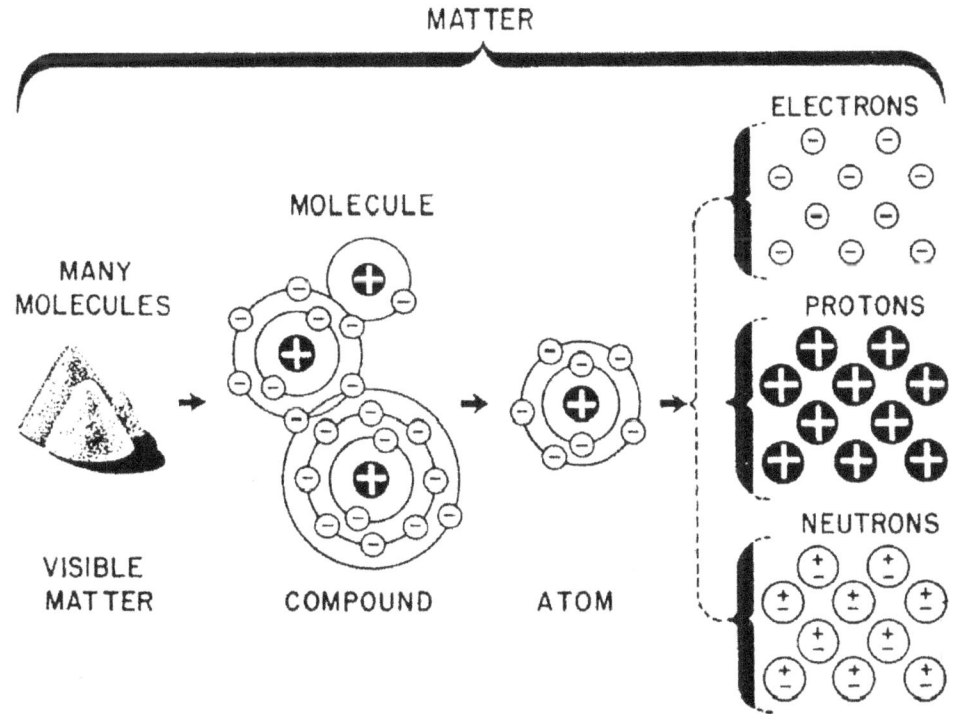

Figure 1-3.—Breakdown of visible matter to electric particles.

If the internal energy of an atom is raised above its normal state, the atom is said to be EXCITED. Excitation may be produced by causing the atoms to collide with particles that are impelled by an electric force. In this way, energy is transferred from the electric source to the atom. The excess energy absorbed by an atom may become sufficient to cause loosely bound outer electrons to leave the atom against the force that acts to hold them within. An atom that has thus lost or gained one or more electrons is said to be IONIZED. If the atom loses electrons it becomes positively charged and is referred to as a POSITIVE ION. Conversely, if the atom gains electrons, it becomes negatively charged and is referred to as a NEGATIVE ION. Actually then, an ion is a small particle of matter having a positive or negative charge.

Conductors and Insulators

Substances that permit the free motion of a large number of electrons are called CONDUCTORS. Copper wire is considered a good conductor because it has many free electrons. Electrical energy is transferred through conductors by means of the movement of free electrons that migrate from atom to atom inside the conductor. Each electron moves a very short distance to the neighboring atom where it replaces one or more electrons by forcing them out of their orbits. The replaced electrons repeat the process in other nearby atoms until the movement is transmitted throughout the entire length of the conductor. The greater the number of electrons that can be made to move in a material under the application of a given force the better are the conductive qualities of that material. A good conductor is said to have a low opposition or low resistance to the current (electron) flow.

In contrast to good conductors, some substances such as rubber, glass, and dry wood have very few free electrons. In these materials large amounts of energy must be expended in order to break the electrons loose from the influence of the nucleus. Substances containing very few free electrons are called POOR CONDUCTORS, NON-CONDUCTORS, or INSULATORS. Actually, there is no sharp dividing line between conductors and insulators, since electron motion is known to exist to some extent in all matter. Electricians simply use the best conductors as wires to carry current and the poorest conductors as insulators to prevent the current from being diverted from the wires.

Listed below are some of the best conductors and best insulators arranged in accordance with their respective abilities to conduct or to resist the flow of electrons.

Conductors	Insulators
Silver	Dry air
Copper	Glass
Aluminum	Mica
Zinc	Rubber
Brass	Asbestos
Iron	Bakelite

Static Electricity

In a natural, or neutral state, each atom in a body of matter will have the proper number of electrons in orbit around it. Consequently, the whole body of matter comprised of the neutral atoms will also be electrically neutral. In this state, it is said to have a "zero charge," and will neither attract nor repel other matter in its vicinity. Electrons will neither leave nor enter the neutrally charged body should it come in contact with other neutral bodies. If, however, any number of electrons are removed from the atoms of a body of matter, there will remain more protons than electrons, and the whole body of matter will become electrically positive. Should the positively charged body come in contact with another body having a normal charge, or having a negative (too many electrons) charge, an electric current will flow between them. Electrons will leave the more negative body and enter the positive body. This electron flow will continue until both bodies have equal charges.

When two bodies of matter have unequal charges, and are near one another, an electric force is exerted between them because of their unequal charges. However, since they are not in contact, their charges cannot equalize. The existence of such an electric force, where current cannot flow, is referred to as static electricity. "Static" means "not moving." This is also referred to as an ELECTROSTATIC FORCE.

One of the easiest ways to create a static charge is by the friction method. With the friction method, two pieces of matter are rubbed together and electrons are "wiped off" one onto the other. If materials that are good conductors are used, it is quite difficult to obtain a detectable charge on either. The reason for this is that equalizing currents will flow easily in and between the conducting materials. These currents equalize the charges almost as fast as they are created. A static charge is easier to obtain by rubbing a hard nonconducting material against a soft, or fluffy, nonconductor. Electrons are rubbed off one material and onto the other material. This is illustrated in figure 1-4.

When the hard rubber rod is rubbed in the fur, the rod accumulates electrons. Since both fur and rubber are poor conductors, little equalizing current can flow, and an electrostatic charge is built up. When the charge is great enough, equalizing currents will flow in spite of the material's poor conductivity. These currents will cause visible sparks, if viewed in darkness, and will produce a crackling sound.

CHARGED BODIES

One of the fundamental laws of electricity is that LIKE CHARGES REPEL EACH OTHER and UNLIKE CHARGES ATTRACT EACH OTHER. A positive charge and negative charge, being unlike, tend to move toward each other. In the atom the negative electrons are drawn toward the positive protons in the nucleus. This attractive force is balanced by the electron's centrifugal force caused by its rotation about the nucleus. As a result, the electrons remain in orbit and are not drawn into the nucleus. Electrons repel each other because of their like negative charges, and protons repel each other because of their like positive charges.

The law of charged bodies may be demonstrated by a simple experiment. Two pith (paper pulp) balls are suspended near one another by threads, as shown in figure 1-5.

If the hard rubber rod is rubbed to give it a negative charge, and then held against the right-hand ball in part (A), the rod will impart a negative charge to the ball. The right-hand ball will be charged negative with respect to the left-hand ball. When released, the two balls will be drawn together, as shown in figure 1-5 (A). They will touch and remain in contact until the left-hand ball acquires a portion of the negative charge of the right-hand ball, at which time they will swing apart as shown in figure 1-5 (C). If. positive charges are placed on both balls (fig. 1-5 (B)), the balls will also be repelled from each other.

COULOMB'S LAW OF CHARGES

The amount of attracting or repelling force which acts between two electrically charged bodies in free space depends on two things(1) their charges, and (2) the distance between them. The relationship of charge and distance to electrostatic force was first discovered and written by a French scientist named Charles A. Coulomb. Coulomb's Law states that CHARGED BODIES ATTRACT OR REPEL EACH OTHER WITH A FORCE THAT IS DIRECTLY PROPORTIONAL TO THE PRODUCT OF THEIR CHARGES, AND IS INVERSELY PROPORTIONAL TO THE SQUARE OF THE DISTANCE BETWEEN THEM.

ELECTRIC FIELDS

The space between and around charged bodies in which their influence is felt is called an ELECTRIC FIELD OF FORCE. The electric field is always terminated on material objects and extends between positive and negative charges. It can exist in air, glass, paper, or a vacuum. ELECTROSTATIC FIELDS and DIELECTRIC FIELDS are other names used to refer to this region of force.

Fields of force spread out in the space surrounding their point of origin and, in general, DIMINISH IN PROPORTION TO THE SQUARE OF THE DISTANCE FROM THEIR SOURCE.

The field about a charged body is generally represented by lines which are

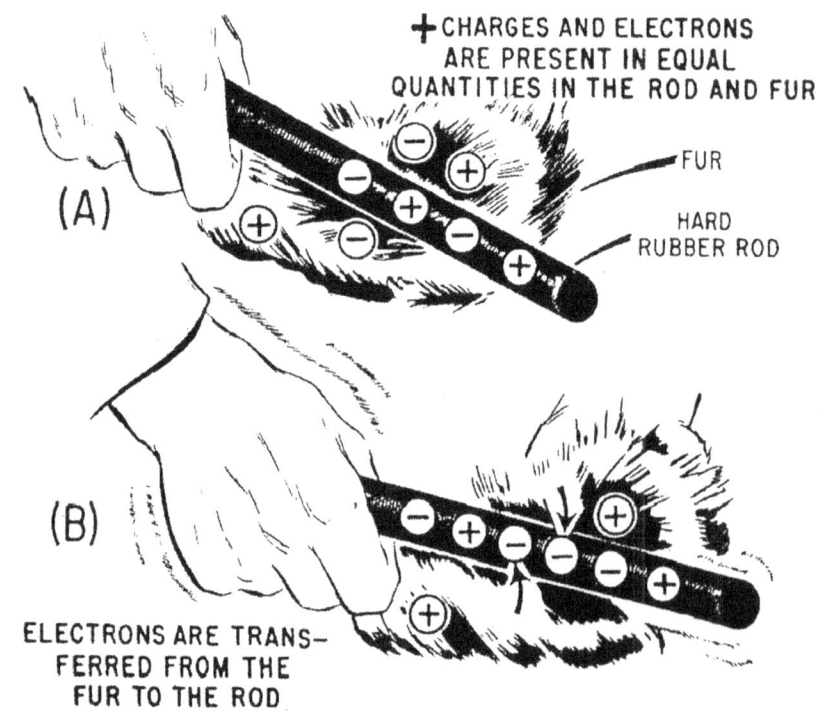

Figure 1-4.—Producing static electricity by friction.

referred to as ELECTROSTATIC LINES OF FORCE. These lines are imaginary and are used merely to represent the direction and strength of the field. To avoid confusion, the lines of force exerted by a positive charge are always shown leaving the charge, and for a negative charge they are shown as entering. Figure 1-6 illustrates the use of lines to represent the field about charged bodies.

Figure 1-6 (A) represents the repulsion of like-charged bodies and their associated fields. Part (B) represents the attraction between unlike-charged bodies and their associated fields.

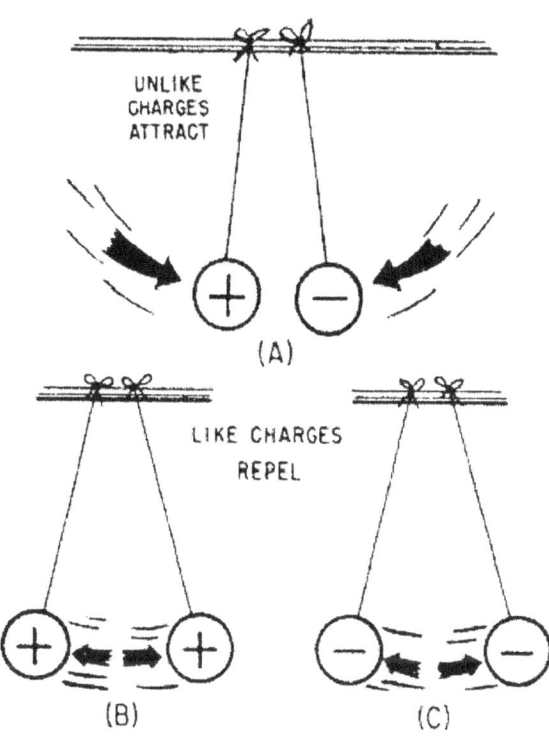

Figure 1-5.—Reaction between charged bodies.

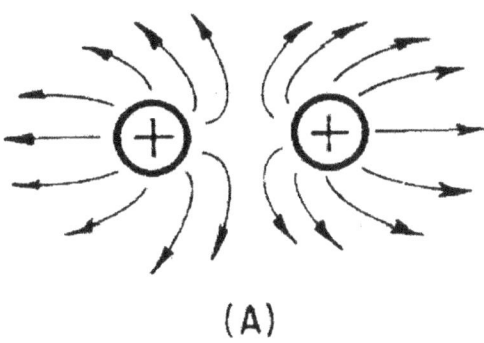

(A)

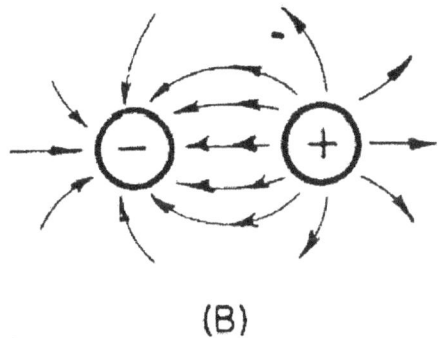

(B)

Figure 1-6.—Electrostatic lines of force.

Magnetism

A substance is said to be a magnet if it has the property of magnetism-that is, if it has the power to attract such substances as iron, steel, nickel, or cobalt, which are known as MAGNETIC MATERIALS. A steel knitting needle, magnetized by a method to be described later, exhibits two points of maximum attraction (one at each end) and no attraction at its center. The points of maximum attraction are called MAGNETIC POLES. All magnets have at least two poles. If the needle is suspended by its middle so that it rotates freely in a horizontal plane about its center, the needle comes to rest in an approximately north-south line of direction. The same pole will always point to the north, and the other will always point toward the south. The magnetic pole that points northward is called the NORTH POLE, and the other the SOUTH POLE.

A MAGNETIC FIELD exists around a simple bar magnet. The field consists of imaginary lines along which a MAGNETIC FORCE acts. These lines emanate from the north pole of the magnet, and enter the south pole, returning to the north pole through the magnet itself, thus forming closed loops.

A MAGNETIC CIRCUIT is a complete path through which magnetic lines of force may be established under the influence of a magnetizing force. Most magnetic circuits are composed largely of magnetic materials in order to contain the magnetic flux. These circuits are similar to the ELECTRIC CIRCUIT, which is a complete path through which current is caused to flow under the influence of an electromotive force.

Magnets may be conveniently divided into three groups.

1. NATURAL MAGNETS, found in the natural state in the form of a mineral called magnetite.

2. PERMANENT MAGNETS, bars of hardened steel (or some form of alloy such as alnico) that have been permanently magnetized.

3. ELECTROMAGNETS, composed of soft-iron cores around which are wound coils of insulated wire. When an electric current flows through the coil, the core becomes magnetized. When the current ceases to flow, the core loses most of its magnetism.

Permanent magnets and electromagnets are sometimes called ARTIFICIAL MAGNETS to further distinguish them from natural magnets.

NATURAL MAGNETS

For many centuries it has been known that certain stones (magnetite, Fe_3O_4) have the ability to attract small pieces of iron. Because many of the best of these stones (natural magnets) were found near Magnesia in Asia Minor, the Greeks called the substance MAGNETITE, or MAGNETIC.

Before this, ancient Chinese observed that when similar stones were suspended freely, or floated on a light substance in a container of water, they tended to assume a nearly north-and-south position. Probably Chinese navigators used bits of magnetite floating on wood in a liquid-filled vessel as crude compasses. At that time it was not known that the earth itself acts like a magnet, and these stones were regarded with considerable superstitious awe. Because bits of this substance were used as compasses they were called LOADSTONES (or lodestones), which means "leading stones."

Natural magnets are also found in the United States, Norway, and Sweden. A natural magnet, demonstrating the attractive force at the poles, is shown in figure 1-7 (A).

ARTIFICIAL MAGNETS

Natural magnets no longer have any practical value because more powerful and more conveniently shaped permanent magnets can be produced artificially. Commercial magnets are made from special steels and alloys for example, alnico, made principally of aluminum, nickel, and cobalt. The name is derived from the first two letters of the three principal elements of which it is composed. An artificial magnet is shown in figure 1-7 (B).

An iron, steel, or alloy bar can be magnetized by inserting the bar into a coil of insulated wire and passing a heavy direct current through the coil, as shown in figure 1-8 (A). This aspect of magnetism is

Artificial magnets may be classified as "permanent" or "temporary" depending on their ability to retain their magnetic strength after the magnetizing force has been removed. Hardened steel and certain alloys are relatively difficult to magnetize and are said to have a LOW PERMEABILITY because the magnetic lines of force do not easily permeate, or distribute themselves readily through the steel. Once magnetized, however, these materials retain a large part of their magnetic strength and are called PERMANENT MAGNETS. Permanent magnets are used extensively in electric instruments, meters, telephone receivers, permanent-magnet loudspeakers, and magnetos. Conversely, substances

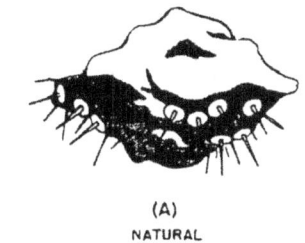

(A) NATURAL

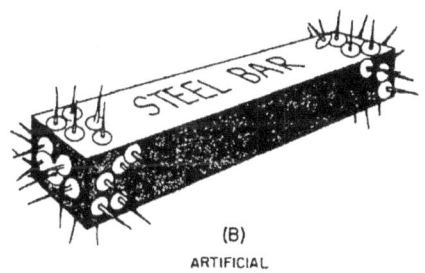

(B) ARTIFICIAL

Figure 1-7.—(A) Natural magnet; (B) artificial magnet.

treated later in the chapter. The same bar may also be magnetized if it is stroked with a bar magnet, as shown in figure 1-8 (B). It will then have the same magnetic property that the magnet used to induce the magnetism-has namely, there will be two poles of attraction, one at either end. This process produces a permanent magnet by INDUCTION-that is, the magnetism is induced in the bar by the influence of the stroking magnet.

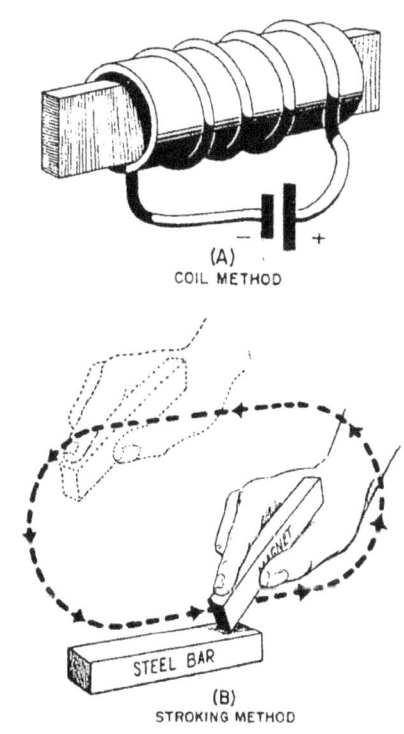

Figure 1-8. Methods of producing artificial magnets.

that are relatively easy to magnetize such as soft iron and annealed silicon steel are said to have a HIGH PERMEABILITY. Such substances retain only a small part of their magnetism after the magnetizing force is removed and are called TEMPORARY MAGNETS. Silicon steel and similar materials are used in transformers where the magnetism is constantly changing and in generators and motors where the strengths of the fields can be readily changed.

The magnetism that remains in a temporary magnet after the magnetizing force is removed is called RESIDUAL MAGNETISM. The fact that temporary magnets retain even a small amount of magnetism is an important factor in the buildup of voltage in self-excited d-c generators.

NATURE OF MAGNETISM

Weber's theory of the nature of magnetism is based on the assumption that each of the molecules of a magnet is itself a tiny magnet. The molecular magnets that compose an unmagne-tized bar of iron or steel are arranged at random, as shown by the simplified diagram of figure 1-9 (A). With this arrangement, the magnetism of each of the molecules is neutralized by that of adjacent molecules, and no external magnetic effect is produced. When a magnetizing force is applied to an unmagnetized iron or steel bar, the molecules become alined so that the north poles point one way and the south poles point the other way, as shown in figure 1-9 (B).

same. If this breaking process could be continued, smaller and smaller pieces would retain their magnetism until each part was reduced to a molecule. It is therefore logical to assume that each of these molecules is a magnet.

A further justification for this assumption results from the fact that when a bar magnet is held out of alinement with the earth's field and is repeatedly jarred, heated, or exposed to a powerful alternating field, the molecular alinement is disarranged and the magnet becomes demagnetized. For example, electric measuring instruments become inaccurate if their permanent magnets lose some of their magnetism because of severe jarring or exposure to opposing magnetic fields.

A theory of magnetism that is perhaps more adequate than the MOLECULAR theory is the DOMAIN theory. Much simplified, this theory may be stated as follows:

In magnetic substances the "atomic" magnets, produced by the movement of the planetary electrons around the nucleus, have a strong tendency to line up together in groups of from 10^{14} to 10^{15} atoms. This occurs without the influence of any external magnetic field. These groups of atoms having their poles orientated in the same direction are called DOMAINS. Therefore,

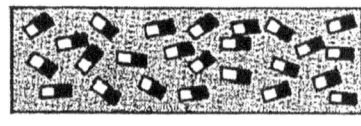
UNMAGNETIZED STEEL
(A)

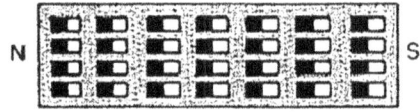
MAGNETIZED STEEL
(B)

Figure 1-9.—Molecular theory of magnetism.

If a bar magnet is broken into several parts, as in figure 1-10, each part constitutes a magnet. The north and south poles of these small magnets are in the same respective directions as those of the original magnet. If each of these parts is again broken, the resulting parts are likewise magnets, and the magnetic orientation is the

throughout each domain an intense magnetic field is produced. These fields are normally in a miscellaneous arrangement so that no external field is apparent when the substance as a whole is unmagnetized.

Each tiny domain (10^6 of them may be contained in 1 cubic millimeter) is always magnetized to saturation, and the addition of an external magnetic field does not increase the inherent magnetism of the individual domains.

However, if an external field that is gradually increased in strength is applied to the magnetic substance the domains will line up one by one (or perhaps several at a time) with the external field.

MAGNETIC FIELDS AND LINES OF FORCE

If a bar magnet is dipped into iron filings, many of the filings are attracted to the ends of the magnet, but none are attracted to the center of the magnet. As mentioned previously, the ends of the magnet where the attractive force is the greatest are called the POLES of the magnet. By using a compass, the line of direction of the magnetic force at various points near the magnet may be observed. The compass needle itself is a magnet. The north end of the compass needle always points toward the south pole, S, as shown in figure 1-11 (A), and thus the sense of direction (with respect to the polarity of the bar magnet) is also indicated. At the center, the compass needle points in a direction that is parallel to the bar magnet.

When the compass is placed successively at several points in the vicinity of the bar magnet the compass needle alines itself with the field at each position. The direction of the field is indicated by the arrows and represents the direction in which the north pole of the compass needle will point when the compass is placed in this field. Such a line along which a compass needle alines itself is called a MAGNETIC LINE OF FORCE. As mentioned previously, the magnetic lines of force are assumed to emanate from the north pole of a magnet, pass through the surrounding space, and enter the south pole. The lines of force then pass from the south pole to the north pole inside the magnet to form a closed loop. Each line of force forms an independent closed loop and does not merge with or cross other lines of force. The lines of force between the poles of a horseshoe magnet are shown in figure 1-11 (B).

The space surrounding a magnet, in which the magnetic force acts, is called a MAGNETIC FIELD. Michael Faraday was the first scientist to visualize the magnet field as being in a state of stress and consisting of uniformly distributed lines of force. The entire quantity of magnetic lines surrounding a magnet is called MAGNETIC FLUX. Flux in a magnetic circuit corresponds to current in an electric circuit.

The number of lines of force per unit area is called FLUX DENSITY and is measured in lines per square inch or lines per square centimeter. Flux density is expressed by the equation

$$B = \frac{\phi}{A}$$

where B is the flux density, ϕ (Greek phi) is the total number of lines of flux, and A is the cross-sectional area of the magnetic circuit. If A is in square centimeters, B is in lines per square centimeter, or GAUSS. The terms FLUX and FLOW of magnetism are frequently used in textbooks. However, magnetism itself is not thought to be a stream of particles in motion, but is simply a field of force exerted in space. A visual representation pf the magnetic field around a magnet can be obtained by placing a plate of glass over a magnet and sprinkling iron filings onto

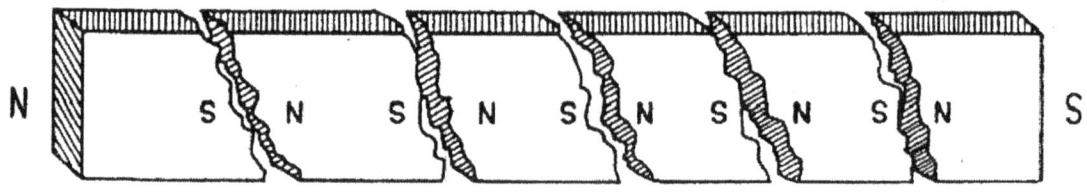

Figure 1-10.—Magnetic poles of a broken magnet.

the glass. The filings arrange themselves in definite paths between the poles.

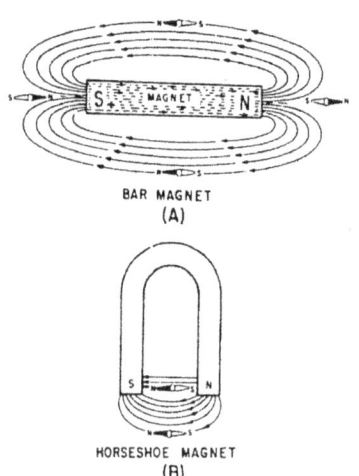

Figure 1-11.—Magnetic lines of force.

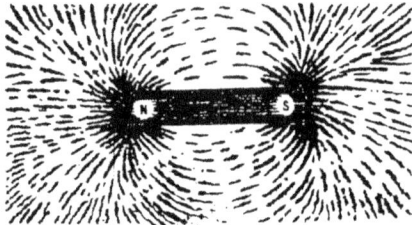

Figure 1-12.—Magnetic field pattern around a magnet.

This arrangement of the filings shows the pattern of the magnetic field around the magnet, as in figure 1-12.

The magnetic field surrounding a symmetrically shaped magnet has the following properties:

1. The field is symmetrical unless disturbed by another magnetic substance.

2. The lines of force have direction and are represented as emanating from the north pole and entering the south pole.

LAWS OF ATTRACTION AND REPULSION

If a magnetized needle is suspended near a bar magnet, as in figure 1-13, it will be seen that a north pole repels a north pole and a south pole repels a south pole. Opposite poles, however, will attract each other.

Thus, the first two laws of magnetic attraction and repulsion are:

1. LIKE magnetic poles REPEL each other.

2. UNLIKE magnetic poles ATTRACT each other.

The flux patterns between adjacent UNLIKE poles of bar magnets, as indicated by lines, are shown in figure 1-14 (A). Similar patterns for adjacent LIKE poles are shown in figure 1-14 (B). The lines do not cross at any point and they act as if they repel each other.

Figure 1-15 shows the flux pattern (indicated by lines) around two bar magnets placed close together and parallel with each other. Figure 1-15 (A) shows the flux pattern when opposite poles are adjacent; and figure 1-15 (B) shows the flux pattern when like poles are adjacent.

The THIRD LAW of magnetic attraction and repulsion states in effect that the force of attraction or repulsion existing between two magnetic poles decreases rapidly as the poles are separated from each other. Actually, the force of attraction or repulsion varies directly as the product of the separate pole strengths and inversely as the square of the distance separating the magnetic poles, provided the poles are small enough to be considered as points. For example, if the distance between two north poles is increased from 2 feet to 4 feet, the force of

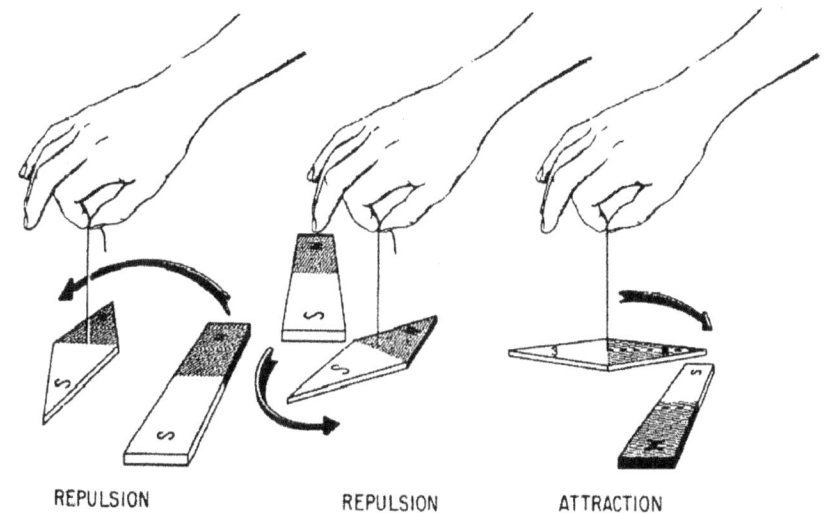

REPULSION   REPULSION   ATTRACTION

Figure 1-13.—Laws of attraction and repulsion.

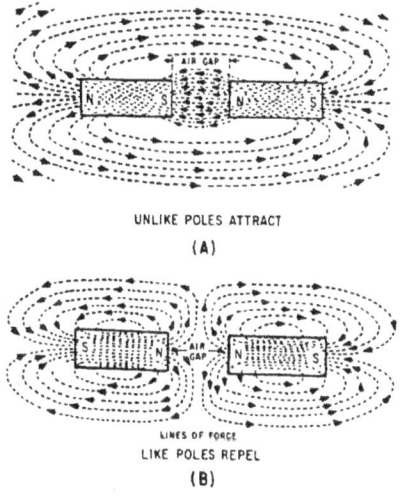

UNLIKE POLES ATTRACT
(A)

LINES OF FORCE
LIKE POLES REPEL
(B)

Figure 1-14.—Lines of force between unlike and like poles.

repulsion between them is decreased to one-fourth of its original value. If either pole strength is doubled, the distance remaining the same, the force between the poles will be doubled.

THE EARTH'S MAGNETISM

As has been stated, the earth is a huge magnet; and surrounding the earth is the magnetic field produced by the earth's magnetism. The magnetic polarities of the earth are as indicated in figure 1-16. The geographic poles are also shown at each end of the axis of rotation of the earth. The magnetic axis does not coincide with the geographic axis, and therefore the magnetic and geographic poles are not at the same place on the surface of the earth.

The early users of the compass regarded the end of the compass needle that points in a northerly direction as being a north pole. The other end was regarded as a south pole. On some maps the magnetic pole of the earth towards which the north pole of the compass pointed was designated a north magnetic pole. This magnetic pole was obviously called a north pole because of its proximity to the north geographic pole.

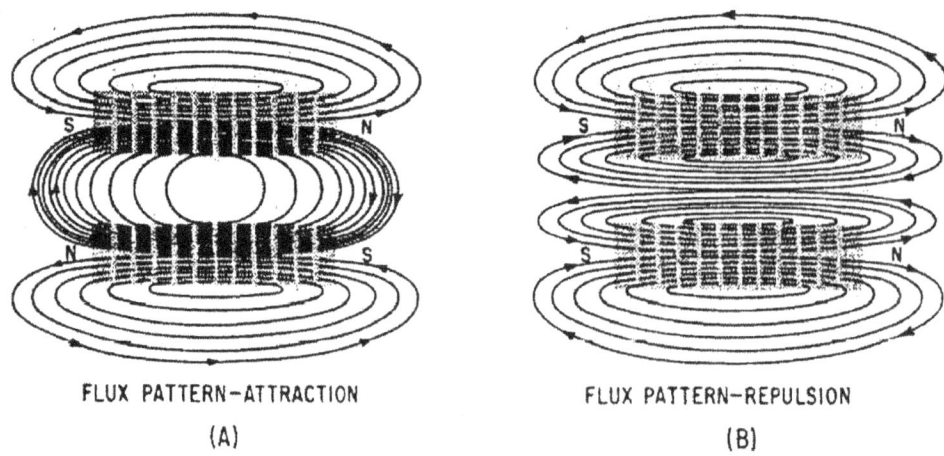

FLUX PATTERN—ATTRACTION
(A)

FLUX PATTERN—REPULSION
(B)

Figure 1-15.—Flux patterns of adjacent parallel bar magnets.

When it was learned that the earth is a magnet and that opposite poles attract, it was necessary to call the magnetic pole located in the northern hemisphere a SOUTH MAGNETIC POLE and the magnetic pole located in the southern hemisphere a NORTH MAGNETIC POLE. The matter of naming the poles was arbitrary. Obviously, the polarity of the compass needle that points toward the north must be opposite to the polarity of the earth's magnetic pole located there.

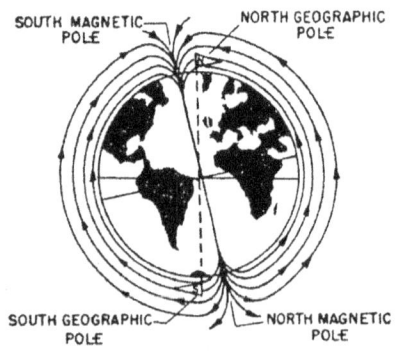

Figure 1-16.—Earth's magnetic poles.

As has been stated, magnetic lines of force are assumed to emanate from the north pole of a magnet and to enter the south pole as closed loops. Because the earth is a magnet, lines of force emanate from its north magnetic pole and enter the south magnetic pole as closed loops. The compass needle alines itself in such a way that the earth's lines of force enter at its south pole and leave at its north pole. Because the north pole of the needle is defined as the end that points in a northerly direction it follows that the magnetic pole in the vicinity of the north geographic pole is in reality a south magnetic pole, and vice versa.

Because the magnetic poles and the geographic poles do not coincide, a compass will not (except at certain positions on the earth) point in a true (geographic) north-south direction-that is, it will not point in a line of direction that passes through the north and south geographic poles, but in a line of direction that makes an angle with it. This angle is called the angle of VARIATION OR DECLINATION.

MAGNETIC SHIELDING

There is not a known INSULATOR for magnetic flux. If a nonmagnetic material is placed in a magnetic field, there is no appreciable change in flux-that is, the flux penetrates the nonmagnetic material. For example, a glass plate placed between the poles of a horseshoe magnet will have no appreciable effect on the field although glass itself is a good insulator in an electric circuit. If a magnetic material (for example, soft iron) is placed in a magnetic field, the flux may be redirected to take advantage of the greater permeability of the magnetic material as shown in figure 1-17. Permeability is the quality of a substance which determines the ease with which it can be magnetized.

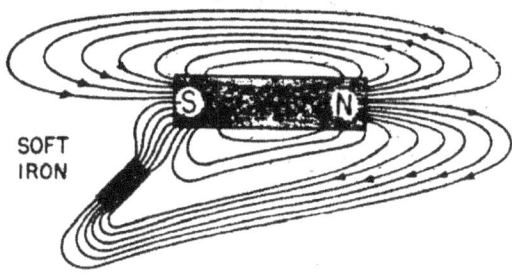

Figure 1-17.—Effects of a magnetic substance in a magnetic field.

The sensitive mechanism of electric instruments and meters can be influenced by stray magnetic fields which will cause errors in their readings. Because instrument mechanisms cannot be insulated against magnetic flux, it is necessary to employ some means of directing the flux around the instrument. This is accomplished by placing a soft-iron case, called a MAGNETIC SCREEN OR SHIELD, about the instrument. Because the flux *is* established more readily through the iron (even though the path is longer) than through the air inside the case, the instrument is effectively shielded, as shown by the watch and soft-iron shield in figure 1-18.

The study of electricity and magnetism, and how they affect each other, is given more thorough coverage in later chapters of this course.

The discussion of magnetism up to this point has been mainly intended to clarify terms and meanings, such as "polarity," "fields," "lines of force," and so forth. Only one fundamental relationship between magnetism and electricity is discussed in this chapter. This relationship pertains to magnetism as used to generate a voltage and it is discussed under the headings that follows.

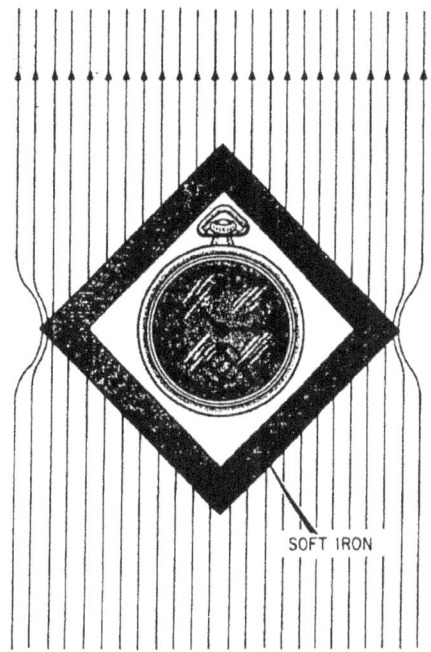

Figure 1-18.—Magnetic shield.

Difference in Potential

The force that causes free electrons to move in a conductor as an electric current is called (1) an electromotive force (e.m.f.), (2) a voltage, or (3) a difference in potential. When a difference in potential exists between two charged bodies that are connected by a conductor, electrons will flow along the conductor. This flow will be from the negatively charged body to the positively charged body until the two charges are equalized and the potential difference no longer exists.

An analogy of this action is shown in the two water tanks connected by a pipe and valve in figure 1-19. At first the valve is closed and all the water is in tank A. Thus, the water pressure across the valve is at maximum. When the valve is opened, the water flows through the pipe from A to B until the water level becomes the same in both tanks. The water then stops flowing in the pipe, because there is no longer a difference in water pressure between the two tanks.

Current flow through an electric circuit is directly proportional to the difference in potential across the circuit, just as the flow of water through the pipe in figure 1-19 is directly proportional to the difference in water level in the two tanks.

A fundamental law of current electricity is that the CURRENT IS DIRECTLY PROPORTIONAL TO THE APPLIED VOLTAGE.

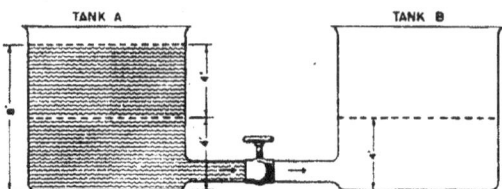

Figure 1-19.—Water analogy of electric difference in potential.

Primary Methods of Producing a Voltage

Presently, there are six commonly used methods of producing a voltage. Some of these methods are much more widely used than others. The methods of utilizing each source will be discussed, and their most common applications will be included. The following is a list of the six most common methods of producing a voltage.

1. FRICTION.-Voltage produced by rubbing two materials together.

2. PRESSURE (Piezoelectricity).- Voltage produced by squeezing crystals of certain substances.

3. HEAT (Thermoelectricity).-Voltage produced by heating the joint (junction) where two unlike metals are joined.

4. LIGHT (Photoelectricity).-Voltage produced by light striking photosensitive (light sensitive) substances.

5. CHEMICAL ACTION.-Voltage produced by chemical reaction in a battery cell.

6. MAGNETISM.-Voltage produced in a conductor when the conductor moves through a magnetic field, or a magnetic field moves through the conductor in such a manner as to cut the magnetic lines of force of the field.

VOLTAGE PRODUCED BY FRICTION

This is the least used of the six methods of producing voltages. Its main application is in Van de Graf generators, used by some laboratories to produce high voltages. As a rule, friction electricity (often referred to as static electricity) is a nuisance. For instance, a flying aircraft accumulates electric charges from the friction between its skin and the passing air.

These charges often interfere with radio communication, and under some circumstances can even cause physical damage to the aircraft. You have probably received unpleasant shocks from friction electricity upon sliding across dry seat covers or walking across dry carpets, and then coming in contact with some other object.

VOLTAGE PRODUCED BY PRESSURE

This action is referred to as piezoelectricity. It is produced by compressing or decompressing crystals of certain substances. To study this form of electricity, you must first understand the meaning of the word "crystal." In a crystal, the molecules are arranged in an orderly and uniform manner. A substance in its crystallized state and in its noncrystallized state is shown in figure 1-20.

For the sake of simplicity, assume that the molecules of this particular substance are spherical (ball-shaped). In the noncrystallized state, in part (A), note that the molecules are arranged irregularly. In the crystallized state, part (B), the molecules are arranged in a regular and uniform manner. This illustrates the major physical difference between crystal and noncrystal forms of matter. Natural crystalline matter is rare; an example of matter that is crystalline in its natural form is diamond, which is crystalline carbon. Most crystals are manufactured.

Crystals of certain substances, such as Rochelle salt or quartz, exhibit peculiar electrical characteristics. These characteristics, or effects, are referred to as "piezoelectric." For instance, when a crystal of quartz is compressed, as in figure 1-20 (C), electrons tend

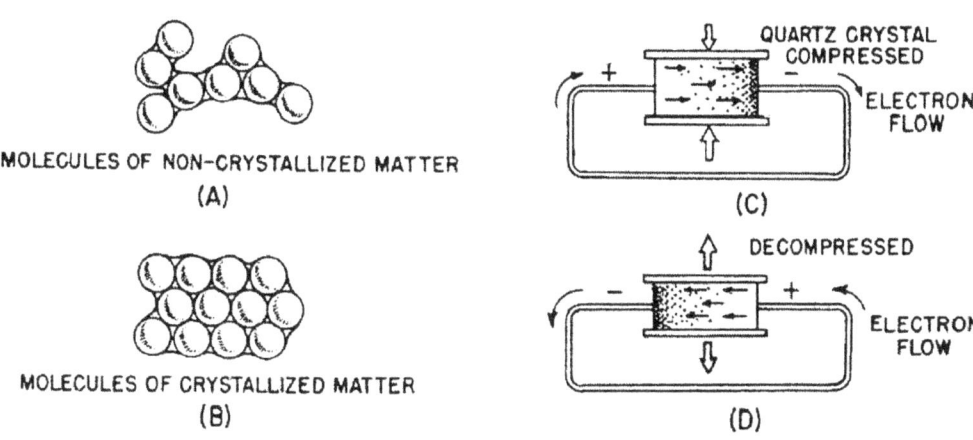

Figure 1-20.—(A) Noncrystallized structure, (B) crystallized structure, (C) compression of a crystal, (D) decompression of a crystal.

to move through the crystal as shown. This tendency creates an electric difference of potential between the two opposite faces of the crystal. (The fundamental reasons for this action are not known. However, the action is predictable, and therefore useful.) If an external wire is connected while the pressure and e.m.f. are present, electrons will flow. If the pressure is held constant, the electron flow will continue until the charges are equalized. When the force is removed, the crystal is decompressed, and immediately causes an electric force in the opposite direction, as shown in part (D). Thus, the crystal is able to convert mechanical force, either pressure or tension, to electrical force.

The power capacity of a crystal is extremely small. However, they are useful because of their extreme sensitivity to changes of mechanical force or changes in temperature. Due to other characteristics not mentioned here, crystals are most widely used in radio communication equipment. The more complicated study of crystals, as they are used for practical applications, is left for those courses that pertain to the special ratings concerned with them.

VOLTAGE PRODUCED BY HEAT

When a length of metal, such as copper, is heated at one end, electrons tend to move away from the hot end toward the cooler end. This is true of most metals. However, in some metals, such as iron, the opposite takes place and electrons tend to move TOWARD the hot end. These characteristics are illustrated in figure 1-21. The negative charges (electrons) are moving through the copper away from the heat and through the iron toward the heat. They cross from the iron to the copper at the hot junction, and from the copper through the current meter to the iron at the cold junction. This device is generally referred to as a thermocouple.

Thermocouples have somewhat greater power capacities than crystals, but their capacity is still very small if compared to some other sources. The thermoelectric voltage in a thermocouple depends mainly on the difference in temperature between the hot and cold junctions. Consequently, they are widely used to measure temperature, and as heat-sensing devices in automatic temperature control equipment. Thermocouples generally can be subjected to much greater temperatures than ordinary thermometers, such as the mercury or alcohol types.

VOLTAGE PRODUCED BY LIGHT

When light strikes the surface of a substance, it may dislodge electrons from their orbits around the surface atoms of the substance. This occurs because light has energy, the same as any moving force.

Some substances, mostly metallic ones, are far more sensitive to light than others. That is, more electrons will be dislodged and emitted from the surface of a highly sensitive metal, with a given amount of light, than will be emitted from a less sensitive

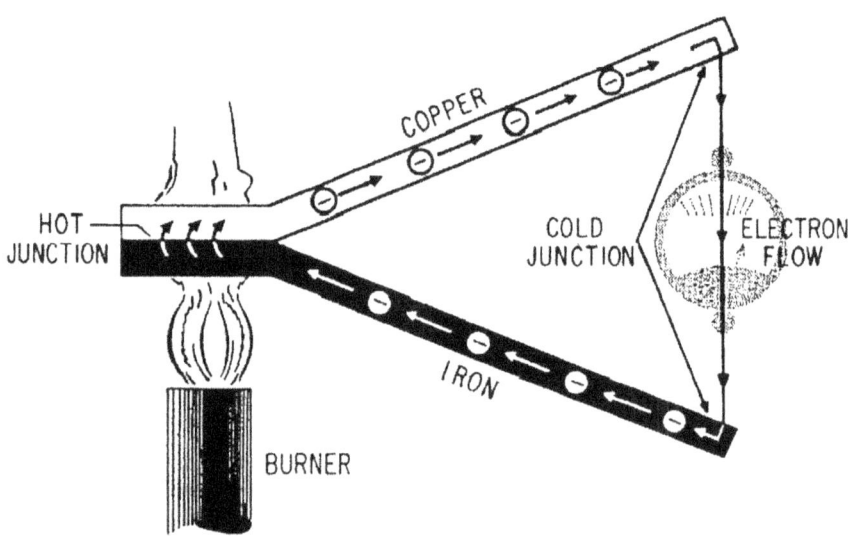

Figure 1-21.—Voltage produced by heat.

substance. Upon losing electrons, the photosensitive (light sensitive) metal becomes positively charged, and an electric force is created. Voltage produced in this manner is referred to as "a photoelectric voltage."

The photosensitive materials most commonly used to produce a photoelectric voltage are various compounds of silver oxide or copper oxide. A complete device which operates on the photoelectric principle is referred to as a "photoelectric cell." There are many sizes and types of photoelectric cells in use, each of which serves the special purpose for which it was designed. Nearly all, however, have some of the basic features of the photoelectric cells shown in figure 1-22.

The cell shown in part (A) has a curved light-sensitive surface focused on the central anode. When light from the direction shown strikes the sensitive surface, it emits electrons toward the anode. The more intense the light, the greater is the number of electrons emitted. When a wire is connected between the filament and the back, or dark side, the accumulated electrons will flow to the dark side. These electrons will eventually

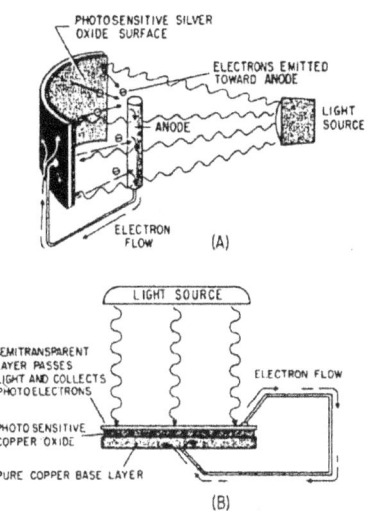

Figure 1-22.—Voltage produced by light.

pass through the metal of the reflector and replace the electrons leaving the light-sensitive surface. Thus, light energy is converted to a flow of electrons, and a usable current is developed.

The cell shown in part (B) is constructed in layers. A base plate of pure copper is coated with light-sensitive copper oxide. An additional layer of metal is put over the copper oxide. This additional layer serves two purposes:

1. It is EXTREMELY thin to permit the penetration of light to the copper oxide.

2. It also accumulates the electrons emitted by the copper oxide.

An externally connected wire completes the electron path, the same as in the reflector type cell. The photocell's voltage is utilized as needed by connecting the external wires to some other device, which amplifies (enlarges) it to a usable level.

A photocell's power capacity is very small. However, it reacts to light-intensity variations in an extremely short time. This characteristic makes the photocell very useful in detecting or accurately controlling a great number of processes or operations. For instance, the photoelectric cell, or some form of the photoelectric principle, is used in television cameras, automatic manufacturing process controls, door openers, burglar alarms, and so forth.

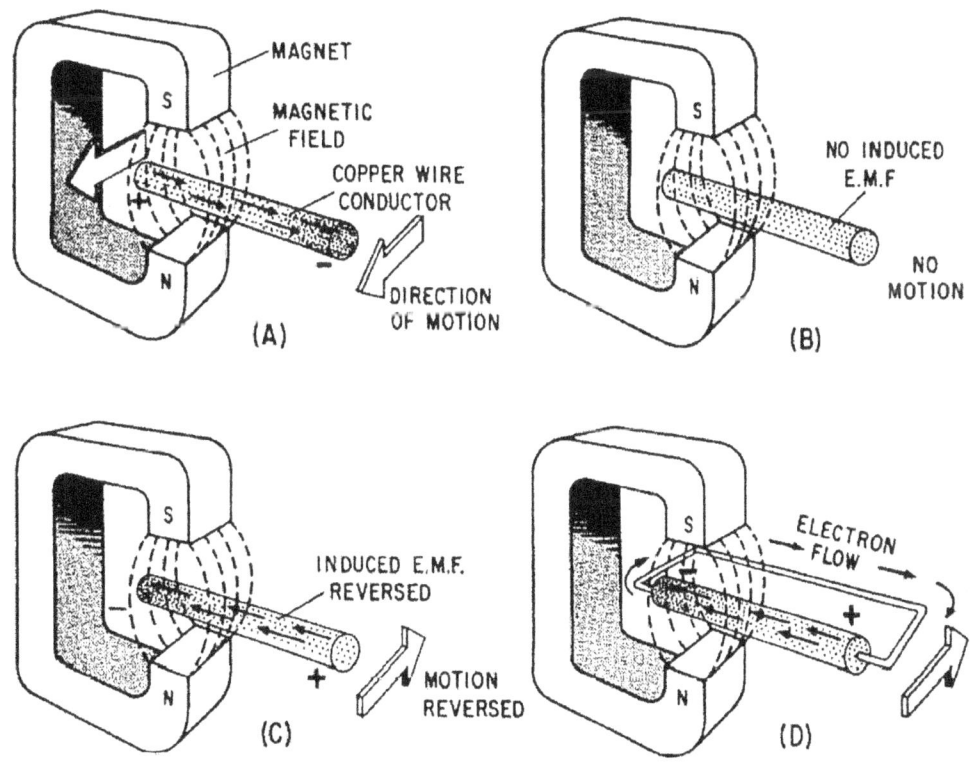

Figure 1-23.—Voltage produced by magnetism.

VOLTAGE PRODUCED BY CHEMICAL ACTION

Up to this point, it has been shown that electrons may be removed from their parent atoms and set in motion by energy derived from a source of friction, pressure, heat, or light. In general, these forms of energy do not alter the molecules of the substances being acted upon. That is, molecules are not usually added, taken away, or split-up when subjected to these four forms of energy. Only electrons are involved. When the molecules of a substance are altered, the action is referred to as CHEMICAL. For instance, if the molecules of a substance combines with atoms of another substance, or gives up atoms of its own, the action is chemical in nature. Such action always changes the , chemical name and characteristics of the substance affected. For instance, when atoms of oxygen from the air come in contact with bare iron, they merge with the molecules of iron. This iron is "oxidized." It has changed chemically from iron to iron oxide, or "rust." Its molecules have been altered by chemical action.

In some cases, when atoms are added to or taken away from the molecules of a substance, the chemical change will cause the substance to take on an electric charge. The process of producing a voltage by chemical action is used in batteries and is explained in chapter 2.

VOLTAGE PRODUCED BY MAGNETISM

Magnets or magnetic devices are used for thousands of different jobs. One of the most useful and widely employed applications of magnets is in the production of vast quantities of electric power from mechanical sources. The mechanical power may be provided by a number of different sources, such as gasoline or diesel engines, and water or steam turbines. However, the final conversion of these source energies to electricity is done by generators employing the principle of electromagnetic induction. These generators, of many types and sizes, are discussed in later chapters of this course. The important subject to be discussed here is the fundamental operating principle of ALL such electromagnetic-induction generators.

To begin with, there are three fundamental conditions which must exist before a voltage can be produced by magnetism. You should learn them well, because they will be encountered again and again. They are:

1. There must be a CONDUCTOR, in which the voltage will be produced.

2. There must be a MAGNETIC FIELD in the conductor's vicinity.

3. There must be relative motion between the field and the conductor. The conductor must be moved so as to cut across the magnetic lines of force, or the field must be moved so that the lines of force are cut by the conductor.

In accordance with these conditions, when a conductor or conductors MOVE ACROSS a magnetic field so as to cut the lines of force, electrons WITHIN THE CONDUCTOR are impelled in one direction or another. Thus, an electric force, or voltage, is created.

In figure 1-23, note the presence of the three conditions needed for creating an induced voltage:

1. A magnetic field exists between the poles of the C-shaped magnet.

2. There is a conductor (copper wire).

3. There is relative motion. The wire is moved back and forth ACROSS the magnetic field.

In part (A) the conductor is moving TOWARD you. This occurs because of the magnetically induced electromotive force (e.m.f.) acting on the electrons in the copper. The right-hand end becomes negative, and the left-hand end positive. In part (B) the conductor is stopped. This eliminates motion, one of the three required conditions, and there is no longer an induced e.m.f. Consequently, there is no longer any difference in potential between the two ends of the wire. In part (C) the conductor is moving AWAY from you. An induced e.m.f. is again created. However, note carefully that the REVERSAL OF MOTION has caused a REVERSAL OF DIRECTION in the induced e.m.f.

If a path for electron flow is provided between the ends of the conductor, electrons will leave the negative end and flow to the positive end. This condition is shown in part (D). Electron flow will continue as long as the e.m.f. exists. In studying figure 1-23, it should be noted that the induced e.m.f. could also have been created by holding the conductor stationary and moving the magnetic field back and forth.

In later chapters of this course, under the heading "Generators," you will study the more complex aspects of power generation by use of mechanical motion and magnetism.

Electric Current

The drift or flow of electrons through a conductor is called ELECTRIC CURRENT. In order to determine the amount (number) of electrons flowing in a given conductor, it is necessary to adopt a unit of measurement of current flow. The term AMPERE is used to define the unit of measurement of the rate at which current flows (electron flow). The symbol for the ampere is I. One ampere may be defined as the fow of 6.28×10^{18} electrons per second past a fixed point in a conductor

A unit quantity of electricity is moved through an electric circuit when one ampere of current flows for one second of time. This unit is equivalent to 6.28×10^{18} electrons, and is called the COULOMB. The coulomb is to electricity as the gallon is to water. The symbol for the coulomb is Q. The rate of flow of current in amperes and the quantity of electricity moved through a circuit are related by the common factor of time. Thus, the quantity of electric charge, in coulombs, electricity moved through a circuit are is equal to the product of the current in amperes, I, and the duration of flow in seconds, t. Expressed as an equation, $Q = It$.

For example, if a current of 2 amperes flows through a circuit for 10 seconds the quantity of electricity moved through the circuit is 2 x 10, or 20 coulombs. Conversely, current flow may be expressed in terms of coulombs and time in seconds. Thus, if 20 coulombs are moved through a circuit in 10 seconds, the average current flow is 20/10, or 2 amperes. Note that the current flow in amperes implies the rate of flow of coulombs per second without indicating either coulombs or seconds. Thus a current flow of 2 amperes is equivalent to a rate of flow of 2 coulombs per second.

Resistance

Every material offers some resistance, or opposition, to the flow of electric current through it. Good conductors, such as copper, silver, and aluminum, offer very little resistance. Poor conductors, or insulators, such as glass, wood, and paper, offer a high resistance to current flow.

The size and type of material of the wires in an electric circuit are chosen so as to keep the electrical resistance as low as possible. In this way, current can flow easily through the conductors, just as water flows through the pipe between the tanks in figure 1-19. If the water pressure remains constant the flow of water in the pipe will depend on how far the valve is opened. The smaller the opening, the greater the opposition to the flow, and the smaller will be the rate of flow in gallons per second.

In the electric circuit, the larger the diameter of the wires, the lower will be their electrical resistance (opposition) to the flow of current through them. In the water analogy, pipe friction opposes the flow of water between the tanks. This friction is similar to electrical resistance. The resistance of the pipe to the flow of water through it depends upon (1) the length of the pipe, (2) the diameter of the pipe, and (3) the nature of the inside walls (rough or smooth). Similarly, the electrical resistance of the conductors depends upon (1) the length of the wires, (2) the diameter of the wires, and (3) the material of the wires (copper, aluminum, etc.).

Temperature also affects the resistance of electrical conductors to some extent. In most conductors (copper, aluminum, iron, etc.) the resistance increases with temperature. Carbon is an exception. In carbon the resistance decreases as temperature increases. Certain alloys of metals (manganin and constantan) have resistance that does not change appreciably with temperature.

The relative resistance of several conductors of the same length and cross section is given in the following list with silver as a standard of 1 and the remaining metals arranged in an order of ascending resistance:

Silver	1.0
Copper	1.08
Gold	1.4
Aluminum	1.8
Platinum	7.0
Lead	13.5

The resistance in an electrical circuit is expressed by the symbol R. Manufactured circuit parts containing definite amounts of resistance are called RESISTORS. Resistance (R) is measured in OHMS. One ohm is the resistance of a circuit element, or circuit, that permits a steady current of 1 ampere (1 coulomb per second) to flow when a steady e.m.f. of 1 volt is applied to the circuit.

www.ingramcontent.com/pod-product-compliance
Lightning Source LLC
Chambersburg PA
CBHW082040300426
44117CB00015B/2556